" *MANY there are who 'stead of harmless fun
Can only see perdition in a pun,
And who imagine that they can descry
Contempt for genius in a parody.*"

A Parody Anthology

COLLECTED BY

Carolyn Wells

Dover Publications, Inc.
New York

International Standard Book Number: 0-486-21844-9
Library of Congress Catalog Card Number: 67-24222

Manufactured in the United States of America
Dover Publications, Inc.
180 Varick Street
New York, N.Y. 10014

TO

MRS. THEODORE ROOSEVELT

NOTE

ACKNOWLEDGMENT is hereby gratefully made to the publishers of the various parodies for permission to include them in this compilation.

The parodies from "Diversions of the Echo Club," by Bayard Taylor, and Mary and Her Lamb, from "New Waggings of Old Tales," by Frank Dempster Sherman, are published by permission of Messrs. Houghton, Mifflin & Company.

By the courtesy of John Lane are included the parodies of Anthony C. Deane, from his volume "New Rhymes for Old;" and those of Owen Seaman, from volumes "In Cap and Bells" and "The Battle of the Bays."

Bed During Exams is from "Cap and Gown," published by Messrs. L. C. Page & Company.

The Golfer's Rubaiyat, by H. C. Boynton, is from "A Book of American Humorous Verse," published by Messrs. Herbert S. Stone & Company.

Staccato to O Le Lupe is from "Last Scenes from Vagabondia," by Bliss Carman and Richard Hovey, published by Messrs. Small, Maynard & Company.

The two poems by Ben King are published by Forbes & Co.

The following are published by Charles Scribner's Sons : Song, from "The Book of Joyous Children," by James Whitcomb Riley ; Home Sweet Home, and Imitation, from "Poems" of H. C. Bunner ; and Song of a Heart, and Godiva, from "Overheard in a Garden," by Oliver Herford.

[vi]

CONTENTS

Contents

Contents

[ix]

Contents

[x]

Contents

Contents

Contents

Contents

[xiv]

Contents

[xv]

INTRODUCTION

PARODY AS A FINE ART

THE fact that parody has been ably defended by many of the world's best minds proves that it is an offensive measure, at least from some viewpoints. But an analysis of the arguments for and against seems to show that parody is a true and legitimate branch of art, whose appreciation depends upon the mental bias of the individual.

To enjoy parody, one must have an intense sense of the humorous and a humorous sense of the intense; and this, of course, presupposes a mental attitude of wide tolerance and liberal judgments.

Parodies are not for those who cannot understand that parody is not necessarily ridicule. Like most other forms of literature, unless the intent of the writer be thoroughly understood and appreciated, the work is of little value to the reader.

The defenders of parody have sometimes endeavored to prove that it has an instructive value, and that it has acted as a reforming influence against mannerisms and other glaring defects. One enthusiastic partisan confidently remarks: "It may gently admonish the best and most established writer, when, from haste, from carelessness, from over-confidence, he is in danger of forfeiting his reputation; it may gently lead the tyro, while there is yet time, from the wrong into the right path." But this ethical air-castle is rudely shattered by facts, for what established writer ever changed his characteristic effects as a result of the parodies upon his works, or what tyro was ever parodied?

It has been said, too, that a good parody makes us love the original work better; but this statement seems to lack satisfactory proof except, perhaps, on the principle that a good parody may lead us to know the original work more thoroughly.

Perhaps the farthest fetched argument of the zealous advocates of the moral virtues of parody is found in Lord Jeffrey's review of the well-known "Rejected Addresses," where he says, "The imitation lets us more completely into the secret of the original author, and enables us to understand far more clearly in what the peculiarity of his manner consists than most of us would ever have done without this assistance." If this be true at all, it is exemplified in very few instances, and is one of the least of the minor reasons for the existence of a parody.

The main intent of the vast majority of parodies is simply to amuse; but to amuse intelligently and cleverly. This aim is quite high enough, and is in no way strengthened or improved by the bolstering up qualities of avowed virtuous influences.

The requirements of the best parody are in a general way simply the requirements of the best literature of any sort; but, specifically, the true parodist requires an exact mental balance, a fine sense of proportion and relative values, good-humor, refinement, and unerring taste. Self-control and self-restraint are also needed; a parodist may go to the very edge, but he must not fall over.

The fact that poor parodies outnumber the good ones in the ratio of about ten to one (which is not an unusual percentage in any branch of literature), is because a wide and generous sense of humor is so rarely found in combination with the somewhat circumscribed quality of good taste. It is, therefore, on account of the abuse of parody, and not the use of it, that a defence of the art has been found necessary.

The parody has the sanction of antiquity, and though its absolute origin is uncertain, and various

"Fathers of Parody" have been named, it is safe
to assume that it began with the Greeks. The
Romans, too, indulged in it, and its continuance
has been traced all through the Middle Ages;
but these ancient parodies, however acceptable
in their time, are of little interest to us now,
save as heirlooms. Their wit is coarse, their
humor heavy; they are usually caustic and often
irreverent.

In the seventeenth and eighteenth centuries the
art of parody began to improve, and during the
nineteenth it rose to a height that demanded
recognition from the literary world.

It is interesting to note that the age of English
parody was ushered in by such masterpieces as the
"Rolliad" and the "Anti-Jacobin," followed by
the "Rejected Addresses" and the "Bon Gaultier
Ballads." Later came Thackeray, Calverley, Swinburne and Lewis Carroll, also Bayard Taylor, Bret
Harte, and Phœbe Cary. More modern still is the
work of Rudyard Kipling, Anthony C. Deane,
H. C. Bunner, and Owen Seaman.

Though some of these are classed among the
minor poets, they are all major parodists and approach their work armed at all points.

The casual critic of parodies, as a rule, divides
them into two classes, which, though under various forms of terminology, resolve themselves into

parodies of sound and parodies of sense. But there are really three great divisions, which may be called " word-rendering," " form-rendering," and " sense-rendering."

The first, mere word-rendering, is simply an imitation of the original, and depends for its interest entirely upon the substitution of a trivial or commonplace motive for a lofty one, and following as nearly as possible the original words.

Form-rendering is the imitation of the style of an author, preferably an author given to mannerisms or affectation of some sort. The third division, sense-rendering, is by far the most meritorious, and utilizes not only the original writer's diction and style, but follows a train of thought precisely along the lines that he would have pursued from the given premises.

This class of parody is seen at its best in Catherine Fanshawe's " Imitation of Wordsworth," and Calverley's " The Cock and the Bull."

But though parodies of this sort are of more serious worth, the other classes show examples quite as good in their own way.

Lewis Carroll's immortal parody of Southey's " Father William" is merely a burlesque of the word-rendering type, yet it is perfect of its kind and defies adverse criticism.

Miss Cary was a pioneer of parody in America and one of the few women writers who have done clever work of this sort. Miss Cary's parodies are numerous and uniformly first-class examples of their kind. They are collected in a small book, now out of print, and are well worth reading.

Of course, parodies which burlesque the actual words of the original are necessarily parodies of some particular poem, and often not so good an imitation of the style of the author.

More difficult than the parody of a particular poem is the imitation or burlesque of the literary style of an author. To accomplish this, the parodist must be himself a master of style, a student of language, and possessed of a power of mimicry with an instant appreciation of opportunities.

"Diversions of the Echo Club," by Bayard Taylor, are among the best of this class of parodies. Aside from their cleverness they are marked by good taste, fairness, justice, and a true poetic instinct.

Naturally, parodies of literary style are founded on the works of those authors whose individual characteristics invite imitation.

Parody is inevitable where sense is sacrificed to sound, where affectations of speech are evident, or where unwarrantable extravagance of any sort is indulged in. This explains the numerous (and usually worthless) parodies of Walt Whitman.

Swinburne and Browning are often parodied for these (perhaps only apparent) reasons, and the poets of the æsthetic school of course offered especially fine opportunities.

Parodies of Rossetti and his followers are often exceedingly funny, though not at all difficult to write, as the originals both in manner and matter fairly invite absurd incongruities.

Nursery Rhymes seem to find favor with the parodists as themes to work upon. A collection of Mother Goose's Melodies as they have been reset by clever pens, would be both large and interesting.

The masters of parody, however, are as a rule to be found among the master poets. Thackeray turned his genius to imitative account; Swinburne parodied himself as well as his fellow-poets; Rudyard Kipling has done some of the best parodies in the language, and C. S. Calverley's burlesques are classics. The work of these writers may be said to be in the third class; for not only do they preserve the diction and style of the author imitated, but they seem to go beyond that, and, assimilating for the moment his very mentality, caricature not only his expressed thoughts but his abstract cerebrations.

It is easy to understand how Swinburne with his facile fancy and wonderful command of words could be among the best parodists. In his " Heptalogia " are long and careful parodies of no less than seven prominent poets, each of which is a masterpiece, and the parody of Browning is especially good. Browning, of course, has always been a tempting mark for the parodists, but though it is easy to imitate his eccentricities superficially, it is only the greater minds that have parodied his subtler peculiarites. Among the best are Calverley's and Kipling's.

Kipling's parodies, written in his early days, and not often to be found in editions of his collected works, rank with the highest. His parody of Swinburne, while going to the very limit of legitimate imitation, is restrained by a powerful hand, and so kept within convincing bounds. The great fault with most parodies of Swinburne is that exaggeration is given play too freely, and the result is merely a meaningless mass of sound. Clever in a different way is Owen Seaman's parody of Swinburne. Mr. Seaman is one of the most brilliant of modern parodists and his parodies, though long, are perfect in all respects.

Among the most exquisite parodies we have ever read must be counted those of Anthony C. Deane, originally published in various London

papers, and Calverley's works are too well known
even to require mention.

The Rubaiyat of Omar Khayyam is often
parodied, but rarely worthily. One reason for
this lies in the fact that it is not Omar who is
parodied at all, but Fitzgerald; consequently, the
imitation is merely a form-rendering and more
often only lines in the Rubaiyat metre.

Shakespeare, with the exception of one or two
of his most hackneyed speeches, is rarely parodied;
doubtless owing to the fact that his harmonious
work shows no incongruities of matter or manner,
and strikes no false notes for the parodists to
catch at.

The extent of the domain of parody is vastly
larger than is imagined by the average reader, and
its already published bibliographies show thousands
of collected parodies of varying degrees of merit.

Of all the poets Tennyson has probably been
parodied the most; followed closely in this respect
by Edgar Allan Poe. After these, Browning,
Swinburne, and Walt Whitman; then Moore,
Wordsworth, Longfellow, and Thomas Campbell.

Of single poems the one showing the greatest
number of parodies is "My Mother," by Ann
Taylor; after this those most used for the purpose
have been "The Raven," Gray's "Elegy," "The
Song of the Shirt," "The May Queen," "Locksley

Hall," " The Burial of Sir John Moore," and Kingsley's " Three Fishers."

Parody, then, is a tribute to popularity, and consequently to merit of one sort or another, and in the hands of the initiate may be considered a touch-stone that proves true worth.

A PARODY ANTHOLOGY

A Parody Anthology

AFTER OMAR KHAYYAM

THE GOLFER'S RUBAIYAT

WAKE! for the sun has driven in equal flight
The stars before him from the Tee of Night,
    And holed them every one without a
        Miss,
Swinging at ease his gold-shod Shaft of Light.

Now, the fresh Year reviving old Desires,
The thoughtful Soul to Solitude retires,
    Pores on this Club and That with anxious eye,
And dreams of Rounds beyond the Rounds of Liars.

Come, choose your Ball, and in the fire of Spring,
Your Red Coat and your wooden Putter fling;
    The Club of Time has but a little while
To waggle, and the Club is on the swing.

A Bag of Clubs, a Silver Town or two,
A Flask of Scotch, a Pipe of Shag, and Thou
    Beside me caddying in the Wilderness —
Ah, Wilderness were Paradise enow.

Myself, when young, did eagerly frequent
Jamie and His, and heard great argument
   Of Grip, and Stance, and Swing; but evermore
Found at the Exit but a Dollar spent.

With them the seed of Wisdom did I sow,
And with mine own hand sought to make it grow;
   And this was all the Harvest that I reap'd:
" You hold it in this Way, and you swing it So."

The swinging Brassie strikes; and, having struck,
Moves on; nor all your Wit or future Luck
   Shall lure it back to cancel half a Stroke,
Nor from the Card a single Seven pluck.

No hope by Club or Ball to win the Prize;
The batter'd, blacken'd Remade sweetly flies,
   Swept cleanly from the Tee; this is the Truth:
Nine-tenths is Skill, and all the rest is Lies.

And that inverted Ball they call the High,
By which the Duffer thinks to live or die,
   Lift not your hands to It for help, for it
As impotently froths as you or I.

Yon rising Moon that leads us home again,
How oft hereafter will she wax and wane;
   How oft hereafter rising, wait for us
At this same Turning — and for One in vain.

And when, like her, my Golfer, I have been
And am no more above the pleasant Green,
   And you in your mild Journey pass the Hole
I made in One — ah, pay my Forfeit then!
H. W. Boynton.

AN OMAR FOR LADIES *

ONE for her Club and her own Latch-key fights,
   Another wastes in Study her good Nights.
      Ah, take the Clothes and let the Culture go,
Nor heed the grumble of the Women's Rights!

Look at the Shop-girl all about us — " Lo,
The Wages of a month," she says, "I blow
   Into a Hat, and when my hair is waved,
Doubtless my Friend will take me to the Show."

And she who saved her coin for Flannels red,
And she who caught Pneumonia instead,
   Will both be Underground in Fifty Years,
And Prudence pays no Premium to the dead.

Th' exclusive Style you set your heart upon
Gets to the Bargain counters — and anon
   Like monograms on a Saleslady's tie
Cheers but a moment — soon for you 't is gone.

Think, on the sad Four Hundred's gilded halls,
Whose endless Leisure ev'n themselves appalls,
   How Ping-pong raged so high — then faded out
To those far Suburbs that still chase its Balls.

* Copyright, 1903, by Harper & Brothers.

They say Sixth Avenue and the Bowery keep
The *dernier cri* that once was far from cheap;
   Green Veils, one season chic — Department stores
Mark down in vain — no profit shall they reap.

I sometimes think that never lasts so long
The Style as when it starts a bit too strong;
   That all the Pompadours the parterre boasts
Some Chorus-girl began, with Dance and Song.

And this Revival of the Chignon low
That fills the most of us with helpless Woe,
   Ah, criticise it Softly! for who knows
What long-necked Peeress had to wear it so!

Ah, my beloved, try each Style you meet;
To-day brooks no loose ends, you must be neat.
   To-morrow! why, to-morrow you may be
Wearing it down your back like Marguerite!

For some we once admired, the Very Best
That ever a French hand-boned Corset prest,
   Wore what they used to call Prunella Boots,
And put on Nightcaps ere they went to rest.

And we that now make fun of Waterfalls
They wore, and whom their Crinoline appalls,
   Ourselves shall from old dusty Fashion plates
Assist our Children in their Costume balls.

Ah, make the most of what we yet may wear,
Before we grow so old that we don't care!
　　Before we have our Hats made all alike,
Sans Plumes, sans Wings, sans Chiffon, and —
　　　　sans Hair!

Josephine Daskam Bacon.

THE MODERN RUBAIYAT

(Dobley's Version)

HARK! for the message cometh from the
　　　King!
　　Winter, thy doom is spoke; thy dirges ring,
Thy time is o'er — and through the Palace door
Enter the Princess! Hail the new-crowned Spring!

Comes she all rose-crowned, glowing with the Joy
Of Laughter and of Cupid, the God-Boy;
　　Buds bursting on the bough in welcoming
To Her we Love, whose loving will not cloy!

List! from the organ rippling in the Street
Come sounds rejoicing, glad Her reign to greet.
　　The Shad is smiling in the Market Place
And eke the Little Neck! Ah — Life is Sweet!

Come, let us lilt a Merry Little Song
And in an Automobile glide along
　　Into the glory of the Year's new Birth.
Hasten! Oh, haste! For this is Spring, I Think!

[7]

Come where the Bonnets bloom within the Grove
And let us pluck them for the One we Love;
  Violets and Things and chiffon-nested Birds.
Tell me — didst ever see a Glass-Eyed Dove?

Think you how many Springs will go and come
When We are Dead Ones — and the busy Hum
  Of life will never reach us — Nothing Done
And Nothing Doing in the Silence Glum!

Listen! the cable car's Gay Gong has rang,
The Elevated on its perch, A-clang
  Like to a District Messenger astir.
Thought you, it was a Nightingale that sang?

Ah! my Beloved, when it's Really Spring
We know it by the Buds a-blossoming,
  Signals from earth to sky — Tremendous Sounds
That might to Some mean any Ancient Thing!

Then let us to the Caravan at Once,
The Sawdust where the Peanut haunts
  The air with strange sweet Odors
And the Elephant does Wild and Woolly Stunts!

Asparagus is glowing on the Stall,
The Spring lamb cavorts on the Menu tall;
  Strawberries ripe — a Dollar for the Box:
Would n't it jar You somehow, After all?

[8]

A Book of Coon Songs underneath the Bough,
A Jug of Wine, a Dozen Buns, and Thou
   Beside me singing rag-time?   I don't know?
I wonder would a dozen be enow?

I sent my soul afling through Joy and Pain
For Information that the Winds might deign:
   Softly the breezes pitched it, Russie-curved,
And whispered slowly — sadly — " Guess Again."

Sometimes I think the Glories that they Sing
Are like the grape-vine the Fox tried to cling;
   But take To-day — and make the Most of It,
I think it 's Just Too Sweet for anything!

What of To-morrow — say you?   Oh, my
     Friend —
To-morrow 's Not been Touched.   It 's yet to
     Spend.
   I often wonder if we should expire
If we could but Collect the Gold we Lend!

Ah, Love! could Thou and I Creation run,
How Different our Scheme! The Summer's sun
   Would see another Springtime blossoming,
Another Summer's Rose to Follow On!

And Leaning from the Sky a Little Star
Would Tell Us from the Canopy afar
   What now we Grope for in the Dinky-dink,
And wonder blindly, vaguely, What we Are!

And when Alone you dream your fancies ripe,
Thyself all Hasheesh-fed — My Prototype!
 Smoke Up — and when you gather with the
  Group
Where I made One — Turn Down an Empty Pipe!
Kate Masterson.

LINES WRITTEN (" BY REQUEST ") FOR A DINNER OF THE OMAR KHAYYAM CLUB

MASTER, in memory of that Verse of Thine,
 And of Thy rather pretty taste in Wine,
 We gather at this jaded Century's end,
Our Cheeks, if so we may, to incarnadine.

Thou hast the kind of Halo which outstays
Most other Genii's.   Though a Laureate's bays
 Should slowly crumple up, Thou livest on,
Having survived a certain Paraphrase.

The Lion and the Alligator squat
In Dervish Courts — the Weather being hot —
 Under Umbrellas.   Where is Mahmud now?
Plucked by the Kitchener and gone to Pot!

Not so with thee; but in Thy place of Rest,
Where East is East and never can be West,
 Thou art the enduring Theme of dining Bards;
O make allowances; they do their Best.

Our Health — Thy Prophet's health — is but so-so;
Much marred by men of Abstinence who know
   Of Thee and all Thy loving Tavern-lore
Nothing, nor care for it one paltry Blow.

Yea, we ourselves, who beam around Thy Bowl,
Somewhat to dull Convention bow the Soul,
   We sit in sable Trouserings and Boots,
Nor do the Vine-leaves deck a single Poll.

How could they bloom in uncongenial air?
Nor, though they bloomed profusely, should we
     wear
   Upon our Heads — so tight is Habit's hold —
Aught else beside our own unaided Hair.

The Epoch curbs our Fancy.   What is more
To BE, in any case, is now a Bore.
   Even in Humor there is nothing new;
There is no Joke that was not made before.

But Thou! with what a fresh and poignant sting
Thy Muse remarked that Time was on the Wing!
   Ah, Golden Age, when Virgin was the Soil,
And Decadence was deemed a newish Thing.

These picturesque departures now are stale;
The noblest Vices have their vogue and fail;
   Through some inherent Taint or lack of Nerve
We cease to sin upon a generous scale.

This hour, though drinking at my Host's expense,
I fear to use a fine Incontinence,
   For terror of the Law and him that waits
Outside, the unknown X, to hale us hence.

For, should he make of us an ill Report
As pipkins of the more loquacious Sort,
   We might be lodged, the Lord alone knows
      where,
Save Peace were purchased with a pewter Quart.

And yet, O Lover of the purple Vine,
Haply Thy Ghost is watching how we dine;
   Ah, let the Whither go; we 'll take our chance
Of fourteen days with option of a Fine.

Master, if we, Thy Vessels, staunch and stout,
Should stagger, half-seas-over, blind with Doubt,
   In sound of that dread moaning of the Bar,
Be near, be very near, to bail us out!

                    Owen Seaman.

THE BABY'S OMAR

OMAR 'S the fad!   Well then, let us indite
   The shape of verse old Omar used to write;
      And Juveniles are up.   So we opine
A *Baby's Omar* would be out of sight!

Methinks the stunt is easy.   Stilted style,
A misplaced Capital once in a while, —
   Other verse writers do it like a shot;
And can't I do it too?   Well, I should Smile!

            But how I ramble on.   I must dismiss
            Dull Sloth, and set to Work at once, I wis;
               I sometimes think there's nothing quite
                  so hard
            As a Beginning.   Say we start like this:

Indeed, indeed my apron oft before
I tore, but was I naughty when I tore?
   And then, and then came Ma, and thread in hand
Repaired the rent in my small pinafore.

            A Penny Trumpet underneath the Bough,
            A Drum that's big enough to make a Row;
               A Toy Fire-Engine, and a squeaking Doll,
            Oh, Life were Pandemonium enow.

            Come, fill the Cup, then quickly on the floor
            Your portion of the Porridge gaily pour.
               The Nurse will Spank you, and she'll be
                  discharged, —
            Ah, but of Nurses there be Plenty more.

            Yes, I can do it!   Now, if but my Purse
            Some kindly Editor will reimburse,
               I'll write a Baby's Omar; for I'm sure
            These Sample Stanzas here are not so
               worse.

                                             Carolyn Wells.

AFTER CHAUCER

YE CLERKE OF YE WETHERE

A CLERKE ther was, a puissant wight was hee,
    Who of ye wethere hadde ye maisterie;
Alway it was his mirthe and his solace —
To put eche seson's wethere oute of place.

Whanne that Aprille shoures wer our desyre,
He gad us Julye sonnes as hotte as fyre;
But sith ye summere togges we donned agayne,
Eftsoons ye wethere chaunged to cold and rayne.

Wo was that pilgrimme who fared forth a-foote,
Without ane gyngham that him list uppe-putte;
And gif no mackyntosches eke had hee,
A parlous state that wight befelle — pardie!

We wist not gif it nexte ben colde or hotte,
Cogswounds! ye barde a grewsome colde hath gotte!
Certes, that clerke's ane mightie man withalle,
Let non don him offence, lest ille befalle.

Anonymous.

AFTER SPENSER

A PORTRAIT

HE is to weet a melancholy carle:
   Thin in the waist, with bushy head of hair,
   As hath the seeded thistle, when a parle
It holds with Zephyr, ere it sendeth fair
Its light balloons into the summer air;
Thereto his beard had not begun to bloom.
No brush had touched his cheek, or razor sheer;
No care had touched his cheek with mortal doom,
But new he was and bright, as scarf from Persian
    loom.

Ne carèd he for wine, or half and half;
Ne carèd he for fish, or flesh, or fowl;
And sauces held he worthless as the chaff;
He 'sdeigned the swine-head at the wassail-bowl:
Ne with lewd ribbalds sat he cheek by jowl;
Ne with sly lemans in the scorner's chair;
But after water-brooks this pilgrim's soul
Panted and all his food was woodland air;
Though he would oft-times feast on gilliflowers rare.

The slang of cities in no wise he knew,
Tipping the wink to him was heathen Greek;
He sipped no " olden Tom," or " ruin blue,"
Or Nantz, or cherry-brandy, drunk full meek

By many a damsel brave and rouge of cheek ;
Nor did he know each aged watchman's beat,
Nor in obscurèd purlieus would he seek
For curlèd Jewesses, with ankles neat,
Who, as they walk abroad, make tinkling with their
    feet.

John Keats.

AFTER SHAKESPEARE

THE BACHELOR'S SOLILOQUY

TO wed, or not to wed? That is the question
Whether 't is nobler in the mind to suffer
The pangs and arrows of outrageous love
Or to take arms against the powerful flame
And by oppressing quench it.
                    To wed — to marry —
And by a marriage say we end
The heartache and the thousand painful shocks
Love makes us heir to — 't is a consummation
Devoutly to be wished! to wed — to marry —
Perchance a scold! aye, there 's the rub!
For in that wedded life what ills may come
When we have shuffled off our single state
Must give us serious pause. There 's the respect
That makes us Bachelors a numerous race.
For who would bear the dull unsocial hours
Spent by unmarried men, cheered by no smile
To sit like hermit at a lonely board
In silence? Who would bear the cruel gibes
With which the Bachelor is daily teased
When he himself might end such heart-felt griefs
By wedding some fair maid? Oh, who would live
Yawning and staring sadly in the fire
Till celibacy becomes a weary life

But that the dread of something after wed-lock
(That undiscovered state from whose strong chains
No captive can get free) puzzles the will
And makes us rather choose those ills we have
Than fly to others which a wife may bring.
Thus caution doth make Bachelors of us all,
And thus our natural taste for matrimony
Is sicklied o'er with the pale cast of thought.
And love adventures of great pith and moment
With this regard their currents turn away
And lose the name of Wedlock.

Anonymous.

POKER

TO draw, or not to draw, — that is the question : —
    Whether 't is safer in the player to take
The awful risk of skinning for a straight,
Or, standing pat, to raise 'em all the limit
And thus, by bluffing, get in. To draw, — to skin ;
No more — and by that skin to get a full,
Or two pairs, or the fattest bouncing kings
That luck is heir to — 't is a consummation
Devoutly to be wished. To draw — to skin ;
To skin ! perchance to burst — ay, there 's the rub !
For in the draw of three what cards may come,
When we have shuffled off th' uncertain pack,
Must give us pause. There 's the respect
That makes calamity of a bobtail flush ;
For who would bear the overwhelming blind,

The reckless straddle, the wait on the edge,
The insolence of pat hands and the lifts
That patient merit of the bluffer takes,
When he himself might be much better off
By simply passing?   Who would trays uphold,
And go out on a small progressive raise,
But that the dread of something after call —
The undiscovered ace-full, to whose strength
Such hands must bow, puzzles the will,
And makes us rather keep the chips we have
Than be curious about the hands we know not of.
Thus bluffing does make cowards of us all:
And thus the native hue of a four-heart flush
Is sicklied with some dark and cussed club,
And speculators in a jack-pot's wealth
With this regard their interest turn away
And lose the right to open.

Anonymous.

TOOTHACHE

TO have it out or not. That is the question —
    Whether 't is better for the jaws to suffer
    The pangs and torments of an aching tooth,
Or to take steel against a host of troubles,
And, by extracting them, end them?   To pull —
        to tug! —
No more: and by a tug to say we end
The toothache and a thousand natural ills
The jaw is heir to.   'T is a consummation
Devoutly to be wished!   To pull — to tug! —

[19]

To tug — perchance to break !   Ay, there's the rub,
For in that wrench what agonies may come
When we have half dislodged the stubborn foe,
Must give us pause.   There's the respect
That makes an aching tooth of so long life.
For who would bear the whips and stings of pain,
The old wife's nostrum, dentist's contumely ;
The pangs of hope deferred, kind sleep's delay ;
The insolence of pity, and the spurns,
That patient sickness of the healthy takes,
When he himself might his quietus make
For one poor shilling ?   Who would fardels bear,
To groan and sink beneath a load of pain ? —
But that the dread of something lodged within
The linen-twisted forceps, from whose pangs
No jaw at ease returns, puzzles the will,
And makes it rather bear the ills it has
Than fly to others that it knows not of.
Thus dentists do make cowards of us all,
And thus the native hue of resolution
Is sicklied o'er with the pale cast of fear ;
And many a one, whose courage seeks the door,
With this regard his footsteps turns away,
Scared at the name of dentist.

Anonymous.

A DREARY SONG

WELL, don't cry, my little tiny boy,
     With hey, ho, the wind and the rain
     Amuse yourself, and break some toy,
For the rain it raineth every day.

Alas, for the grass on Papa's estate,
   With hey, ho, the wind and the rain,
He'll have to buy hay at an awful rate,
   For the rain it raineth every day.

Mamma, she can't go out for a drive,
   With hey, ho, the wind and the rain,
How cross she gets about four or five,
   For the rain it raineth every day.

If I were you I'd be off to bed,
   With hey, ho, the wind and the rain,
Or the damp will give you a cold in the head,
   For the rain it raineth every day.

A great while ago this song was done,
   With hey, ho, the wind and the rain,
And I, for one, cannot see it's fun,
   But the Dyces and the Colliers can — they say.
                    Shirley Brooks.

TO THE STALL-HOLDERS AT A FANCY FAIR

WITH pretty speech accost both old and
        young,
    And speak it trippingly upon the tongue;
But if you mouth it with a hoyden laugh,
With clumsy ogling and uncomely chaff —
As I have oft seen done at fancy fairs,
I had as lief a huckster sold my wares,

Avoid all so-called beautifying, dear.
Oh! it offends me to the soul to hear
The things that men among themselves will say
Of some *soi-disant* " beauty of the day,"
Whose face, when she with cosmetics has cloyed it,
Out-Rachels Rachel! pray you, girls, avoid it.
Neither be you too tame — but, ere you go,
Provide yourselves with sprigs of mistletoe;
Offer them coyly to the Roman herd —
But don't you suit " the action to the word,"
For in that very torrent of your passion
Remember modesty is still in fashion.
Oh, there be ladies whom I 've seen hold stalls —
Ladies of rank, my dear — to whom befalls
Neither the accent nor the gait of ladies;
So clumsily made up with Bloom of Cadiz,
Powder-rouge — lip-salve — that I 've fancied then
They were the work of Nature's journeymen.

W. S. Gilbert.

SONG

WITH a hey! and a hi! and a hey-ho rhyme!
  Oh, the shepherd lad
  He is ne'er so glad
As when he pipes, in the blossom-time,
  So rare!
While Kate picks by, yet looks not there.
  So rare! so rare!
With a hey! and a hi! and a ho!
The grasses curdle where the daisies blow!

With a hey! and a hi! and a hey-ho vow!
     Then he sips her face
     At the sweetest place —
And ho! how white is the hawthorn now! —
     So rare! —
And the daisied world rocks round them there.
     So rare! so rare!
With a hey! and a hi! and a ho!
The grasses curdle where the daisies blow!

               James Whitcomb Riley.

THE WHIST-PLAYER'S SOLILOQUY

TO trump, or not to trump, — that is the ques-
       tion:
   Whether 't is better in this case to notice
The leads and signals of outraged opponents,
Or to force trumps against a suit of diamonds,
And by opposing end them? To trump, — to
     take, —
No more; and by that trick to win the lead
And after that, return my partner's spades
For which he signalled, — 't is a consummation
Devoutly to be wished. To trump — to take, —
To take! perchance to win! Ay, there's the rub;
For if we win this game, what hands may come
When we have shuffled up these cards again.
Play to the score? ah! yes, there's the defect
That makes this Duplicate Whist so much like
     work.

For who would heed the theories of Hoyle,
The laws of Pole, the books of Cavendish,
The Short-Suit system, Leads American,
The Eleven Rule Finesse, The Fourth-best play,
The Influence of signals on The Ruff,
When he himself this doubtful trick might take
With a small two-spot ?   Who would hesitate,
But that the dread of something afterwards,
An undiscovered discard or forced lead
When playing the return, puzzles the will,
And makes us rather lose the tricks we have
To win the others that we know not of ?
Thus Duplicate Whist makes cowards of us all ;
And thus the native hue of Bumblepuppy
Is sicklied o'er with the pale cast of thought.
And good whist-players of great skill and judg-
          ment,
With this regard their formulas defy,
And lose the game by ruffing.

Carolyn Wells.

AFTER WITHER

ANSWER TO MASTER WITHER'S SONG, "SHALL I, WASTING IN DESPAIR?"

SHALL I, mine affections slack,
　　'Cause I see a woman's black?
　　Or myself, with care cast down,
'Cause I see a woman brown?
Be she blacker than the night,
Or the blackest jet in sight!
　　If she be not so to me,
　　What care I how black she be?

Shall my foolish heart be burst,
'Cause I see a woman's curst?
Or a thwarting hoggish nature
Joined in as bad a feature?
Be she curst or fiercer than
Brutish beast, or savage man!
　　If she be not so to me,
　　What care I how curst she be?

Shall a woman's vices make
Me her vices quite forsake?
Or her faults to me made known,
Make me think that I have none?

Be she of the most accurst,
And deserve the name of worst!
   If she be not so to me,
   What care I how bad she be?

'Cause her fortunes seem too low,
Shall I therefore let her go?
He that bears an humble mind
And with riches can be kind,
Think how kind a heart he'd have,
If he were some servile slave!
   And if that same mind I see
   What care I how poor she be?

Poor, or bad, or curst, or black,
I will ne'er the more be slack!
If she hate me (then believe!)
She shall die ere I will grieve!
If she like me when I woo
I can like and love her too!
   If that she be fit for me!
   What care I what others be?

Ben Jonson.

AFTER HERRICK

SONG

GATHER Kittens while you may,
    Time brings only Sorrow;
And the Kittens of To-day
Will be Old Cats To-morrow.

Oliver Herford.

TO JULIA UNDER LOCK AND KEY

(*A form of betrothal gift in America is an anklet
    secured by a padlock, of which the other party
    keeps the key*)

WHEN like a bud my Julia blows
    In lattice-work of silken hose,
    Pleasant I deem it is to note
How, 'neath the nimble petticoat,
Above her fairy shoe is set
The circumvolving zonulet.
And soothly for the lover's ear
A perfect bliss it is to hear
About her limb so lithe and lank
My Julia's ankle-bangle clank.

[27]

Not rudely tight, for 't were a sin
To corrugate her dainty skin;
Nor yet so large that it might fare
Over her foot at unaware;
But fashioned nicely with a view
To let her airy stocking through:
So as, when Julia goes to bed,
Of all her gear disburdenèd,
This ring at least she shall not doff
Because she cannot take it off.
And since thereof I hold the key,
She may not taste of liberty,
Not though she suffer from the gout,
Unless I choose to let her out.

Owen Seaman.

AFTER NURSERY RHYMES

AN IDYLL OF PHATTE AND LEENE

THE hale John Sprat — oft called for shortness,
    Jack —
    Had married — had, in fact, a wife — and she
Did worship him with wifely reverence.
He, who had loved her when she was a girl,
Compass'd her, too, with sweet observances;
E'en at the dinner table did it shine.
For he — liking no fat himself — he never did,
With jealous care piled up her plate with lean,
Not knowing that all lean was hateful to her.
And day by day she thought to tell him o 't,
And watched the fat go out with envious eye,
But could not speak for bashful delicacy.

At last it chanced that on a winter day,
The beef — a prize joint! — little was but fat;
So fat, that John had all his work cut out,
To snip out lean fragments for his wife,
Leaving, in very sooth, none for himself;
Which seeing, she spoke courage to her soul,
Took up her fork, and, pointing to the joint
Where 't was the fattest, piteously she said;
" Oh, husband! full of love and tenderness!
What is the cause that you so jealously

Pick out the lean for me.   I like it not!
Nay, loathe it—'t is on the fat that I would feast;
O me, I fear you do not like my taste!"

Then he, dropping his horny-handled carving knife,
Sprinkling therewith the gravy o'er her gown,
Answer'd, amazed: "What! you like fat, my wife!
And never told me.   Oh, this is not kind!
Think what your reticence has wrought for us;
How all the fat sent down unto the maid —
Who likes not fat — for such maids never do —
Has been put in the waste-tub, sold for grease,
And pocketed as servant's perquisite!
Oh, wife! this news is good; for since, perforce,
A joint must be not fat nor lean, but both;
Our different tastes will serve our purpose well;
For, while you eat the fat — the lean to me
Falls as my cherished portion.   Lo! 't is good!"
So henceforth — he that tells the tale relates —
In John Sprat's household waste was quite un-
    known;
For he the lean did eat, and she the fat,
And thus the dinner-platter was all cleared.

Anonymous.

NURSERY SONG IN PIDGIN ENGLISH

SINGEE a songee sick a pence,
    Pockee muchee lye;
Dozen two time blackee bird
    Cookee in e pie.

[30]

When him cutee topside
   Birdee bobbery sing;
Himee tinkee nicey dish
   Setee foree King!
Kingee in a talkee loom
   Countee muchee money;
Queeny in e kitchee,
   Chew-chee breadee honey.
Servant galo shakee,
   Hangee washee clothes;
Cho-chop comee blackie bird,
   Nipee off her nose!

Anonymous.

THE HOUSE THAT JACK BUILT

AND this reft house is that the which he built,
   Lamented Jack! and here his malt he piled.
   Cautious in vain! these rats that squeak so
      wild,
Squeak not unconscious of their father's guilt.
Did he not see her gleaming through the glade!
Belike 't was she, the maiden all forlorn.
What though she milked no cow with crumpled
   horn,
Yet, aye she haunts the dale where erst she strayed:
And aye before her stalks her amorous knight!
Still on his thighs their wonted brogues are worn,
And through those brogues, still tattered and betorn,
His hindward charms gleam an unearthly white.

Samuel Taylor Coleridge.

BOSTON NURSERY RHYMES

RHYME FOR A GEOLOGICAL BABY

TRILOBITE, Graptolite, Nautilus pie ;
  Seas were calcareous, oceans were dry.
  Eocene, miocene, pliocene Tuff,
Lias and Trias and that is enough.

RHYME FOR ASTRONOMICAL BABY

BYE Baby Bunting,
  Father 's gone star-hunting ;
  Mother 's at the telescope
Casting baby's horoscope.
Bye Baby Buntoid,
Father 's found an asteroid ;
Mother takes by calculation
The angle of its inclination.

RHYME FOR BOTANICAL BABY

LITTLE bo-peepals
  Has lost her sepals,
  And can't tell where to find them ;
In the involucre
By hook or by crook or
She 'll make up her mind not to mind them.

RHYME FOR A CHEMICAL BABY

OH, sing a song of phosphates,
　　Fibrine in a line,
　　Four-and-twenty follicles
In the van of time.

When the phosphorescence
　　Evoluted brain,
Superstition ended,
　　Men began to reign.

Rev. Joseph Cook.

A SONG OF A HEART

UPON a time I had a Heart,
　　And it was bright and gay;
　　And I gave it to a Lady fair
To have and keep alway.

She soothed it and she smoothed it
And she stabbed it till it bled;
She brightened it and lightened it
And she weighed it down with lead.

She flattered it and battered it
And she filled it full of gall;
Yet had I Twenty Hundred Hearts,
Still should she have them all.

Oliver Herford.

[33]

THE DOMICILE OF JOHN

BEHOLD the mansion reared by Daedal Jack!
　　See the malt stored in many a plethoric sack,
　　　In the proud cirque of Ivan's Bivouac!

Mark how the rat's felonious fangs invade
　　The golden stores in John's pavilion laid!

Anon, with velvet foot and Tarquin strides,
　　Subtle Grimalkin to his quarry glides;
Grimalkin grim, that slew the fierce rodent,
　　Whose tooth insidious Johann's sackcloth rent!

Lo! Now the deep-mouthed canine foe's assault!
　　That vexed the avenger of the stolen malt,
Stored in the hallowed precincts of that hall,
　　That rose complete at Jack's creative call.

Here stalks the impetuous cow with the crumpled
　　　horn,
　　Whereon the exacerbating hound was torn
Who bayed the feline slaughter-beast that slew
　　The rat predaceous, whose keen fangs ran
　　　through
The textile fibres that involved the grain
　　That lay in Hans' inviolate domain.

Here walks forlorn the damsel crowned with rue,
　　Lactiferous spoils from vaccine dugs who drew
Of that corniculate beast whose tortuous horn
　　Tossed to the clouds, in fierce vindictive scorn,

The baying hound whose braggart bark and stir
   Arched the lithe spine and reared the indignant
      fur
Of puss, that, with verminicidal claw,
   Struck the weird rat, in whose insatiate maw
Lay reeking malt, that erst in Juan's courts we saw.

Robed in senescent garb, that seems, in sooth,
   Too long a prey to Chronos' iron tooth,
Behold the man whose amorous lips incline
   Full with young Eros' osculative sign,
To the lorn maiden whose lactalbic hands
   Drew albulactic wealth from lacteal glands
Of that immortal bovine, by whose horn
   Distort, to realms ethereal was borne
The beast catulean, vexer of that sly
   Ulysses quadrupedal, who made die
The old mordaceous rat that dared devour
   Antecedaneous ale in John's domestic bower.

Lo! Here, with hirsute honors doffed, succinct
   Of saponaceous locks, the priest who linked
In Hymen's golden bands the man unthrift
   Whose means exiguous stared from many a rift,
E'en as he kissed the virgin all forlorn
   Who milked the cow with implicated horn,
Who in fierce wrath the canine torturer skied,
   That dared to vex the insidious muricide,
Who let auroral effluence through the pelt
   Of that sly rat that robbed the palace that Jack
      built.

The loud cantankerous Shanghai comes at last,
  Whose shouts aroused the shorn ecclesiast,
Who sealed the vows of Hymen's sacrament
  To him who, robed in garments indigent,
Exosculates the damsel lachrymose,
  The emulgator of the horned brute morose
That on gyrated horn, to heaven's high vault
  Hurled up, with many a tortuous somersault,
The low bone-cruncher, whose hot wrath pursued
  The scratching sneak, that waged eternal feud
With long-tailed burglar, who his lips would smack
    On farinaceous wealth, that filled the halls of
      Jack.

Vast limbed and broad the farmer comes at length,
  Whose cereal care supplied the vital strength
Of chanticleer, whose matutinal cry
  Roused the quiescent form and ope'd the eye
Of razor-loving cleric, who in bands
  Connubial linked the intermixed hands
Of him, whose rent apparel gaped apart,
  And the lorn maiden with lugubrious heart,
Her who extraught the exuberant lactic flow
  Of nutriment from that cornigerent cow,
Eumenidal executor of fate,
  That to sidereal altitudes elate
Cerberus, who erst with fang lethiferous
  Left lacerate Grimalkin latebrose —
That killed the rat
  That ate the malt
    That lay in the house that Jack built.

                              A. Pope.

MARY AND THE LAMB

MARY, — what melodies mingle
    To murmur her musical name!
    It makes all one's finger-tips tingle
Like fagots, the food of the flame;
About her an ancient tradition
    A romance delightfully deep
Has woven in juxtaposition
    With one little sheep, —

One dear little lamb that would follow
    Her footsteps, unwearily fain.
Down dale, over hill, over hollow,
    To school and to hamlet again;
A gentle companion, whose beauty
    Consisted in snow-driven fleece,
And whose most imperative duty
    Was keeping the peace.

His eyes were as beads made of glassware,
    His lips were coquettishly curled,
His capers made many a lass swear
    His caper-sauce baffled the world;
His tail had a wag when it relished
    A sip of the milk in the pail, —
And this fact has largely embellished
    The wag of this tale.

One calm summer day when the sun was
    A great golden globe in the sky,
One mild summer morn when the fun was
    Unspeakably clear in his eye,
He tagged after exquisite Mary,
    And over the threshold of school
He tripped in a temper contrary,
    And splintered the rule.

A great consternation was kindled
    Among all the scholars, and some
Confessed their affection had dwindled
    For lamby, and looked rather glum;
But Mary's schoolmistress quick beckoned
    The children away from the jam,
And said, *sotto voce*, she reckoned
    That Mame loved the lamb.

Then all up the spine of the rafter
    There ran a most risible shock,
And sorrow was sweetened with laughter
    At this little lamb of the flock;
And out spoke the schoolmistress Yankee,
    With rather a New Hampshire whine,
" Dear pupils, sing Moody and Sankey,
    Hymn ' Ninety and Nine.' "

Now after this music had finished,
    And silence again was restored,
The ardor of lamby diminished,
    His quips for a moment were floored.

Then cried he, " Bah-ed children, you blundered
  When singing that psalmistry, quite.
I 'm labelled by Mary, ' Old Hundred,'
  And I 'm labelled right."

Then vanished the lambkin in glory,
  A halo of books round his head :
What furthermore happened the story,
  Alackaday ! cannot be said.
And Mary, the musical maid, is
  To-day but a shadow in time ;
Her epitaph, too, I 'm afraid is
  Writ only in rhyme.

She 's sung by the cook at her ladle
  That stirs up the capering sauce ;
She 's sung by the nurse at the cradle
  When ba-ba is restless and cross ;
And lamby, whose virtues were legion,
  Dwells ever in songs that we sing,
He makes a nice dish in this region
  To eat in the spring!
                                        Frank Dempster Sherman.

AFTER WALLER

THE AESTHETE TO THE ROSE

GO, flaunting Rose!
    Tell her that wastes her love on thee,
        That she nought knows
Of the New Cult, Intensity,
If sweet and fair to her you be.

    Tell her that's young,
Or who in health and bloom takes pride,
    That bards have sung
Of a new youth — at whose sad side
Sickness and pallor aye abide.

    Small is the worth
Of Beauty in crude charms attired.
    She must shun mirth,
Have suffered, fruitlessly desired,
And wear no flush by hope inspired.

    Then die, that she
May learn that Death is passing fair;
    May read in thee
How little of Art's praise they share,
Who are not sallow, sick, and spare!

Punch.

[40]

AFTER DRYDEN

THREE BLESSINGS

THREE brightest blessings of this thirsty race,
  (Whence sprung and when I don't propose
    to trace);
Pale brandy, potent spirit of the night,
Brisk soda, welcome when the morn is bright;
To make the third, combine the other two,
The force of nature can no further go.

Anonymous.

OYSTER-CRABS

THREE viands in three different courses
    served,
  Received the commendation they deserved.
The first in succulence all else surpassed;
The next in flavor; and in both, the last.
For Nature's forces could no further go;
To make the third, she joined the other two.

Carolyn Wells.

AFTER DR. WATTS

THE VOICE OF THE LOBSTER

" 'TIS the voice of the Lobster: I heard him
declare
'You have baked me too brown, I must
sugar my hair.'
As a duck with its eyelids, so he with his nose
Trims his belt and his buttons, and turns out
his toes.
When the sands are all dry, he is gay as a lark,
And will talk in contemptuous tones of the
Shark:
But, when the tide rises and sharks are around,
His voice has a timid and tremulous sound.

" I passed by his garden, and marked, with one eye,
How the Owl and the Panther were sharing a pie;
The Panther took pie-crust, and gravy, and meat,
While the Owl had the dish as its share of the
treat.
When the pie was all finished, the Owl, as a
boon,
Was kindly permitted to pocket the spoon;
While the Panther received knife and fork with
a growl,
And concluded the banquet by —— "

Lewis Carroll.

[42]

THE CROCODILE

HOW doth the little crocodile
   Improve his shining tail,
    And pour the waters of the Nile
On every golden scale!

How cheerfully he seems to grin,
   How neatly spreads his claws,
And welcomes little fishes in,
   With gently smiling jaws!

Lewis Carroll.

AFTER GOLDSMITH

WHEN LOVELY WOMAN

WHEN lovely woman wants a favor,
    And finds, too late, that man won't
        bend,
What earthly circumstance can save her
    From disappointment in the end?

The only way to bring him over,
    The last experiment to try,
Whether a husband or a lover,
    If he have feeling is — to cry.

Phœbe Cary.

AFTER BURNS

GAELIC SPEECH; OR, "AULD LANG SYNE" DONE UP IN TARTAN

SHOULD Gaelic speech be e'er forgot,
　　And never brocht to min',
　　For she'll be spoke in Paradise
In the days of auld lang syne.
When Eve, all fresh in beauty's charms,
　　First met fond Adam's view,
The first word that he'll spoke till her
　　Was, "*cumar achum dhu.*"

And Adam in his garden fair,
　　Whene'er the day did close,
The dish that he'll to supper teuk
　　Was always Athole brose.
When Adam from his leafy bower
　　Cam oot at broke o' day,
He'll always for his morning teuk
　　A quaich o' usquebae.

An' when wi' Eve he'll had a crack,
　　He'll teuk his sneeshin' horn,
An' on the tap ye'll well mitch mark
　　A pony praw Cairngorm.

[45]

The sneeshin' mull is fine, my friens —
  The sneeshin' mull is gran';
We'll teukta hearty sneesh, my friens,
  And pass frae han' to han'.

When man first fan the want o' claes,
  The wind an' cauld to fleg.
He twisted roon' about his waist
  The tartan philabeg.
An' music first on earth was heard
  In Gaelic accents deep,
When Jubal in his oxter squeezed
  The blether o' a sheep.

The praw bagpipes is gran', my friens,
  The praw bagpipes is fine;
We'll teukta nother pibroch yet,
  For the days o' auld lang syne!

Anonymous.

MY FOE

JOHN ALCOHOL, my foe, John,
    When we were first acquaint,
  I'd siller in my pockets, John,
  Which noo, ye ken, I want;
I spent it all in treating, John,
  Because I loved you so;
But mark ye, how you've treated me,
  John Alcohol, my foe.

[46]

John Alcohol, my foe, John,
  We 've been ower lang together,
Sae ye maun tak' ae road, John,
  And I will take anither;
Foe we maun tumble down, John,
  If hand in hand we go;
And I shall hae the bill to pay,
  John Alcohol, my foe.

John Alcohol, my foe, John,
  Ye 've blear'd out a' my een,
And lighted up my nose, John,
  A fiery sign atween!
My hands wi' palsy shake, John,
  My locks are like the snow;
Ye 'll surely be the death of me,
  John Alcohol, my foe.

John Alcohol, my foe, John,
  'T was love to you, I ween,
That gart me rise sae ear', John,
  And sit sae late at e'en;
The best o' friens maun part, John,
  It grieves me sair, ye know;
But "we 'll nae mair to yon town,"
  John Alcohol, my foe.

John Alcohol, my foe, John,
  Ye 've wrought me muckle skaith;
And yet to part wi' you, John,
  I own I 'm unko' laith;

But I 'll join the temperance ranks, John,
  Ye needna say me no;
It 's better late than ne'er do weel,
  John Alcohol, my foe.

Anonymous.

RIGID BODY SINGS

GIN a body meet a body
      Flyin' through the air,
    Gin a body hit a body,
  Will it fly? and where?
Ilka impact has its measure,
  Ne'er a' ane hae I,
Yet a' the lads they measure me,
  Or, at least, they try.

Gin a body meet a body
  Altogether free,
How they travel afterwards
  We do not always see.
Ilka problem has its method
  By analytics high;
For me, I ken na ane o' them,
  But what the waur am I?

J. C. Maxwell.

AFTER
CATHERINE FANSHAWE

COCKNEY ENIGMA ON THE
LETTER H

I DWELLS in the Herth and I breathes in the
     Hair;
   If you searches the Hocean you'll find that I'm
     there;
The first of all Hangels in Holympus am Hi,
Yet I'm banished from 'Eaven, expelled from on
     'Igh.
But tho' on this Horb I am destined to grovel,
I'm ne'er seen in an 'Ouse, in an 'Ut, nor an
     'Ovel;
Not an 'Oss nor an 'Unter e'er bears me, alas!
But often I'm found on the top of a Hass.
I resides in a Hattic and loves not to roam,
And yet I'm invariably habsent from 'Ome.
Tho' 'ushed in the 'Urricane, of the Hatmosphere
     part,
I enters no 'Ed, I creeps into no 'Art,
But look and you'll see in the Heye I appear.
Only 'ark and you'll 'ear me just breathe in the
     Hear;
Tho' in sex not an 'E, I am (strange paradox!),
Not a bit of an 'Effer, but partly a Hox.

[49]

Of Heternity Hi'm the beginning! and mark,
Tho' I goes not with Noar, I'm the first in the
    Hark.
I'm never in 'Elth — have with Fysic no power;
I dies in a Month, but comes back in a Hour.

Horace Mayhew.

AFTER WORDSWORTH

ON WORDSWORTH

HE lived amidst th' untrodden ways
    To Rydal Lake that lead;
  A bard whom there was none to praise
And very few to read.

Behind a cloud his mystic sense,
  Deep hidden, who can spy?
Bright as the night when not a star
  Is shining in the sky.

Unread his works — his "Milk White Doe"
  With dust is dark and dim;
It's still in Longmans' shop, and oh!
  The difference to him.

                                Anonymous.

JACOB

HE dwelt among "Apartments let,"
    About five stories high;
  A man, I thought, that none would get,
And very few would try.

A boulder, by a larger stone
　Half hidden in the mud,
Fair as a man when only one
　Is in the neighborhood.

He lived unknown, and few could tell
　When Jacob was not free;
But he has got a wife — and O!
　The difference to me!

Phœbe Cary.

FRAGMENT IN IMITATION OF WORDSWORTH

THERE is a river clear and fair,
　　'T is neither broad nor narrow;
　　It winds a little here and there —
It winds about like any hare;
And then it holds as straight a course
As, on the turnpike road, a horse,
Or, through the air, an arrow.

The trees that grow upon the shore
Have grown a hundred years or more;
So long there is no knowing:
Old Daniel Dobson does not know
When first those trees began to grow;
But still they grew, and grew, and grew,
As if they 'd nothing else to do,
But ever must be growing.

[52]

The impulses of air and sky
Have reared their stately heads so high,
And clothed their boughs with green;
Their leaves the dews of evening quaff, —
And when the wind blows loud and keen,
I 've seen the jolly timbers laugh,
And shake their sides with merry glee —
Wagging their heads in mockery.

Fixed are their feet in solid earth
Where winds can never blow;
But visitings of deeper birth
Have reached their roots below.
For they have gained the river's brink,
And of the living waters drink.

There 's little Will, a five years' child —
He is my youngest boy;
To look on eyes so fair and wild,
It is a very joy.
He hath conversed with sun and shower,
And dwelt with every idle flower,
As fresh and gay as them.
He loiters with the briar-rose, —
The blue-bells are his play-fellows,
That dance upon their slender stem.

And I have said, my little Will,
Why should he not continue still
A thing of Nature's rearing?
A thing beyond the world's control —
A living vegetable soul, —
No human sorrow fearing.

[53]

It were a blessed sight to see
That child become a willow-tree,
His brother trees among.
He 'd be four times as tall as me,
And live three times as long.

Catherine M. Fanshawe.

JANE SMITH

I JOURNEYED, on a winter's day,
Across the lonely wold;
No bird did sing upon the spray,
And it was very cold.

I had a coach with horses four,
Three white (though one was black),
And on they went the common o'er,
Nor swiftness did they lack.

A little girl ran by the side,
And she was pinched and thin.
"Oh, please, sir, do give me a ride!
I 'm fetching mother's gin."

"Enter my coach, sweet child," said I,
"For you shall ride with me;
And I will get you your supply
Of mother's eau-de-vie."

[54]

The publican was stern and cold,
    And said: " Her mother's score
Is writ, as you shall soon behold,
    Behind the bar-room door ! "

I blotted out the score with tears,
    And paid the money down;
And took the maid of thirteen years
    Back to her mother's town.

And though the past with surges wild
    Fond memories may sever,
The vision of that happy child
    Will leave my spirits never !
                        Rudyard Kipling.

ONLY SEVEN

(*A Pastoral Story after Wordsworth*)

I MARVELLED why a simple child,
        That lightly draws its breath,
    Should utter groans so very wild,
And look as pale as Death.

Adopting a parental tone,
    I ask'd her why she cried;
The damsel answered with a groan,
    " I 've got a pain inside !

"I thought it would have sent me mad
    Last night about eleven."
Said I, "What is it makes you bad?
How many apples have you had?"
    She answered, "Only seven!"

"And are you sure you took no more,
    My little maid?" quoth I;
"Oh, please, sir, mother gave me four,
    But they were in a pie!"

"If that's the case," I stammer'd out,
    "Of course you've had eleven."
The maiden answered with a pout,
    "I ain't had more nor seven!"

I wonder'd hugely what she meant,
    And said, "I'm bad at riddles;
But I know where little girls are sent
    For telling taradiddles.

"Now, if you won't reform," said I,
    "You'll never go to Heaven."
But all in vain; each time I try,
That little idiot makes reply,
    "I ain't had more nor seven!"

POSTSCRIPT

To borrow Wordsworth's name was wrong,
    Or slightly misapplied;
And so I'd better call my song,
    "Lines after Ache-Inside."

                  Henry S. Leigh.

LUCY LAKE

POOR Lucy Lake was overgrown,
   But somewhat underbrained.
   She did not know enough, I own,
To go in when it rained.

Yet Lucy was constrained to go;
   Green bedding, — you infer.
Few people knew she died, but oh,
   The difference to her!

Newton Mackintosh.

AFTER SIR WALTER SCOTT

YOUNG LOCHINVAR

(*The true story in blank verse*)

OH! young Lochinvar has come out of the
West,
  Thro' all the wide border his horse has no
    equal,
Having cost him forty-five dollars at the market,
Where good nags, fresh from the country,
With burrs still in their tails are selling
For a song; and save his good broadsword
He weapon had none, except a seven shooter
Or two, a pair of brass knuckles, and an Arkansaw

Toothpick in his boot, so, comparatively speaking,
He rode all unarmed, and he rode all alone,
Because there was no one going his way.
He stayed not for brake, and he stopped not for
Toll-gates; he swam the Eske River where ford
There was none, and saved fifteen cents
In ferriage, but lost his pocket-book, containing
Seventeen dollars and a half, by the operation.

Ere he alighted at the Netherby mansion
He stopped to borrow a dry suit of clothes,
And this delayed him considerably, so when

He arrived the bride had consented — the gallant
Came late — for a laggard in love and a dastard in
    war
Was to wed the fair Ellen, and the guests had
    assembled.

So boldly he entered the Netherby Hall
Among bridesmen and kinsmen and brothers and
Brothers-in-law and forty or fifty cousins;
Then spake the bride's father, his hand on his sword
(For the poor craven bridegroom ne'er opened his
    head):

"Oh, come ye in peace here, or come ye in anger,
Or to dance at our bridal, young Lord Lochinvar?"
"I long wooed your daughter, and she will tell you
I have the inside track in the free-for-all
For her affections!   My suit you denied; but let
That pass, while I tell you, old fellow, that love
Swells like the Solway, but ebbs like its tide,
And now I am come with this lost love of mine
To lead but one measure, drink one glass of beer;
There are maidens in Scotland more lovely by far
That would gladly be bride to yours very truly."

The bride kissed the goblet, the knight took it up,
He quaffed off the nectar and threw down the mug,
Smashing it into a million pieces, while
He remarked that he was the son of a gun
From Seven-up and run the Number Nine.
She looked down to blush, but she looked up again
For she well understood the wink in his eye;

He took her soft hand ere her mother could
Interfere, "Now tread we a measure; first four
Half right and left; swing," cried young Lochinvar.

One touch to her hand and one word in her ear,
When they reached the hall-door and the charger
Stood near on three legs eating post-hay;
So light to the croup the fair lady he swung,
Then leaped to the saddle before her.
"She is won! we are gone! over bank! bush, and
    spar,
They 'll have swift steeds that follow " — but in
    the

Excitement of the moment he had forgotten
To untie the horse, and the poor brute could
Only gallop in a little circus around the
Hitching-post; so the old gent collared
The youth and gave him the awfullest lambasting
That was ever heard of on Canobie Lee;
So dauntless in war and so daring in love,
Have ye e'er heard of gallant like young Lochinvar?

Anonymous.

AFTER COLERIDGE

THE ANCIENT MARINER

*(The Wedding Guest's Version of the Affair from His
Point of View)*

IT is an Ancient Mariner,
   And he stoppeth one of three —
   In fact he coolly took my arm —
" There was a ship," quoth he.

" Bother your ships ! " said I, " is this
   The time a yarn to spin ?
This is a wedding, don't you see,
   And I am next of kin.

" The wedding breakfast has begun,
   We 're hungry as can be —
Hold off !   Unhand me, longshore man ! "
   With that his hand dropt he.

But there was something in his eye,
   That made me sick and ill,
Yet forced to listen to his yarn —
   The Mariner 'd had his will.

While Tom and Harry went their way
　　I sat upon a stone —
So queer on Fanny's wedding day
　　Me sitting there alone !

Then he began, that Mariner,
　　To rove from pole to pole,
In one long-winded, lengthened-out,
　　Eternal rigmarole,

About a ship in which he 'd sailed,
　　Though whither, goodness knows,
Where "ice will split with a thunder-fit,"
　　And every day it snows.

And then about a precious bird
　　Of some sort or another,
That — was such nonsense ever heard ? —
　　Used to control the weather !

Now, at this bird the Mariner
　　Resolved to have a shy,
And laid it low with his cross-bow —
　　And then the larks ! My eye !

For loss of that uncommon fowl,
　　They could n't get a breeze ;
And there they stuck, all out of luck,
　　And rotted on the seas.

The crew all died, or seemed to die,
    And he was left alone
With that queer bird.   You never heard
    What games were carried on!

At last one day he stood and watched
    The fishes in the sea,
And said, " I'm blest! " and so the ship
    Was from the spell set free.

And it began to rain and blow,
    And as it rained and blew,
The dead got up and worked the ship —
    That was a likely crew!

However, somehow he escaped,
    And got again to land,
But mad as any hatter, say,
    From Cornhill to the Strand.

For he believes that certain folks
    Are singled out by fate,
To whom this cock-and-bull affair
    Of his he must relate.

Describing all the incidents,
    And painting all the scenes,
As sailors will do in the tales
    They tell to the Marines.

Confound the Ancient Mariner!
   I knew I should be late;
And so it was; the wedding guests
   Had all declined to wait.

Another had my place, and gave
   My toast; and sister Fan
Said " 'T was a shame.   What could you want
   With that seafaring man?"

I felt like one that had been stunned
   Through all this wrong and scorn;
A sadder and a later man
   I rose the morrow morn.   *Anonymous.*

STRIKING

IT was a railway passenger,
   And he lept out jauntilie.
     " Now up and bear, thou stout portèr,
My two chattèls to me.

" Bring hither, bring hither my bag so red,
   And portmanteau so brown;
(They lie in the van, for a trusty man
   He labelled them London town:)

" And fetch me eke a cabman bold,
   That I may be his fare, his fare;
And he shall have a good shilling,
If by two of the clock he do me bring
   To the Terminus, Euston Square."

"Now, — so to thee the saints alway,
  Good gentleman, give luck, —
As never a cab may I find this day,
  For the cabman wights have struck.

And now, I wis, at the Red Post Inn,
  Or else at the Dog and Duck,
Or at Unicorn Blue, or at Green Griffin,
The nut-brown ale and the fine old gin
  Right pleasantly they do suck."

"Now rede me aright, thou stout portèr,
  What were it best that I should do :
For woe is me, an' I reach not there
  Or ever the clock strike two."

"I have a son, a lytel son ;
  Fleet is his foot as the wild roebuck's :
Give him a shilling, and eke a brown,
And he shall carry thy fardels down
To Euston, or half over London town,
  On one of the station trucks."

Then forth in a hurry did they twain fare,
The gent and the son of the stout portèr,
Who fled like an arrow, nor turned a hair,
  Through all the mire and muck :
"A ticket, a ticket, sir clerk, I pray :
For by two of the clock must I needs away."
"That may hardly be," the clerk did say,
  "For indeed — the clocks have struck."

Charles S. Calverley.

AFTER SOUTHEY

THE OLD MAN'S COLD AND HOW HE GOT IT

(By Northey-Southey-Eastey-Westey)

" YOU are cold, Father William," the young
man cried,
        " You shake and you shiver, I say;
You 've a cold, Father William, your nose it is red,
    Now tell me the reason, I pray."

" In the days of my youth," Father William
    replied —
    (He was a dissembling old man)
" I put lumps of ice in my grandpapa's boots,
    And snowballed my Aunt Mary Ann."

" Go along, Father William," the young man cried,
    " You are trying it on, sir, to-day;
What makes your teeth chatter like bone casta-
    nets?
    Come tell me the reason, I pray."

" In the days of my youth," Father William replied,
    " I went to the North Pole with Parry;
And now, my sweet boy, the Arc-tic doloreaux
    Plays with this old man the Old Harry."

[66]

"Get out! Father William," the young man cried.
"Come, you should n't go on in this way;
You are funny, but still you 've a frightful bad cold —
Now tell me the reason, I pray."

"I am cold, then, dear youth," Father William
replied;
"I 've a cold, my impertinent son,
Because for some weeks my coals have been bought
At forty-eight shillings a ton!"

FATHER WILLIAM

"YOU are old, Father William," the young
man said,
"And your hair has become very white;
And yet you incessantly stand on your head —
Do you think, at your age, it is right?"

"In my youth," Father William replied to his son,
"I feared it might injure the brain;
But now that I 'm perfectly sure I have none,
Why, I do it again and again."

"You are old," said the youth, "as I mentioned
before,
And grown most uncommonly fat;
Yet you turned a back-somersault in at the door —
Pray what is the reason of that?"

"In my youth," said the sage, as he shook his gray
    locks,
" I kept all my limbs very supple
By the use of this ointment — one shilling the box —
    Allow me to sell you a couple."

" You are old," said the youth, " and your jaws are
    too weak
    For anything tougher than suet;
Yet you finished the goose, with the bones and the
    beak;
    Pray, how did you manage to do it?"

" In my youth," said his father, " I took to the law,
    And argued each case with my wife;
And the muscular strength which it gave to my jaw,
    Has lasted the rest of my life."

" You are old," said the youth, " one would hardly
    suppose
    That your eye was as steady as ever;
Yet you balanced an eel on the end of your nose —
    What made you so awfully clever?"

" I have answered three questions and that is
    enough,"
    Said his father; " don't give yourself airs!
Do you think I can listen all day to such stuff?
    Be off, or I 'll kick you downstairs!"

Lewis Carroll.

LADY JANE

(Sapphics)

DOWN the green hill-side fro' the castle
    window
    Lady Jane spied Bill Amaranth a-workin';
Day by day watched him go about his ample
        Nursery garden.

Cabbages thriv'd there, wi' a mort o' green-stuff —
Kidney beans, broad beans, onions, tomatoes,
Artichokes, seakale, vegetable marrows,
        Early potatoes.

Lady Jane cared not very much for all these:
What she cared much for was a glimpse o' Willum
Strippin' his brown arms wi' a view to horti-
        Cultural effort.

Little guessed Willum, never extra-vain, that
Up the green hill-side, i' the gloomy castle,
Feminine eyes could so delight to view his
        Noble proportions.

Only one day while, in an innocent mood,
Moppin' his brow (cos 'twas a trifle sweaty)
With a blue kerchief — lo, he spies a white un
        Coyly responding.

Oh, delightsome Love! Not a jot do *you* care
For the restrictions set on human inter-
Course by cold-blooded social refiners;
    Nor do I, neither.

Day by day, peepin' fro' behind the bean-sticks,
Willum observed that scrap o' white a-wavin',
Till his hot sighs out-growin' all repression
    Busted his weskit.

Lady Jane's guardian was a haughty Peer, who
Clung to old creeds and had a nasty temper;
Can we blame Willum that he hardly cared to
    Risk a refusal?

Year by year found him busy 'mid the bean-sticks,
Wholly uncertain how on earth to take steps.
Thus for eighteen years he beheld the maiden
    Wave fro' her window.

But the nineteenth spring, i' the castle post-bag,
Came by book-post Bill's catalogue o' seedlings
Mark'd wi' blue ink at " Paragraphs relatin'
    Mainly to Pumpkins."

" W. A. can," so the Lady Jane read,
" Strongly commend that very noble Gourd, the
Lady Jane, first-class medal, ornamental;
    Grows to a great height."

Scarce a year arter, by the scented hedgerows —
Down the mown hill-side, fro' the castle gateway —
Came a long train and, i' the midst, a black bier,
                    Easily shouldered.

"Whose is yon corse that, thus adorned wi' gourd
        leaves
Forth ye bear with slow step?"   A mourner
        answer'd,
"'T is the poor clay-cold body Lady Jane grew
                    Tired to abide in."

"Delve my grave quick, then, for I die to-morrow.
Delve it one furlong fro' the kidney bean-sticks,
Where I may dream she's goin' on precisely
                    As she was used to."

Hardly died Bill when, fro' the Lady Jane's grave,
Crept to his white death-bed a lovely pumpkin:
Climb'd the house wall and over-arched his head wi'
                    Billowy verdure.

Simple this tale! — but delicately perfumed
As the sweet roadside honeysuckle.   That's why,
Difficult though its metre was to tackle,
                    I'm glad I wrote it.
                              A. T. Quiller-Couch.

AFTER CAMPBELL

THE NEW ARRIVAL

THERE came to port last Sunday night
    The queerest little craft,
    Without an inch of rigging on;
I looked and looked — and laughed!
It seemed so curious that she
    Should cross the Unknown water,
And moor herself within my room —
    My daughter! Oh, my daughter!

Yet by these presents witness all
    She's welcome fifty times,
And comes consigned in hope and love —
    And common-metre rhymes.
She has no manifest but this,
    No flag floats o'er the water;
She's too new for the British Lloyds —
    My daughter! Oh, my daughter!

Ring out, wild bells — and tame ones too,
    Ring out the lover's moon;
Ring in the little worsted socks,
    Ring in the bib and spoon.
Ring out the muse, ring in the nurse,
    Ring in the milk and water;
Away with paper, pen, and ink —
    My daughter! Oh, my daughter!
George Washington Cable.

JOHN THOMPSON'S DAUGHTER

A FELLOW near Kentucky's clime
    Cries, " Boatman, do not tarry,
    And I 'll give thee a silver dime
To row us o'er the ferry."

" Now, who would cross the Ohio,
    This dark and stormy water ? "
" O, I am this young lady's beau,
    And she, John Thompson's daughter.

" We 've fled before her father's spite
    With great precipitation;
And should he find us here to-night,
    I 'd lose my reputation.

" They 've missed the girl and purse beside,
    His horsemen hard have pressed me;
And who will cheer my bonny bride,
    If yet they shall arrest me ? "

Out spoke the boatman then in time,
    " You shall not fail, don't fear it ;
I 'll go, not for your silver dime,
    But for your manly spirit.

" And by my word, the bonny bird
    In danger shall not tarry;
For though a storm is coming on,
    I 'll row you o'er the ferry."

[73]

By this the wind more fiercely rose,
    The boat was at the landing;
And with the drenching rain their clothes
    Grew wet where they were standing.

But still, as wilder rose the wind,
    And as the night grew drearer;
Just back a piece came the police,
    Their tramping sounded nearer.

" Oh, haste thee, haste!" the lady cries,
    " It's anything but funny;
I'll leave the light of loving eyes,
    But not my father's money!"

And still they hurried in the face
    Of wind and rain unsparing;
John Thompson reached the landing place —
    His wrath was turned to swearing.

For by the lightning's angry flash,
    His child he did discover;
One lovely hand held all the cash,
    And one was round her lover!

" Come back, come back!" he cried in woe,
    Across the stormy water;
" But leave the purse, and you may go,
    My daughter, oh, my daughter!"

'T was vain ; they reached the other shore
　　(Such doom the Fates assign us) ;
The gold he piled went with his child,
　　And he was left there *minus*.
Phœbe Cary.

AFTER THOMAS MOORE

THE LAST CIGAR

'TIS a last choice Havana
    I hold here alone;
      All its fragrant companions
In perfume have flown.
No more of its kindred
    To gladden the eye,
So my empty cigar case
    I close with a sigh.

I 'll not leave thee, thou lone one,
    To pine; but the stem
I 'll bite off and light thee
    To waft thee to them.
And gently I 'll scatter
    The ashes you shed,
As your soul joins its mates in
    A cloud overhead.

All pleasure is fleeting,
    It blooms to decay;
From the weeds' glowing circle
    The ash drops away.
A last whiff is taken,
    The butt-end is thrown,
And with empty cigar-case,
    I sit all alone.   *Anonymous.*

'TWAS EVER THUS

I NEVER bought a young gazelle,
　　To glad me with its soft black eye,
　But, when it came to know me well,
　'T was sure to butt me on the sly.

I never drilled a cockatoo,
　　To speak with almost human lip,
But, when a pretty phrase it knew,
　　'T was sure to give some friend a nip.

I never trained a collie hound
　　To be affectionate and mild,
But, when I thought a prize I 'd found,
　　'T was sure to bite my youngest child.

I never kept a tabby kit
　　To cheer my leisure with its tricks,
But, when we all grew fond of it,
　　'T was sure to catch the neighbor's chicks.

I never reared a turtle-dove,
　　To coo all day with gentle breath,
But, when its life seemed one of love,
　　'T was sure to peck its mate to death

I never — well I never yet —
　　And I have spent no end of pelf —
Invested money in a pet
　　That did n't misconduct itself.

Anonymous.

"THERE'S A BOWER OF BEAN-VINES"

THERE'S a bower of bean-vines in Benjamin's yard,
 And the cabbages grow round it, planted for
  greens;
In the time of my childhood 't was terribly hard
 To bend down the bean-poles, and pick off the
  beans.

That bower and its products I never forget,
 But oft, when my landlady presses me hard,
I think, are the cabbages growing there yet,
 Are the bean-vines still bearing in Benjamin's
  yard?

No, the bean-vines soon withered that once used
  to wave,
 But some beans had been gathered, the last that
  hung on;
And a soup was distilled in a kettle, that gave
 All the fragrance of summer when summer was
  gone.

Thus memory draws from delight, ere it dies,
 An essence that breathes of it awfully hard;
As thus good to my taste as 't was then to my eyes,
 Is that bower of bean-vines in Benjamin's yard.
     Phœbe Cary.

DISASTER

’TWAS ever thus from childhood’s hour!
   My fondest hopes would not decay;
   I never loved a tree or flower
Which was the first to fade away!
The garden, where I used to delve
   Short-frock’d, still yields me pinks in plenty;
The pear-tree that I climbed at twelve
   I see still blossoming, at twenty.

I never nursed a dear gazelle;
   But I was given a parroquet —
(How I did nurse him if unwell!)
   He’s imbecile, but lingers yet.
He’s green, with an enchanting tuft;
   He melts me with his small black eye;
He’d look inimitable stuffed,
   And knows it — but he will not die!

I had a kitten — I was rich
   In pets — but all too soon my kitten
Became a full-sized cat, by which
   I’ve more than once been scratched and bitten.
And when for sleep her limbs she curl’d
   One day beside her untouch’d plateful,
And glided calmly from the world,
   I freely own that I was grateful.

[79]

And then I bought a dog — a queen !
    Ah, Tiny, dear departing pug !
She lives, but she is past sixteen
    And scarce can crawl across the rug.
I loved her beautiful and kind ;
    Delighted in her pert bow-wow ;
But now she snaps if you don't mind ;
    'T were lunacy to love her now.

I used to think, should e'er mishap
    Betide my crumple-visaged Ti,
In shape of prowling thief, or trap,
    Or coarse bull-terrier — I should die.
But ah ! disasters have their use,
    And life might e'en be too sunshiny ;
Nor would I make myself a goose,
    If some big dog should swallow Tiny.

               Charles S. Calverley.

SARAH'S HALLS

THE broom that once through Sarah's halls,
    In hole and corner sped,
    Now useless leans 'gainst Sarah's walls
And gathers dust instead.
So sweeps the slavey now-a-days
    So work is shifted o'er,
And maids that once gained honest praise
    Now earn that praise no more !

No more the cobweb from its height
　　The broom of Sarah fells;
The fly alone unlucky wight
　　Invades the spider's cells.
Thus energy so seldom wakes,
　　All sign that Sarah gives
Is when some dish or platter breaks,
　　To show that still she lives.

Judy.

'TWAS EVER THUS

I NEVER rear'd a young gazelle,
　　(Because, you see, I never tried);
　　But had it known and loved me well,
　No doubt the creature would have died.
My rich and aged Uncle John
　　Has known me long and loves me well
But still persists in living on —
　　I would he were a young gazelle.

I never loved a tree or flower;
　　But, if I had, I beg to say
The blight, the wind, the sun, or shower
　　Would soon have withered it away.
I've dearly loved my Uncle John,
　　From childhood to the present hour,
And yet he will go living on —
　　I would he were a tree or flower!

Henry S. Leigh.

AFTER JANE TAYLOR

THE BAT

TWINKLE, twinkle, little bat!
  How I wonder what you 're at!

Up above the world you fly,
Like a tea-tray in the sky.

Lewis Carroll.

AFTER BARRY CORNWALL

THE TEA

THE tea! The tea! The beef, beef-tea!
The brew from gravy-beef for me!
Without a doubt, as I 'll be bound,
The best for an invalid 't is found;
It 's better than gruel; with sago vies;
Or with the cradled babe's supplies.

I like beef-tea! I like beef-tea,
I 'm satisfied, and aye shall be,
With the brew I love, and the brew I know,
And take it wheresoe'er I go.
If the price should rise, or meat be cheap,
No matter. I 'll to beef-tea keep.

I love — oh, how I love to guide
The strong beef-tea to its place inside,
When round and round you stir the spoon
Or whistle thereon to cool it soon.
Because one knoweth — or ought to know,
That things get cool whereon you blow.

I never have drunk the dull souchong
But I for my loved beef-tea did long,
And inly yearned for that bountiful zest,
Like a bird. As a child on that I messed —
And a mother it was and is to me,
For I was weaned on the beef — beef-tea!

Tom Hood, Jr.

AFTER BYRON

THE ROUT OF BELGRAVIA

THE Belgravians came down on the Queen in
    her hold,
    And their costumes were gleaming with pur-
ple and gold,
And the sheen of their jewels was like stars on the
    sea,
As their chariots rolled proudly down Piccadill-ee.

Like the leaves of *Le Follet* when summer is green,
That host in its glory at noontide was seen;
Like the leaves of a toy-book all thumb-marked
    and worn,
That host four hours later was tattered and torn.

For the rush of the crowd, which was eager and
    vast,
Had rumpled and ruined and wrecked as it passed;
And the eyes of the wearer waxed angry in haste,
As a dress but once worn was dragged out at the
    waist.

And there lay the feather and fan side by side,
But no longer they nodded or waved in their pride;
And there lay lace flounces and ruching in slips,
And spur-torn material in plentiful strips.

[84]

And there were odd gauntlets and pieces of hair;
And fragments of back-combs and slippers were
    there;
And the gay were all silent, their mirth was all
    hushed,
Whilst the dewdrops stood out on the brows of
    the crushed.

And the dames of Belgravia were loud in their wail,
And the matrons of Mayfair all took up the tale;
And they vow as they hurry unnerved from the scene,
That it's no trifling matter to call on the Queen.
                                        Jon Duan.

A GRIEVANCE

DEAR Mr. Editor: I wish to say —
        If you will not be angry at my writing
            it —
But I've been used, since childhood's happy day,
    When I have thought of something, to inditing
        it;
I seldom think of things; and, by the way,
    Although this metre may not be exciting, it
Enables one to be extremely terse,
Which is not what one always is in verse.

I used to know a man, such things befall
    The observant wayfarer through Fate's domain
He was a man, take him for all in all,
    We shall not look upon his like again;

[85]

I know that statement 's not original;
    What statement is, since Shakespere? or, since
        Cain,
What murder? I believe 't was Shakespere said
        it, or
Perhaps it may have been your Fighting Editor.

Though why an Editor should fight, or why
    A Fighter should abase himself to edit,
Are problems far too difficult and high
    For me to solve with any sort of credit.
Some greatly more accomplished man than I
        Must tackle them: let 's say then Shakespere
            said it;
And, if he did not, Lewis Morris may
(Or even if he did). Some other day,

When I have nothing pressing to impart,
    I should not mind dilating on this matter.
I feel its import both in head and heart,
    And always did, — especially the latter.
I could discuss it in the busy mart
    Or on the lonely housetop; hold! this chatter
Diverts me from my purpose. To the point:
The time, as Hamlet said, is out of joint,

And perhaps I was born to set it right, —
    A fact I greet with perfect equanimity.
I do not put it down to " cursed spite,"
    I don't see any cause for cursing in it. I

Have always taken very great delight
   In such pursuits since first I read divinity.
Whoever will may write a nation's songs
As long as I 'm allowed to right its wrongs.

What's Eton but a nursery of wrong-righters,
   A mighty mother of effective men;
A training ground for amateur reciters,
   A sharpener of the sword as of the pen;
A factory of orators and fighters,
   A forcing-house of genius?   Now and then
The world at large shrinks back, abashed and
     beaten,
Unable to endure the glare of Eton.

I think I said I knew a man : what then ?
   I don't suppose such knowledge is forbid.
We nearly all do, more or less, know men, —
   Or think we do ; nor will a man get rid
Of that delusion, while he wields a pen.
   But who this man was, what, if aught, he did,
Nor why I mentioned him, I do not know ;
Nor what I " wished to say " a while ago.
J. K. Stephen.

AFTER CHARLES WOLFE

THE BURIAL OF THE BACHELOR

NOT a laugh was heard, not a frivolous note,
   As the groom to the wedding we carried;
   Not a jester discharged his farewell shot
As the bachelor went to be married.

We married him quickly that morning bright,
   The leaves of our prayer-books turning,
In the chancel's dimly religious light,
   And tears in our eyelids burning.

No useless nosegay adorned his chest,
   Not in chains but in laws we bound him;
And he looked like a bridegroom trying his best
   To look used to the scene around him.

Few and small were the fees it cost,
   And we spoke not a word of sorrow,
But we silently gazed on the face of the lost
   And we bitterly thought of the morrow.

We thought as we hurried him home to be fed,
   And tried our low spirits to rally,
That the weather looked very like squalls overhead
   For the passage from Dover to Calais.

Lightly they'll talk of the bachelor gone,
  And o'er his frail fondness upbraid him;
But little he'll reck if they let him alone,
  With his wife that the parson hath made him.

But half of our heavy task was done,
  When the clock struck the hour for retiring;
And we judged by the knocks which had now begun
  That their cabby was rapidly tiring.

Slowly and sadly we led them down,
  From the scene of his lame oratory;
We told the four-wheeler to drive them to town,
  And we left them alone in their glory.

                                        Anonymous.

NOT A SOU HAD HE GOT

NOT a sou had he got—not a guinea or note,
      And he looked confoundedly flurried
      As he bolted away without paying his shot,
And the Landlady after him hurried.

We saw him again at dead of night,
  When home from the club returning;
We twigged the Doctor beneath the light
  Of the gas-lamp brilliantly burning.

All bare and exposed to the midnight dews,
  Reclined in the gutter we found him;
And he look'd like a gentleman taking a snooze,
  With his Marshal cloak around him.

"The Doctor's as drunk as the d——," we said,
  And we managed a shutter to borrow;
We raised him, and sighed at the thought that his
    head
  Would "consumedly ache" on the morrow.

We bore him home, and we put him to bed,
  And we told his wife and his daughter
To give him, next morning, a couple of red
  Herrings, with soda-water.

Loudly they talked of his money that's gone
  And his lady began to upbraid him;
But little he reck'd, so they let him snore on
  'Neath the counterpane just as we laid him.

We tucked him in, and had hardly done
  When, beneath the window calling,
We heard the rough voice of a son of a gun
  Of a watchman "One o'clock!" bawling.

Slowly and sadly we all walk'd down
  From his room in the uppermost story;
A rushlight was placed on the cold hearth-stone,
  And we left him alone in his glory!

                                    R. Harris Barham.

THE MARRIAGE OF SIR JOHN SMITH

NOT a sigh was heard, nor a funeral tone,
     As the man to his bridal we hurried;
     Not a woman discharged her farewell groan,
On the spot where the fellow was married.

We married him just about eight at night,
   Our faces paler turning,
By the struggling moonbeam's misty light,
   And the gas-lamp's steady burning.

No useless watch-chain covered his vest,
   Nor over-dressed we found him;
But he looked like a gentleman wearing his best,
   With a few of his friends around him.

Few and short were the things we said,
   And we spoke not a word of sorrow,
But we silently gazed on the man that was wed,
   And we bitterly thought of the morrow.

We thought, as we silently stood about,
   With spite and anger dying,
How the merest stranger had cut us out,
   With only half our trying.

[91]

Lightly we'll talk of the fellow that's gone,
　And oft for the past upbraid him;
But little he'll reck if we let him live on,
　In the house where his wife conveyed him.

But our heavy task at length was done,
　When the clock struck the hour for retiring;
And we heard the spiteful squib and pun
　The girls were sullenly firing.

Slowly and sadly we turned to go, —
　We had struggled, and we were human;
We shed not a tear, and we spoke not our woe,
　But we left him alone with his woman.

Phœbe Cary.

AFTER MRS. HEMANS

THE THYROID GLAND

"WE hear thee speak of the thyroid gland,
But what thou say'st we don't understand;
Professor, where does the acinus dwell?
We hashed our dissection and can't quite tell.
Is it where the mascula lutea flows,
And the suprachordial tissue grows?"
   " Not there, not there, my class ! "

" Is it far away where the bronchi part
And the pneumogastric controls the heart?
Where endothelium encardium lines,
And a subpericardial nerve intertwines?
Where the subpleural plexus of lymphatics expand?
Is it there, Professor, that gruesome gland?"
   " Not there, not there, my class ! "

" I have not seen it, my gentle youths,
My myxoedemia, I'm told, it soothes.
Landois says stolidly ' functions unknown ; '
Foster adopts an enquiring tone.
Duct does not lead to its strange recess,
Far below the vertex, above the pes,
   It is there, I am told, my class ! "

        R. M.

AFTER KEATS

ODE ON A JAR OF PICKLES

A SWEET, acidulous, down-reaching thrill
    Pervades my sense.   I seem to see or hear
    The lushy garden-grounds of Greenwich Hill
In autumn, where the crispy leaves are sere ;
And odors haunt me of remotest spice
    From the Levant or musky-aired Cathay,
Or from the saffron-fields of Jericho,
        Where everything is nice.
    The more I sniff, the more I swoon away,
And what else mortal palate craves, forego.

II.

Odors unsmelled are keen, but those I smell
    Are keener ; wherefore let me sniff again !
Enticing walnuts, I have known ye well
    In youth, when pickles were a passing pain ;
Unwitting youth, that craves the candy stem,
    And sugar plums to olives doth prefer,
And even licks the pots of marmalade
        When sweetness clings to them.
    But now I dream of ambergris and myrrh,
Tasting these walnuts in the poplar shade.

[94]

III.

Lo ! hoarded coolness in the heart of noon,
    Plucked with its dew, the cucumber is here,
As to the Dryad's parching lips a boon,
    And crescent bean-pods, unto Bacchus dear;
And, last of all, the pepper's pungent globe,
    The scarlet dwelling of the sylph of fire,
Provoking purple draughts; and, surfeited,
            I cast my trailing robe
O'er my pale feet, touch up my tuneless lyre,
And twist the Delphic wreath to suit my head.

IV.

Here shall my tongue in otherwise be soured
    Than fretful men's in parched and palsied days;
And, by the mid-May's dusky leaves embowered,
    Forget the fruitful blame, the scanty praise.
No sweets to them who sweet themselves were born,
    Whose natures ooze with lucent saccharine;
Who, with sad repetition soothly cloyed,
            The lemon-tinted morn
Enjoy, and find acetic twilight fine.
Wake I, or sleep ?   The pickle-jar is void.

Bayard Taylor.

AFTER HEINE

IMITATION

MY love she leans from the window
    Afar in a rosy land ;
    And red as a rose are her blushes,
And white as a rose her hand.

And the roses cluster around her,
    And mimic her tender grace ;
And nothing but roses can blossom
    Wherever she shows her face.

I dwell in a land of winter,
    From my love a world apart, —
But the snow blooms over with roses
    At the thought of her in my heart.

This German style of poem
    Is uncommonly popular now ;
For the worst of us poets can do it —
    Since Heine showed us how.

H. C. Bunner.

COMMONPLACES

RAIN on the face of the sea,
   Rain on the sodden land,
    And the window-pane is blurred with rain
    As I watch it, pen in hand.

Mist on the face of the sea,
   Mist on the sodden land,
Filling the vales as daylight fails,
   And blotting the desolate sand.

Voices from out of the mist,
   Calling to one another :
" Hath love an end, thou more than friend,
   Thou dearer than ever brother ? "

Voices from out of the mist,
   Calling and passing away ;
But I cannot speak, for my voice is weak,
   And . . . this is the end of my lay.
                     Rudyard Kipling.

AFTER HOOD

SONG OF THE SHEET

THE DRIPPING SHEET

This sheet wrung out of cold or tepid water is thrown around the body. Quick rubbing follows, succeeded by the same operation with a dry sheet. Its operation is truly shocking. Dress after to prevent remarks.

WITH nerves all shattered and worn,
  With shouts terrific and loud,
    A patient stood in a cold wet sheet —
A Grindrod's patent shroud.
Wet, wet, wet,
  In douche and spray and sleet,
And still, with a voice I shall never forget,
  He sang the song of the sheet.

" Drip, drip, drip,
  Dashing, and splashing, and dipping;
And drip, drip, drip,
  Till your fat all melts to dripping.
It's oh, for dry deserts afar,
  Or let me rather endure
Curing with salt in a family jar,
  If this is the water cure.

[98]

" Rub, rub, rub,
    He 'll rub away life and limb;
Rub, rub, rub.
    It seems to be fun for him.
Sheeted from head to foot,
    I 'd rather be covered with dirt;
I 'll give you the sheet and the blankets to
        boot,
    If you 'll only give me my shirt.

" Oh, men, with arms and hands,
    Oh, men, with legs and shins,
It is not the sheet you 're wearing out,
    But human creatures' skins.
Rub, rub, rub,
    Body, and legs, and feet;
Rubbing at once with a double rub,
    A skin as well as a sheet.

" My wife will see me no more —
    She 'll see the bone of her bone,
But never will see the flesh of her flesh,
    For I 'll have no flesh of my own.
The little that was my own,
    They won't allow me to keep;
It 's a pity that flesh should be so dear,
    And water so very cheap.

" Pack, pack, pack,
    Whenever your spirit flags,
You 're doomed by hydropathic laws
    To be packed in cold water rags;

Rolled up on bed or on floor,
    Or sweated to death in a chair;
But my chairman's rank — my shadow I 'd thank
    For taking my place in there.

" Slop, slop, slop,
    Never a moment of time;
Slop, slop, slop,
    Slackened like mason's lime.
Stand and freeze and steam —
    Steam or freeze and stand;
I wish those friends had their tongues benumbed,
    That told me to leave dry land.

" Up, up, up,
    In the morn before daylight,
The bathman cries ' Get up,'
    (I wish he were up for a fight).
While underneath the eaves,
    The dry snug swallows cling;
But give them a cold wet sheet to their backs,
    And see if they 'll come next spring.

" Oh! oh! it stops my breath,
    (He calls it short and sweet),
Could they hear me underneath
    I 'll shout them from the street!
He says that in half an hour
    A different man I 'll feel;
That I 'll jump half over the moon and want
    To walk into a meal!

"I feel more nerve and power,
   And less of terror and grief;
I 'm thinking now of love and hope —
   And now of mutton and beef.
This glorious scene will rouse my heart,
   Oh, who would lie in bed?
I cannot stop, but jump and hop,
   Going like needle and thread."

With buoyant spirit upborne,
   With cheeks both healthy and red,
The same man ran up the Malvern Crags,
   Pitying those in bed.
Trip, trip, trip,
   Oh, life with health is sweet;
And still in a voice both strong and quick,
Would that its tones could reach the sick,
   He sang the Song of the Sheet.

Anonymous.

I REMEMBER, I REMEMBER

I REMEMBER, I remember,
   The house where I was wed,
   And the little room from which that night
My smiling bride was led.
She did n't come a wink too soon,
   Nor make too long a stay;
But now I often wish her folks
   Had kept the girl away!

I remember, I remember,
　Her dresses, red and white,
Her bonnets and her caps and cloaks,—
　They cost an awful sight!
The " corner lot " on which I built,
　And where my brother met
At first my wife, one washing-day,—
　That man is single yet!

I remember, I remember,
　Where I was used to court,
And thought that all of married life
　Was just such pleasant sport: —
My spirit flew in feathers then,
　No care was on my brow;
I scarce could wait to shut the gate, —
　I 'm not so anxious now!

I remember, I remember,
　My dear one's smile and sigh;
I used to think her tender heart
　Was close against the sky.
It was a childish ignorance,
　But now it soothes me not
To know I 'm farther off from Heaven
　Than when she was n't got!

Phœbe Cary.

AFTER ALFRED BUNN

A YULE–TIDE PARODY

WHEN other wits and other bards,
      Their tales at Christmas tell,
      Or praise on cheap and colored cards
The time they love so well,
Secure from scorn and ridicule
   I hope my verse may be,
If I can still remember Yule,
   And Yule remember me.

The days are dark, the days are drear,
   When dull December dies;
But, while we mourn an ended year,
   Another's star will rise.
I hail the season formed by rule
   For merriment and glee;
So let me still remember Yule,
   And Yule remember me.

The rich plum-pudding I enjoy,
   I greet the pie of mince;
And loving both while yet a boy,
   Have loved them ever since.

More dull were I than any mule
   That eyes did ever see,
If I should not remember Yule,
   And Yule remember me.

Anonymous.

SELF–EVIDENT

WHEN other lips and other eyes
   Their tales of love shall tell,
   Which means the usual sort of lies
You 've heard from many a swell;
When, bored with what you feel is bosh,
   You 'd give the world to see
A friend, whose love you know will wash,
   Oh, then remember me !

When Signor Solo goes his tours,
   And Captain Craft 's at Ryde,
And Lord Fitzpop is on the moors,
   And Lord knows who besides;
When to exist you feel a task
   Without a friend at tea,
At such a moment I but ask
   That you 'll remember me.

J. R. Planché.

AFTER LORD MACAULAY

THE LAUREATE'S TOURNEY

By the Hon. T — B — M.

FYTTE THE FIRST

"WHAT news, what news, thou pilgrim
gray, what news from the southern
land?
How fare the bold Conservatives, how is it with
Ferrand?
How does the little Prince of Wales — how looks
our lady Queen?
And tell me, is the monthly nurse once more at
Windsor seen?"

"I bring no tidings from the Court, nor from St.
Stephen's hall;
I 've heard the thundering tramp of horse, and the
trumpet's battle-call;
And these old eyes have seen a fight, which Eng-
land ne'er had seen,
Since fell King Richard sobbed his soul through
blood on Bosworth Green.

"'He's dead, he's dead, the Laureate's dead!'
    'T was thus the cry began,
And straightway every garret-roof gave up its
    minstrel man;
From Grub Street, and from Houndsditch, and
    from Farringdon Within,
The poets all towards Whitehall poured on with
    eldritch din.

"Loud yelled they for Sir James the Graham; but
    sore afraid was he;
A hardy knight were he that might face such a
    minstrelsie.
'Now by St. Giles of Netherby, my patron Saint,
    I swear,
I'd rather by a thousand crowns Lord Palmerston
    were here! —

"'What is't ye seek, ye rebel knaves — what
    make you there beneath?'
'The bays, the bays! we want the bays! we seek
    the laureate wreath!
We seek the butt of generous wine that cheers the
    son of song;
Choose thou among us all, Sir Knight — we may
    not tarry long!'

"Loud laughed the good Sir James in scorn —
    'Rare jest it were, I think,
But one poor butt of Xeres, and a thousand rogues
    to drink!

An' if it flowed with wine or beer, 't is easy to be
  seen,
That dry within the hour would be the well of
  Hippocrene.

"' Tell me, if on Parnassus' heights there grow a
  thousand sheaves ;
Or has Apollo's laurel bush yet borne ten hundred
  leaves ?
Or if so many leaves were there, how long would
  they sustain
The ravage and the glutton bite of such a locust
  train ?

"' No ! get ye back into your dens, take counsel
  for the night,
And choose me out two champions to meet in
  deadly fight ;
To-morrow's dawn shall see the lists marked out
  in Spitalfields,
And he who wins shall have the bays, and he shall
  die who yields ! '

" Down went the window with a crash, — in
  silence and in fear
Each ragged bard looked anxiously upon his
  neighbor near ;
Then up and spake young Tennyson — ' Who 's
  here that fears for death ?
'T were better one of us shall die, than England
  lose the wreath !

"' Let's cast the lot among us now, which two
    shall fight to-morrow;
For armor bright we'll club our mite, and horses
    we can borrow;
'T were shame that bards of France should sneer,
    and German Dichters too,
If none of British song might dare a deed of
    derringdo!'

"' The lists of Love are mine,' said Moore, 'and
    not the lists of Mars;'
Said Hunt, 'I seek the jars of wine, but shun the
    combat's jars!'
'I'm old,' quoth Samuel Rogers. — 'Faith,' says
    Campbell, 'so am I!'
'And I'm in holy orders, sir!' quoth Tom of
    Ingoldsby.

"' Now out upon ye, craven loons,' cried Moxon,
    good at need;
'Bide, if ye will, secure at home, and sleep while
    others bleed.
I second Alfred's motion, boys, — let's try the
    chance of lot;
And monks shall sing, and bells shall ring, for him
    that goes to pot.'

"Eight hundred minstrels slunk away — two hun-
    dred stayed to draw;
Now Heaven protect the daring wight that pulls
    the longest straw!

'T is done! 't is done! And who hath won?
    Keep silence one and all, —
The first is William Wordsworth hight, the second
    Ned Fitzball!"

FYTTE THE SECOND

Oh, bright and gay hath dawned the day on lordly
    Spitalfields, —
How flash the rays with ardent blaze from polished
    helms and shields!
On either side the chivalry of England throng the
    green,
And in the middle balcony appears our gracious
    Queen.

With iron fists, to keep the lists, two valiant knights
    appear,
The Marquis Hal of Waterford, and stout Sir
    Aubrey Vere.
"What ho! there, herald, blow the trump! Let's
    see who comes to claim
The butt of golden Xeres, and the Laureate's hon-
    ored name!"

That instant dashed into the lists, all armed from
    head to heel,
On courser brown, with vizor down, a warrior
    sheathed in steel;

Then said our Queen — " Was ever seen so stout a
    knight and tall ?
His name — his race?" — "An't please your grace,
    it is the brave Fitzball.

" Oft in the Melodrama line his prowess hath been
    shown,
And well throughout the Surrey side his thirst for
    blood is known.
But see, the other champion comes!" — Then rang
    the startled air
With shouts of " Wordsworth, Wordsworth, ho !
    the bard of Rydal 's there."

And lo! upon a little steed, unmeet for such a
    course,
Appeared the honored veteran ; but weak seemed
    man and horse.
Then shook their ears the sapient peers, — " That
    joust will soon be done :
My Lord of Brougham, I 'll back Fitzball, and give
    you two to one !"

" Done," quoth the Brougham, — " And done with
    you !"   " Now minstrels, are you ready ?"
Exclaimed the Lord of Waterford, — "You 'd better
    both sit steady.
Blow, trumpets, blow the note of charge! and for-
    ward to the fight !"
" Amen !" said good Sir Aubrey Vere; " Saint
    Schism defend the right !"

As sweeps the blast against the mast when blows
    the furious squall,
So started at the trumpet's sound the terrible Fitz-
    ball;
His lance he bore his breast before,—Saint George
    protect the just!
Or Wordsworth's hoary head must roll along the
    shameful dust!

"Who threw that calthrop? Seize the knave!"
    Alas! the deed is done;
Down went the steed, and o'er his head flew bright
    Apollo's son.
"Undo his helmet! cut the lace! pour water on
    his head!"
"It ain't no use at all, my lord; 'cos vy? the
    covey 's dead!"

Above him stood the Rydal bard — his face was
    full of woe.
"Now there thou liest, stiff and stark, who never
    feared a foe:
A braver knight, or more renowned in tourney and
    in hall,
Ne'er brought the upper gallery down than terrible
    Fitzball!"

They led our Wordsworth to the Queen — she
    crowned him with the bays
And wished him many happy years, and many
    quarter-days;

And if you'd have the story told by abler lips than
    mine,
You've but to call at Rydal Mount, and taste the
    Laureate's wine!

William Aytoun.

AFTER EMERSON

MUTTON

IF the fat butcher thinks he slays,
  Or he — the mutton — thinks he 's slain,
  Why, "troth is truth," the eater says —
"I 'll come, and cut and come again."

To hungry wolves that on him leer
  Mutton is cheap, and sheep the same,
No famished god would at him sneer —
  To famine, chops are more than fame.

Who hiss at him, him but assures
  That they are geese, but wanting wings —
Your coat is his whose life is yours,
  And baa! the hymn the mutton sings.

Ye curs, and gods of grander blood,
  And you, ye Paddies fresh from Cork,
Come taste, ye lovers of the good —
  Eat! Stuff! and turn your back on pork.
Anonymous.

AFTER MARY HOWITT

THE LOBSTER QUADRILLE

"WILL you walk a little faster?" said a
whiting to a snail,
"There's a porpoise close behind us,
and he's treading on my tail.
See how eagerly the lobsters and the turtles all
advance!
They are waiting on the shingle — will you come
and join the dance?
Will you, won't you, will you, won't you, will
you join the dance?
Will you, won't you, will you, won't you, won't
you join the dance?

"You can really have no notion how delightful it
will be
When they take us up and throw us, with the lob-
ters, out to sea!"
But the snail replied "Too far, too far!" and gave
a look askance —
Said he thanked the whiting kindly, but he would
not join the dance.
Would not, could not, would not, could not,
would not join the dance.
Would not, could not, would not, could not,
could not join the dance.

[114]

"What matters it how far we go?" his scaly friend
    replied.
"There is another shore, you know, upon the other
    side.
The further off from England the nearer is to
    France—
Then turn not pale, beloved snail, but come and join
    the dance.
    Will you, won't you, will you, won't you, will
       you join the dance?
    Will you, won't you, will you, won't you, won't
       you join the dance?"

Lewis Carroll.

AFTER MRS. BROWNING

IN THE GLOAMING

IN the gloaming to be roaming, where the crested
  waves are foaming,
 And the shy mermaidens combing locks that
  ripple to their feet;
When the gloaming is, I never made the ghost of
  an endeavor
To discover — but whatever were the hour, it would
  be sweet.

"To their feet," I say, for Leech's sketch indis-
  putably teaches
That the mermaids of our beaches do not end in
  ugly tails,
Nor have homes among the corals; but are shod
  with neat balmorals,
An arrangement no one quarrels with, as many
  might with scales.

Sweet to roam beneath a shady cliff, of course with
  some young lady,
Lalage, Nærea, Haidee, or Elaine, or Mary Ann:
Love, you dear delusive dream, you! Very sweet
  your victims deem you,
When, heard only by the seamew, they talk all the
  stuff one can.

Sweet to haste, a licensed lover, to Miss Pinkerton,
    the glover;
Having managed to discover what is dear Nærea's
    " size ":
P'raps to touch that wrist so slender, as your tiny
    gift you tender,
And to read you're no offender, in those laughing
    hazel eyes.

Then to hear her call you " Harry," when she
    makes you fetch and carry —
O young men about to marry, what a blessed thing
    it is !
To be photograph'd — together — cased in pretty
    Russia leather —
Hear her gravely doubting whether they have
    spoilt your honest phiz !

Then to bring your plighted fair one first a ring —
    a rich and rare one —
Next a bracelet, if she'll wear one, and a heap of
    things beside;
And serenely bending o'er her, to inquire if it would
    bore her
To say when her own adorer may aspire to call her
    bride !

Then, the days of courtship over, with your WIFE
    to start for Dover
Or Dieppe — and live in clover evermore, what e'er
    befalls;

[117]

For I've read in many a novel that, unless they've
  souls that grovel
Folks *prefer* in fact a hovel to your dreary marble
  halls.

To sit, happy married lovers; Phillis trifling with a
  plover's
Egg, while Corydon uncovers with a grace the Sally
  Lunn,
Or dissects the lucky pheasant — that, I think, were
  passing pleasant,
As I sit alone at present, dreaming darkly of a
  Dun.

C. S. Calverley.

GWENDOLINE

'TWAS not the brown of chestnut boughs
    That shadowed her so finely;
  It was the hair that swept her brows,
And framed her face divinely;
Her tawny hair, her purple eyes,
  The spirit was ensphered in,
That took you with such swift surprise,
  Provided you had peered in.

Her velvet foot amid the moss
  And on the daisies patted,
As, querulous with sense of loss,
  It tore the herbage matted.

"And come he early, come he late,"
  She saith, " it will undo me;
The sharp fore-speeded shaft of fate
  Already quivers through me.

" When I beheld his red-roan steed,
  I knew what aim impelled it.
And that dim scarf of silver brede,
  I guessed for whom he held it.
I recked not, while he flaunted by,
  Of Love's relentless vi'lence,
Yet o'er me crashed the summer sky,
  In thunders of blue silence.

" His hoof-prints crumbled down the dale,
  But left behind their lava;
What should have been my woman's mail
  Grew jellied as guava.
I looked him proud, but 'neath my pride
  I felt a boneless tremor;
He was the Beér, I descried,
  And I was but the Seemer!

" Ah, how to be what then I seemed,
  And bid him seem that is so!
We always tangle threads we dreamed,
  And contravene our bliss so,
I see the red-roan steed again!
  He looks as something sought he;
Why, hoity-toity! — *he* is fain,
  So *I*'ll be cold and haughty!"

                              Bayard Taylor.

[119]

AFTER LONGFELLOW

THE MODERN HIAWATHA

HE killed the noble Mudjokivis.
　Of the skin he made him mittens,
　Made them with the fur side inside,
Made them with the skin side outside.
He, to get the warm side inside,
Put the inside skin side outside;
He, to get the cold side outside,
Put the warm side fur side inside.
That's why he put the fur side inside,
Why he put the skin side outside,
Why he turned them inside outside.

Anonymous.

HIGHER

THE shadows of night were a-comin' down
　　　swift,
　And the dazzlin' snow lay drift on drift,
As thro' a village a youth did go,
A-carryin' a flag with this motto, —
　　　　　　　Higher!

[120]

O'er a forehead high curled copious hair,
His nose a Roman, complexion fair,
O'er an eagle eye an auburn lash,
And he never stopped shoutin' thro' his moustache!
"Higher!"

He saw thro' the windows as he kept gettin' upper
A number of families sittin' at supper,
But he eyes the slippery rocks very keen
And fled as he cried, and cried while a fleein' —
"Higher!"

"Take care you there!" said an old woman; "stop!
It's blowing gales up there on top —
You'll tumble off on t' other side!"
But the hurryin' stranger loud replied,
"Higher!"

"Oh! don't you go up such a shocking night,
Come sleep on my lap," said a maiden bright.
On his Roman nose a tear-drop come,
But still he remarked, as he upward clomb,
"Higher!"

"Look out for the branch of that sycamore-tree!
Dodge rolling stones, if any you see!"
Sayin' which the farmer went home to bed
And the singular voice replied overhead,
"Higher!"

About quarter past six the next afternoon,
A man accidentally goin' up soon,
Heard spoken above him as often as twice
The very same word in a very weak voice,
                    " Higher ! "

And not far, I believe, from quarter of seven —
He was slow gettin' up, the road bein' uneven —
Found the stranger dead in the drifted snow,
Still clutchin' the flag with the motto —
                    Higher !

Yes ! lifeless, defunct, without any doubt,
The lamp of life being decidedly out,
On the dreary hillside the youth was a layin' !
And there was no more use for him to be sayin'
                    " Higher ! "

Anonymous.

TOPSIDE GALAH !

THAT nightee teem he come chop, chop,
    One young man walkee, no can stop,
    Colo makee ; icee makee ;
He got flag ; chop b'long welly culio, see —
    Topside Galah !

He too muchee folly ; one piecee eye
Lookee sharp — so fashion — alla same mi ;
He talkee largee, talkee stlong,
To muchee culio ; alla same gong —
    Topside Galah !

[122]

Inside any house he can see light;
Any piecee loom got fire all light;
He lookee see plenty ice more high,
Inside he mouf he plenty cly —
      Topside Galah!

" No can walkee! " olo man speakee he;
" Bimeby lain come, no can see;
Hab got water welly wide! "
Maskee, mi must go topside —
      Topside Galah!

" Man-man," one galo talkee he,
" What for you go topside look see? "
" Nother teem," he makee plenty cly,
Maskee, alla teem walkee plenty high —
      Topside Galah!

" Take care that spilum tlee, young man;
Take care that icee! " he no man-man
That coolie chin-chin he good-night;
He talkee " mi can go all light " —
      Topside Galah!

Joss pidgin man chop-chop begin,
Morning teem that Joss chin-chin,
No see any man, he plenty fear,
Cause some man talkee, he can hear —
      Topside Galah!

Young man makee die; one largee dog see
Too muchee bobbery, findee he.
Hand too muchee colo, inside can stop
Alla same piecee flag, got culio chop —
      Topside Galah!

Anonymous.

EXCELSIOR

THE swampy State of Illinois
    Contained a greenish sort of boy,
    Who read with idiotic joy —
          " Excelsior!"

He tarried not to eat or drink,
    But put a flag of lightish pink,
    And traced on it in violet ink —
          Excelsior!

Though what he meant by that absurd,
    Uncouth, and stupid, senseless word,
    Has not been placed upon record —
          Excelsior!

The characters were very plain,
    In German text, yet he was fain
    With greater clearness to explain —
          Excelsior!

And so he ran, this stupid wight,
    And hollered out with all his might,
    (As to a person out of sight) —
          " Excelsior!"

[124]

And everybody thought the lad
   Within an ace of being mad,
   Who cried in accents stern and sad —
           " Excelsior ! "

" Come to my arms," the maiden cried;
   The youth grinned sheepishly, and sighed,
   And then appropriately replied —
           " Excelsior ! "

The evening sun is in the sky,
   But still the creature mounts on high
   And shouts (nor gives a reason why)
           " Excelsior ! "

And ere he gains the topmost crag
   His feeble legs begin to lag;
   Unsteadily he holds the flag —
           Excelsior !

Now P. C. Nab is on his track !
   He puts him in an empty sack,
   And brings him home upon his back —
           Excelsior !

Nab takes him to a lumber store,
   They toss him in and lock the door,
   Which only makes him bawl the more —
           " Excelsior ! "
               Anonymous.

"THE DAY IS DONE"

THE day is done, and darkness
    From the wing of night is loosed,
    As a feather is wafted downward,
From a chicken going to roost.

I see the lights of the baker,
    Gleam through the rain and mist,
And a feeling of sadness comes o'er me,
    That I cannot well resist.

A feeling of sadness and longing
    That is not like being sick,
And resembles sorrow only
    As a brickbat resembles a brick.

Come, get for me some supper, —
    A good and regular meal —
That shall soothe this restless feeling,
    And banish the pain I feel.

Not from the pastry bakers,
    Not from the shops for cake;
I would n't give a farthing
    For all that they can make.

For, like the soup at dinner,
    Such things would but suggest
Some dishes more substantial,
    And to-night I want the best.

Go to some honest butcher,
  Whose beef is fresh and nice,
As any they have in the city,
  And get a liberal slice.

Such things through days of labor,
  And nights devoid of ease,
For sad and desperate feelings,
  Are wonderful remedies.

They have an astonishing power
  To aid and reinforce,
And come like the " finally, brethren,"
  That follows a long discourse.

Then get me a tender sirloin
  From off the bench or hook.
And lend to its sterling goodness
  The science of the cook.

And the night shall be filled with comfort,
  And the cares with which it begun
Shall fold up their blankets like Indians,
  And silently cut and run.

                         Phœbe Cary.

A PSALM OF LIFE

TELL me not, in idle jingle,
    Marriage is an empty dream,
  For the girl is dead that 's single,
And things are not what they seem.

Married life is real, earnest,
  Single blessedness a fib,
Taken from man, to man returnest,
  Has been spoken of the rib.

Not enjoyment, and not sorrow,
  Is our destined end or way;
But to act, that each to-morrow
  Nearer brings the wedding-day.

Life is long, and youth is fleeting,
  And our hearts, if there we search,
Still like steady drums are beating
  Anxious marches to the Church.

In the world's broad field of battle,
  In the bivouac of life,
Be not like dumb, driven cattle;
  Be a woman, be a wife!

Trust no Future, howe'er pleasant!
  Let the dead Past bury its dead!
Act — act in the living Present.
  Heart within, and Man ahead!

Lives of married folks remind us
  We can live our lives as well,
And, departing, leave behind us; —
  Such examples as will tell; —

Such examples, that another,
  Sailing far from Hymen's port,
A forlorn, unmarried brother,
  Seeing, shall take heart, and court.

Let us then be up and doing,
  With the heart and head begin;
Still achieving, still pursuing,
  Learn to labor, and to win!

Phœbe Cary.

HOW OFTEN

THEY stood on the bridge at midnight,
  In a park not far from the town;
  They stood on the bridge at midnight,
Because they did n't sit down.

The moon rose o'er the city,
  Behind the dark church spire;
The moon rose o'er the city
  And kept on rising higher.

How often, oh, how often!
  They whispered words so soft;
How often, oh, how often;
  How often, oh, how oft!

Ben King.

DESOLATION

SOMEWHAT back from the village street
  Stands the old fashioned country seat.
    Across its antique portico
Tall poplar trees their shadows throw.
And there throughout the livelong day,
Jemima plays the pi-a-na.
        Do, re, mi,
        Mi, re, do.

In the front parlor there it stands,
And there Jemima plies her hands,
While her papa, beneath his cloak,
Mutters and groans: "This is no joke!"
And swears to himself and sighs, alas!
With sorrowful voice to all who pass.
        Do, re, mi,
        Mi, re, do.

Through days of death and days of birth
She plays as if she owned the earth.
Through every swift vicissitude
She drums as if it did her good,
And still she sits from morn till night
And plunks away with main and might
        Do, re, mi,
        Mi, re, do.
          [130]

In that mansion used to be
Free-hearted hospitality;
But that was many years before
Jemima dallied with the score.
When she began her daily plunk,
Into their graves the neighbors sunk.
  Do, re, mi,
  Mi, re, do.

To other worlds they 've long since fled,
All thankful that they 're safely dead.
They stood the racket while alive
Until Jemima rose at five.
And then they laid their burdens down,
And one and all they skipped the town.
  Do, re, mi,
  Mi, re, do.

Tom Masson.

THE BIRDS AND THE PHEASANT

I SHOT a partridge in the air,
 It fell in turnips, "Don" knew where;
For just as it dropped, with my right
I stopped another in its flight.

I killed a pheasant in the copse,
 It fell amongst the fir-tree tops;
For though a pheasant's flight is strong,
 A cock, hard hit, cannot fly long.

Soon, soon afterwards, in a pie,
   I found the birds in jelly lie;
And the pheasant at a fortnight's end,
   I found again in the carte of a friend.

                      Punch.

AFTER WHITTIER

HIRAM HOVER

(*A Ballad of New England life*)

WHERE the Moosatockmaguntic
　　Pours its waters in the Skuntic,
　　　Met, along the forest side
Hiram Hover, Huldah Hyde.

She, a maiden fair and dapper,
He, a red-haired, stalwart trapper,
　　Hunting beaver, mink, and skunk
　　In the woodlands of Squeedunk.

She, Pentucket's pensive daughter,
Walked beside the Skuntic water
　　Gathering, in her apron wet,
　　Snake-root, mint, and bouncing-bet.

" Why," he murmured, loth to leave her,
" Gather yarbs for chills and fever,
　　When a lovyer bold and true,
　　Only waits to gather you ? "

" Go," she answered, " I 'm not hasty,
I prefer a man more tasty ;
　　Leastways, one to please me well
　　Should not have a beasty smell."

" Haughty Huldah ! " Hiram answered,
" Mind and heart alike are cancered ;
    Jest look here ! these peltries give
    Cash, wherefrom a pair may live.

"I, you think, am but a vagrant,
Trapping beasts by no means fragrant ;
    Yet, I'm sure it's worth a thank —
    I've a handsome sum in bank."

Turned and vanished Hiram Hover,
And, before the year was over,
    Huldah, with the yarbs she sold,
    Bought a cape, against the cold.

Black and thick the furry cape was,
Of a stylish cut the shape was ;
    And the girls, in all the town,
    Envied Huldah up and down.

Then at last, one winter morning,
Hiram came without a warning.
    " Either," said he, " you are blind,
    Huldah, or you've changed your mind.

" Me you snub for trapping varmints,
Yet you take the skins for garments ;
    Since you wear the skunk and mink,
    There's no harm in me, I think."

"Well," said she, "we will not quarrel,
  Hiram; I accept the moral,
    Now the fashion's so I guess
    I can't hardly do no less."

Thus the trouble all was over
Of the love of Hiram Hover.
    Thus he made sweet Huldah Hyde
    Huldah Hover as his bride.

Love employs, with equal favor,
Things of good and evil savor;
    That which first appeared to part,
    Warmed, at last, the maiden's heart.

Under one impartial banner,
Life, the hunter, Love the tanner,
    Draw, from every beast they snare,
    Comfort for a wedded pair!

Bayard Taylor.

AFTER MRS. NORTON

THE HORSE AND HIS MASTER

(A panegyric)

MY — anything but beautiful, that standest
"knock-knee'd" by,
"Inverted arch" describes thy back, as
"dismal" doth thine eye.
Fret not — go roam the commons now, limp there
for want of speed;
I dare not mount on thee ('t were pain), thou bag
of bones, indeed.
Fret not with that too patient hoof, puff not with
wheezy wind;
The harder that thou roarest now the more we lag
behind;
The stranger "had" thy master, brute, for twice
ten pounds, all told;
I only wish he had thee back! Too late — I'm
sold! I'm sold!

To-morrow's sun will dawn again, but ah! no ride
for me.
Can I gallop over Rotten Row astride on such as
thee?
'T is evening now, and getting dark, and blowing
up for rain;

[136]

I 'll lead thee then, with slow, slow steps, to some
    " bait stables " plain.
(When a horse dealer cheats, with eyes of clap-
    trap truth and tears,
A hack's form for an instant like a thoroughbred's
    appears.)
And sitting down, I 'll ponder well beside this
    water's brink,
Here — what 's thy name? Come, Rosinante!
    Drink pretty (?) creature, drink!

Drink on, inflate thy skin. Away! this wretched
    farce is o'er;
I could not live a day and know that we must
    meet once more.
I 've tempted thee, in vain (though Sanger's power
    be strong,
They could not tempt this beast to trot), oh, thou
    hast lived too long!
Who says that I 'll give in? Come up! who says
    thou art not old?
Thy faults were faults, poor useless steed, I fear,
    when thou wert foal'd.
Thus, thus I whack upon thy back; go, scour with
    might and main
The asphalt! Ha! who stops thee now may have
    thee for his gain.

               Philip F. Allen.

THE NEW VERSION

A SOLDIER of the Russians
    Lay japanned at Tschrtzvkjskivitch,
    There was lack of woman's nursing
And other comforts which
Might add to his last moments
    And smooth the final way ; —
But a comrade stood beside him
    To hear what he might say.
The japanned Russian faltered
    As he took that comrade's hand,
And he said : " I never more shall see
    My own, my native land ;
Take a message and a token
    To some distant friends of mine,
For I was born at Smnlxzrskgqrxzski,
    Fair Smnlxzrskgqrxzski on the Irkztrvzkimnov."

                   W. J. Lampton.

AFTER POE

WHAT TROUBLED POE'S RAVEN

COULD Poe walk again to-morrow, heavy
    with dyspeptic sorrow,
      While the darkness seemed to borrow dark-
    ness from the night before,
From the hollow gloom abysmal, floating downward,
    grimly dismal,
Like a pagan curse baptismal from the bust above
    the door,
He would hear the Raven croaking from the dusk
    above the door,
      " Never, never, nevermore ! "

And, too angry to be civil, " Raven," Poe would
    cry " or devil,
Tell me why you will persist in haunting Death's
    Plutonian shore ? "
Then would croak the Raven gladly, " I will tell
    you why so sadly,
I so mournfully and madly, haunt you, taunt you,
    o'er and o'er,
Why eternally I haunt you, daunt you, taunt you,
    o'er and o'er —
      Only this, and nothing more.

" Forty-eight long years I 've pondered, forty-eight
    long years I 've wondered,
How a poet ever blundered into a mistake so sore.

How could lamp-light from your table ever in the
    world be able,
From *below*, to throw my sable shadow ' streaming
    on the floor,'
When I perched up here on Pallas, high above
    your chamber-door?
        Tell me that — if nothing more!"

Then, like some wan, weeping willow, Poe would
    bend above his pillow,
Seeking surcease in the billow where mad recollec-
    tions drown,
And in tearful tones replying, he would groan
    " There's no denying
Either I was blindly lying, or the world was upside
    down —
Say, by Joe! — it was just midnight — so the
    world *was* upside down —
        Aye, the world was upside down!"
                John Bennett.

THE AMATEUR FLUTE

HEAR the fluter with his flute,
    Silver flute!
Oh, what a world of wailing is awakened by its toot!
    How it demi-semi quavers
      On the maddened air of night!
    And defieth all endeavors
      To escape the sound or sigh
    Of the flute, flute, flute,
    With its tootle, tootle, toot;

With reiterated tooteling of exasperating toots,
The long protracted tootelings of agonizing toots
    Of the flute, flute, flute, flute,
        Flute, flute, flute,
And the wheezings and the spittings of its toots.
    Should he get that other flute,
        Golden flute,
Oh, what a deeper anguish will his presence institoot!
    How his eyes to heaven he'll raise,
        As he plays,
        All the days!
        How he'll stop us on our ways
        With its praise!
        And the people — oh, the people,
        That don't live up in the steeple,
        But inhabit Christian parlors
Where he visiteth and plays,
        Where he plays, plays, plays
        In the cruellest of ways,
    And thinks we ought to listen,
    And expects us to be mute,
Who would rather have the earache
    Than the music of his flute,
        Of his flute, flute, flute,
        And the tootings of his toot,
Of the toots wherewith he tooteleth its agonizing
    toot,
        Of the flute, flewt, fluit, floot,
        Phlute, phlewt, phlewght,
And the tootle, tootle, tooting of its toot.

                        Anonymous.

SAMUEL BROWN

IT was many and many a year ago,
  In a dwelling down in town,
    That a fellow there lived whom you may know,
  By the name of Samuel Brown;
And this fellow he lived with no other thought
  Than to our house to come down.

I was a child, and he was a child,
  In that dwelling down in town,
But we loved with a love that was more than love,
  I and my Samuel Brown, —
With a love that the ladies coveted,
  Me and Samuel Brown.

And this was the reason that, long ago,
  To that dwelling down in town,
A girl came out of her carriage, courting
  My beautiful Samuel Brown;
So that her high-bred kinsmen came,
  And bore away Samuel Brown,
And shut him up in a dwelling house,
  In a street quite up in the town.

The ladies not half so happy up there,
  Went envying me and Brown;
Yes! that was the reason (as all men know,
  In this dwelling down in town),
That the girl came out of the carriage by night,
  Coquetting and getting my Samuel Brown.

But our love is more artful by far than the love
   Of those who are older than we, —
   Of many far wiser than we, —
And neither the girls that are living above,
   Nor the girls that are down in town,
Can ever dissever my soul from the soul
   Of the beautiful Samuel Brown.

For the morn never shines, without bringing me
      lines,
   From my beautiful Samuel Brown ;
And the night 's never dark, but I sit in the park
   With my beautiful Samuel Brown.
And often by day, I walk down in Broadway,
With my darling, my darling, my life and my stay,
   To our dwelling down in town,
   To our house in the street down town.

Phœbe Cary.

THE PROMISSORY NOTE

IN the lonesome latter years
     (Fatal years !)
  To the dropping of my tears
Danced the mad and mystic spheres
In a rounded, reeling rune,
   'Neath the moon,
To the dripping and the dropping of my tears.

Ah, my soul is swathed in gloom,
    (Ulalume !)
In a dim Titanic tomb,
For my gaunt and gloomy soul
Ponders o'er the penal scroll,
O'er the parchment (not a rhyme),
Out of place, — out of time, —
I am shredded, shorn, unshifty,
    (Oh, the fifty !)
And the days have passed, the three,
    Over me !
And the debit and the credit are as one to him
    and me !

'T was the random runes I wrote
At the bottom of the note,
    (Wrote and freely
    Gave to Greeley)
In the middle of the night,
In the mellow, moonless night,
When the stars were out of sight,
When my pulses, like a knell,
    (Israfel !)
Danced with dim and dying fays
O'er the ruins of my days,
O'er the dimeless, timeless days,
When the fifty, drawn at thirty,
Seeming thrifty, yet the dirty
Lucre of the market, was the most that I could
    raise !

[144]

Fiends controlled it,
(Let him hold it!)
Devils held for me the inkstand and the pen;
Now the days of grace are o'er,
(Ah, Lenore!)
I am but as other men;
What is time, time, time,
To my rare and runic rhyme,
To my random, reeling rhyme,
By the sands along the shore,
Where the tempest whispers, "Pay him!" and I
answer, "Nevermore!"

Bayard Taylor.

THE CANNIBAL FLEA

IT was many and many a year ago
In a District called E. C.,
That a Monster dwelt whom I came to know
By the name of Cannibal Flea,
And the brute was possessed with no other thought
Than to live — and to live on me!

I was in bed, and he was in bed
In the District named E. C.,
When first in his thirst so accurst he burst
Upon me, the Cannibal Flea,
With a bite that felt as if some one had driven
A bayonet into me.

[145]

And this was the reason why long ago
In that District named E. C.
I tumbled out of my bed, willing
To capture the Cannibal Flea,
Who all the night until morning came
Kept boring into me!
It wore me down to a skeleton
In the District hight E. C.

From that hour I sought my bed — eleven —
Till daylight he tortured me.
Yes! — that was the reason (as all men know
In that District named E. C.)
I so often jumped out of my bed by night
Willing the killing of Cannibal Flea.

But his hops they were longer by far than the hops
Of creatures much larger than he —
Of parties more long-legged than he;
And neither the powder nor turpentine drops,
Nor the persons engaged by me,
Were so clever as ever to stop me the hop
Of the terrible Cannibal Flea.

For at night with a scream, I am waked from my
    dream
By the terrible Cannibal Flea;
And at morn I ne'er rise without bites — of such
    size! —
From the terrible Cannibal Flea.

So I'm forced to decide I'll no longer reside
In the District — the District — where he doth
    abide,
The locality known as E. C.
That is postally known as E. C.
                      Tom Hood, Jr.

ANNABEL LEE

'TWAS more than a million years ago,
    Or so it seems to me,
    That I used to prance around and beau
    The beautiful Annabel Lee.
There were other girls in the neighborhood
    But none was a patch to she.

And this was the reason that long ago,
    My love fell out of a tree,
And busted herself on a cruel rock;
    A solemn sight to see,
For it spoiled the hat and gown and looks
    Of the beautiful Annabel Lee.

We loved with a love that was lovely love,
    I and my Annabel Lee,
And we went one day to gather the nuts
    That men call hickoree.
And I stayed below in the rosy glow
    While she shinned up the tree,
But no sooner up than down kerslup
    Came the beautiful Annabel Lee.

[147]

And the pallid moon and the hectic noon
　　Bring gleams of dreams for me,
Of the desolate and desperate fate
　　Of the beautiful Annabel Lee.
And I often think as I sink on the brink
Of slumber's sea, of the warm pink link
　　That bound my soul to Annabel Lee;
And it was n't just best for her interest
　　To climb that hickory tree,
For had she stayed below with me,
　　We 'd had no hickory nuts maybe,
But I should have had my Annabel Lee.
　　　　　　　　　　　　Stanley Huntley.

THE BELLS

HEAR a voice announcing IRVING in The
　　　Bells — sledge's bells !
　　What a scene of wild excitement the adver-
　　　tisement foretells !
　　　　See the rush upon the pay-hole —
　　　　People stand a night and day whole
　　To secure a little corner for The Bells !
To look ghastly pale and shudder, every man and
　　　" every brudder "
　　　　Feels that nothing can be equal to The
　　　　　Bells !
　　　　Bells ! Bells ! Bells ! Bells !
　　　　Too horrified to cheer,
　　　　　Folk will testify by fear

How appalled they are by IRVING in The
Bells ;
While great beads of perspiration will
appear,
For in conscience-stricken terrors he excels !
Gloomy Bells !
Pit and gallery will glory in the weird and frightful
story,
Which may even thrill the bosom of the swells,
For every Yankee " dude "
Unquestionably should
Have nightmare after witnessing The Bells !
Will our cousins all go frantic from Pacific to
Atlantic, or condemn as childish antic
IRVING's dancing, and his gasping, and his
yells !
There's a certain admiration which the strange
impersonation
Still compels,
E'en from those who can't see beauty in The
Bells —
In the play that MR. LEWIS calls The Bells !
Wondrous Bells !
You first made Henry famous, so the stage
historian tells.
Will the scene be now repeated which in London
always greeted
His performance of Mathias in The Bells ?
Or will every sneering Yankee,
In his nasal tones, say " Thankee,
I guess this is just another of your mighty
British ' sells ' " ?

[149]

Let the thought for ever perish, that the actor whom
we cherish
Could fail to lick creation in The Bells!
But if there are detractors
Of this foremost of our actors,
Of the gentlemanly IRVING — friend of Toole's —
"They are neither man nor woman, they are
neither brute nor human,"
They are fools!
Judy.

THE GOBLIN GOOSE

ONCE it happened I'd been dining, on my
couch I slept reclining,
And awoke with moonlight shining brightly
on my bedroom floor,
It was in the bleak December, Christmas night as
I remember,
But I had no dying ember, as Poe had, when near
the door,
Like a gastronomic goblin just beside my chamber
door
Stood a bird, — and nothing more.

And I said, for I'm no craven, "Are you Edgar's
famous raven,
Seeking as with him a haven — were you mixed up
with Lenore?"
Then the bird uprose and fluttered, and this sentence
strange he uttered,

" Hang Lenore," he mildly muttered ; "you have
    seen me once before,
Seen me on this festive Christmas, seen me surely
    once before,
        I 'm the Goose — and nothing more."

Then he murmured, " Are you ready ? " and with
    motion slow and steady,
Straight he leapt upon my bed ; he simply gave a
    stifled roar ;
And I cried, " As I 'm a sinner, at a Goose-Club I
    was winner,
'T is a memory of my dinner, which I ate at half-
    past four,
Goose well-stuffed with sage and onions, which I
    ate at half-past four."
        Quoth he hoarsely, " Eat no more ! "

Said I, " I 've enjoyed your juices, breast and back ;
    but tell me, Goose, is
This revenge, and what the use is of your being
    such a bore ?
For Goose-flesh I will no more ax, if you 'll not
    sit on my thorax,
Go try honey mixed with borax, for I hear your
    throat is sore,
You speak gruffly, though too plainly, and I 'm
    sure your throat is sore."
        Quoth the nightmare, " Eat no more ! "

"Goose!" I shrieked out, "leave, oh, leave me,
    surely you don't mean to grieve me,
You are heavy, pray reprieve me, now my penance
    must be o'er;
Though to-night you 've brought me sorrow, com-
    fort surely comes to-morrow,
Some relief from those I 'd borrow at my doctor's
    ample store."
        Quoth the goblin, "Eat no more!"

And that fat Goose, never flitting, like a night-
    mare still is sitting
With me all the night emitting words that thrill my
    bosom's core,
Now throughout the Christmas season, while I lie
    and gasp and wheeze, on
Me he sits until my reason nothing surely can
    restore,
        While that Goose says, "Eat no more!"
                Punch.

AFTER LORD HOUGHTON

LOVE AND SCIENCE

(The Sphygmophon is an apparatus connected with the telephone, by the help of which the movements of the pulse and heart may be rendered audible)

I WANDERED by the brookside,
　I wandered by the mill;
　The Sphygmophon was fixed there,
　　Its wires ran past the hill.
I heeded not the grasshopper,
　Nor chirp of any bird,
For the beating of my own heart
　Was all the sound I heard.

To test his apparatus,
　One end I closely press'd,
The other at a distance,
　I hoped was next his chest.
I listened for his footfall,
　I listened for his word,
Still the bumping of my own heart
　Was all the sound I heard.

He came not, no he came not,
　The night came on alone;
And thinking he had tricked me,
　I loosed the Sphygmophon.

[153]

The evening air passed by my cheek,
  The leaves above were stirred,
When — the thumping of his own heart
  Was all the sound I heard.

With joy I grasped the magnet,
  When some one stood behind,
His hand was on my shoulder
  (But that I did not mind).
Each spoke then — nearer — nearer,
  We shouted every word;
But the booming of our own hearts
  Was all the sound we heard.

                                        Anonymous.

AFTER TENNYSON

THE BATHER'S DIRGE

BREAK, break, break,
   On thy cold, hard stones, O sea!
   And I hope that my tongue won't utter
The curses that rise in me.

Oh, well for the fisherman's boy,
   If he likes to be soused with the spray!
Oh, well for the sailor lad,
   As he paddles about in the bay!

And the ships swim happily on,
   To their haven under the hill;
But O for a clutch of that vanished hand,
   And a kick — for I'm catching a chill!

Break, break, break,
   At my poor bare feet, O sea!
But the artful scamp who has collar'd my clothes
   Will never come back to me.

                              Tennyson Minor.

LITTLE MISS MUFFET

(Reset as an Arthurian Idyl)

UPON a tuffet of most soft and verdant moss,
   Beneath the spreading branches of an ancient
      oak,
Miss Muffet sat, and upward gazed,
To where a linnet perched and sung,
And rocked him gently, to and fro.
Soft blew the breeze
And mildly swayed the bough,
Loud sung the bird,
And sweetly dreamed the maid;
Dreamed brightly of the days to come —
The golden days, with her fair future blent.
When one — some wondrous stately knight —
Of our great Arthur's " Table Round ; "
One, brave as Launcelot, and
Spotless as the pure Sir Galahad,
Should come, and coming, choose her
For his love, and in her name,
And for the sake of her fair eyes,
Should do most knightly deeds.
And as she dreamed and softly sighed,
She pensively began to stir,
With a tiny golden spoon
Within an antique dish upon her lap,
Some snow-white milky curds;
Soft were they, full of cream and rich,
And floated in translucent whey;

And as she stirred, she smiled,
Then gently tasted them.
And smiling, ate, nor sighed no more.
Lo! as she ate — nor harbored thought of ill —
Near and nearer yet, there to her crept,
A monster great and terrible,
With huge, misshapen body — leaden eyes —
Full many a long and hairy leg,
And soft and stealthy footstep.
Nearer still he came — Miss Muffet yet,
All unwitting his dread neighborhood,
Did eat her curds and dream.
Blithe, on the bough, the linnet sung —
All terrestrial natures, sleeping, wrapt
In a most sweet tranquillity.
Closer still the spider drew, and —
Paused beside her — lifted up his head
And gazed into her face.
Miss Muffet then, her consciousness alive
To his dread eyes upon her fixed,
Turned and beheld him.
Loud screamed she, frightened and amazed,
And straightway sprung upon her feet,
And, letting fall her dish and spoon,
She — shrieking — turned and fled.

Anonymous.

THE MUSICAL PITCH

BREAK, break, break,
　　O voice! — let me urge thy plea!
　　Oh, lower the Pitch, lest utter
Despair be the end of me!

'T is well for the fiddles to squeak,
　　The bassoon to grunt in its play;
'T were well had I lungs of brass,
　　Or that nothing but strings give way!

Break, break, break,
　　O voice! I must urge thy plea,
For the tender skin of my larynx is torn,
　　And I fail in my upper G!

　　　　　　　　　　　　　　Anonymous.

TO AN IMPORTUNATE HOST

(During dinner and after Tennyson)

ASK me no more: I 've had enough Chablis;
　　The wine may come again and take the
　　　　shape
From glass to glass of " Mountain " or of
　　" Cape,"
But my dear boy, when I have answered thee,
　　Ask me no more.

[158]

Ask me no more : what answer should I give,
   I love not pickled pork, nor partridge pie ;
   I feel if I took whiskey I should die !
Ask me no more — for I prefer to live :
     Ask me no more.

Ask me no more : unless my fate is sealed,
   And I have striven against you all in vain.
   Let your good butler bring me " Hock " again ;
Then rest, dear boy.　If for this once I yield,
     Ask me no more.

                    Anonymous.

THE VILLAGE CHOIR

HALF a bar, half a bar,
   Half a bar onward !
   Into an awful ditch
Choir and precentor hitch,
Into a mess of pitch,
   They led the Old Hundred.
Trebles to right of them,
Tenors to left of them,
Basses in front of them,
   Bellowed and thundered.
Oh, that precentor's look,
When the sopranos took
Their own time and hook
   From the Old Hundred !

Screeched all the trebles here,
Boggled the tenors there,

Raising the parson's hair,
　　While his mind wandered;
Theirs not to reason why
This psalm was pitched too high:
Theirs but to gasp and cry
　　Out the Old Hundred.
Trebles to right of them,
Tenors to left of them,
Basses in front of them,
　　Bellowed and thundered.
Stormed they with shout and yell,
Not wise they sang nor well,
Drowning the sexton's bell,
While all the church wondered.

Dire the precentor's glare,
Flashed his pitchfork in air
Sounding fresh keys to bear
　　Out the Old Hundred.
Swiftly he turned his back,
Reached he his hat from rack,
Then from the screaming pack,
　　Himself he sundered.
Tenors to right of him,
Tenors to left of him,
Discords behind him,
　　Bellowed and thundered.
Oh, the wild howls they wrought:
Right to the end they fought!
Some tune they sang, but not,
　　Not the Old Hundred.

Anonymous.

[160]

THE BITER BIT

THE sun is in the sky, mother, the flowers
     are springing fair;
     And the melody of woodland birds is stirring
in the air;
The river, smiling to the sky, glides onward to the
     sea,
And happiness is everywhere, oh, mother, but
     with me !

They are going to the church, mother — I hear
     the marriage bell
It booms along the upland — Oh ! it haunts me
     like a knell ;
He leads her on his arm, mother, he cheers her
     faltering step,
And closely to his side she clings — she does, the
     demirep !

They are crossing by the stile, mother, where we
     so oft have stood,
The stile beside the shady thorn, at the corner of
     the wood ;
And the boughs, that wont to murmur back the
     words that won my ear,
Wave their silver branches o'er him, as he leads
     his bridal fere.

[161]

He will pass beside the stream, mother, where first
    my hand he pressed,
By the meadow where, with quivering lip, his
    passion he confessed ;
And down the hedgerows where we've strayed
    again and yet again ;
But he will not think of me, mother, his broken-
    hearted Jane !

He said that I was proud, mother, that I looked
    for rank and gold,
He said I did not love him — he said my words
    were cold ;
He said I kept him off and on, in hopes of higher
    game —
And it may be that I did, mother ; who has n't
    done the same ?

I did not know my heart, mother — I know it now
    too late ;
I thought that I without a pang could wed some
    nobler mate ;
But no nobler suitor sought me — and he has
    taken wing,
And my heart is gone, and I am left a lone and
    blighted thing.

You may lay me in my bed, mother — my head is
    throbbing sore ;
And, mother, prithee, let the sheets be duly aired
    before ;

And, if you 'd please, my mother dear, your poor
    desponding child,
Draw me a pot of beer, mother, and mother, draw
    it mild !

William Aytoun.

THE LAUREATE

W HO would not be
    The Laureate bold,
     With his butt of sherry
To keep him merry,
And nothing to do but to pocket his gold ?

'T is I would be the Laureate bold !
When the days are hot, and the sun is strong,
I 'd lounge in the gateway all the day long
With her Majesty's footmen in crimson and gold.
I 'd care not a pin for the waiting-lord,
But I 'd lie on my back on the smooth greensward
With a straw in my mouth, and an open vest,
And the cool wind blowing upon my breast,
And I 'd vacantly stare at the clear blue sky,
And watch the clouds that are listless as I,
    Lazily, lazily !
And I 'd pick the moss and the daisies white,
And chew their stalks with a nibbling bite ;
And I 'd let my fancies roam abroad
In search of a hint for a birthday ode,
    Crazily, crazily !

Oh, that would be the life for me,
With plenty to get and nothing to do,
But to deck a pet poodle with ribbons of blue,
And whistle all day to the Queen's cockatoo,
   Trance-somely, trance-somely!
Then the chambermaids, that clean the rooms,
Would come to the windows and rest on their
  brooms,

With their saucy caps and their crispéd hair,
And they 'd toss their heads in the fragrant air,
And say to each other — " Just look down there,
At the nice young man, so tidy and small,
Who is paid for writing on nothing at all,
   Handsomely, handsomely!

They would pelt me with matches and sweet
  pastilles,
And crumpled-up balls of the royal bills,
Giggling and laughing, and screaming with fun,
As they 'd see me start, with a leap and a run,
From the broad of my back to the points of my
  toes,
When a pellet of paper hit my nose,
   Teasingly, sneezingly!

Then I 'd fling them bunches of garden flowers,
And hyacinths plucked from the Castle bowers;
And I 'd challenge them all to come down to me,
And I 'd kiss them all till they kissed me,
   Laughingly, laughingly.

Oh, would not that be a merry life,
Apart from care and apart from strife,
With the Laureate's wine, and the Laureate's pay,
And no deductions at quarter-day?
Oh, that would be the post for me!
With plenty to get and nothing to do,
But to deck a pet poodle with ribbons of blue,
And whistle a tune to the Queen's cockatoo,
And scribble of verses remarkably few,
And empty at evening a bottle or two,
      Quaffingly, quaffingly!

      'T is I would be
      The Laureate bold,
      With my butt of sherry
      To keep me merry,
And nothing to do but to pocket my gold!
                 William Aytoun.

THE LAY OF THE LOVELORN

COMRADES, you may pass the rosy.   With
      permission of the chair,
  I shall leave you for a little, for I'd like to
    take the air.

Whether 't was the sauce at dinner, or that glass
    of ginger-beer,
Or these strong cheroots, I know not, but I feel a
    little queer.

[165]

Let me go. Nay, Chuckster, blow me, 'pon my
    soul, this is too bad!
When you want me, ask the waiter; he knows
    where I 'm to be had.

Whew! This is a great relief now! Let me but
    undo my stock;
Resting here beneath the porch, my nerves will
    steady like a rock.

In my ears I hear the singing of a lot of favorite
    tunes —
Bless my heart, how very odd! Why surely
    there 's a brace of moons!

See! the stars! how bright they twinkle, winking
    with a frosty glare,
Like my faithless cousin Amy when she drove me
    to despair.

Oh, my cousin, spider-hearted! Oh, my Amy!
    No, confound it,
I must wear the mournful willow, — all around my
    heart I 've bound it!

Falser than the bank of fancy, frailer than a shin-
    ing glove,
Puppet to a father's anger, minion to a nabob's
    love!

Is it well to wish thee happy? Having known
    me, could you ever
Stoop to marry half a heart, and a little more than
    half a liver?

Happy! Damme! Thou shalt lower to his level
    day by day,
Changing from the best of china to the commonest
    of clay.

As the husband is, the wife is, — he is stomach-
    plagued and old;
And his curry soups will make thy cheek the color
    of his gold.

When his feeble love is sated, he will hold thee
    surely then
Something lower than his hookah, — something
    less than his cayenne.

What is this? His eyes are pinky. Was 't the
    claret? Oh, no, no, —
Bless your soul! it was the salmon, — salmon
    always makes him so.

Take him to thy dainty chamber — soothe him
    with thy lightest fancies;
He will understand thee, won't he? — pay thee
    with a lover's glances?

[167]

Louder than the loudest trumpet, harsh as harshest
    ophicleide,
Nasal respirations answer the endearments of his
    bride.

Sweet repose, delightful music! Gaze upon thy
    noble charge,
Till the spirit fill thy bosom that inspired the
    meek Laffarge.

Better thou wert dead before me, — better, better
    that I stood,
Looking on thy murdered body, like the injured
    Daniel Good!

Better thou and I were lying, cold and timber-
    stiff and dead,
With a pan of burning charcoal underneath our
    nuptial bed!

Cursed be the Bank of England's notes, that tempt
    the soul to sin!
Cursed be the wants of acres, — doubly cursed the
    want of tin!

Cursed be the marriage-contract, that enslaved thy
    soul to greed!
Cursed be the sallow lawyer that prepared and
    drew the deed!

Cursed be his foul apprentice, who the loathsome
    fees did earn!
Cursed be the clerk and parson, — cursed be the
    whole concern!

Oh, 't is well that I should bluster, — much I 'm
    like to make of that;
Better comfort have I found in singing "All
    Around my Hat."

But that song, so wildly plaintive, palls upon my
    British ears.
'T will not do to pine for ever, — I am getting up
    in years.

Can't I turn the honest penny, scribbling for the
    weekly press,
And in writing Sunday libels drown my private
    wretchedness?

Oh, to feel the wild pulsation that in manhood's
    dawn I knew,
When my days were all before me, and my years
    were twenty-two!

When I smoked my independent pipe along the
    Quadrant wide,
With the many larks of London flaring up on every
    side;

When I went the pace so wildly, caring little what
    might come;
Coffee-milling care and sorrow with a nose-adapted
    thumb;

Felt the exquisite enjoyment, tossing nightly off,
    oh, heavens!
Brandies at the Cider Cellars, kidneys smoking hot
    at Evans'!

Or in the Adelphi sitting, half in rapture, half in
    tears,
Saw the glorious melodrama conjure up the shades
    of years!

Saw Jack Sheppard, noble stripling, act his won-
    drous feats again,
Snapping Newgate's bars of iron, like an infant's
    daisy chain.

Might was right, and all the terrors, which had
    held the world in awe,
Were despised, and priggings prospered, spite of
    Laurie, spite of law.

In such scenes as these I triumphed, ere my pas-
    sion's edge was rusted,
And my cousin's cold refusal left me very much
    disgusted!

Since, my heart is sere and withered, and I do not
    care a curse
Whether worse shall be the better, or the better be
    the worse.

Hark! my merry comrades call me, bawling for
    another jorum;
They would mock me in derision, should I thus
    appear before 'em.

Womankind shall no more vex me, such at least as
    go arrayed
In the most expensive satins and the newest silk
    brocade.

I'll to Afric, lion-haunted, where the giant forest
    yields
Rarer robes and finer tissue than are sold at Spital-
    fields.

Or to burst all chains of habit, flinging habit's self
    aside
I shall walk the tangled jungle in mankind's pri-
    meval pride;

Feeding on the luscious berries and the rich
    cassava root,
Lots of dates and lots of guavas, clusters of for-
    bidden fruit.

[171]

Never comes the trader thither, never o'er the
    purple main
Sounds the oath of British commerce, or the accent
    of Cockaigne.

There, methinks, would be enjoyment, where no
    envious rule prevents;
Sink the Steamboats! cuss the railways! rot, oh,
    rot the Three per Cents!

There the passions, cramped no longer, shall have
    space to breathe, my cousin!
I will wed some savage woman — nay, I'll wed at
    least a dozen.

There I'll rear my young mulattoes, as no Bond
    Street brats are reared;
They shall dive for alligators, catch the wild goats
    by the beard —

Whistle to the cockatoos, and mock the hairy-
    faced baboon,
Worship mighty Mumbo Jumbo in the Mountains
    of the Moon.

I myself, in far Timbuctoo, leopard's blood will
    daily quaff,
Ride a tiger-hunting, mounted on a thorough-bred
    giraffe.

Fiercely shall I shout the war-whoop, as some
  sullen stream he crosses,
Startling from their noonday slumbers iron-bound
  rhinoceroses.

Fool! again the dream, the fancy! But I know
  my words are mad,
For I hold the gray barbarian lower than the
  Christian cad.

I the swell — the city dandy! I to seek such
  horrid places, —
I to haunt with squalid negroes, blubber-lips, and
  monkey-faces.

I to wed with Coromantees! I, who managed —
  very near —
To secure the heart and fortune of the widow
  Shillibeer!

Stuff and nonsense! let me never fling a single
  chance away;
Maids ere now, I know, have loved me, and another maiden may.

Morning Post (*The Times* won't trust me) help me,
  as I know you can;
I will pen an advertisement, — that 's a never fail-
  ing plan.

[173]

" Wanted — by a bard, in wedlock, some young
  interesting woman ;
Looks are not so much an object, if the shiners be
  forthcoming !

" Hymen's chains the advertiser vows shall be but
  silken fetters ;
Please address to A. T., Chelsea.   N. B. — You
  must pay the letters."

That 's the sort of thing to do it.   Now I 'll go
  and taste the balmy, —
Rest thee with thy yellow nabob, spider-hearted
  Cousin Amy !

                                        William Aytoun.

IN IMMEMORIAM

WE seek to know, and knowing seek ;
  We seek, we know, and every sense
  Is trembling with the great Intense
And vibrating to what we speak.

We ask too much, we seek too oft,
We know enough, and should no more ;
And yet we skim through Fancy's lore
And look to earth and not aloft.

A something comes from out the gloom;
I know it not, nor seek to know;
I only see it swell and grow,
And more than this world would presume.

Meseems, a circling void I fill,
And I, unchanged where all is changed;
It seems unreal; I own it strange,
Yet nurse the thoughts I cannot kill.

I hear the ocean's surging tide,
Raise quiring on its carol-tune;
I watch the golden-sickled moon,
And clearer voices call besides.

O Sea! whose ancient ripples lie
On red-ribbed sands where seaweeds shone;
O Moon! whose golden sickle's gone;
O Voices all! like ye I die!

Cuthbert Bede.

SIR EGGNOGG

FORTH from the purple battlements he fared,
Sir Eggnogg of the Rampant Lily, named
From that embrasure of his argent shield
Given by a thousand leagues of heraldry
On snuffy parchments drawn. So forth he fared,
By bosky boles and autumn leaves he fared,

[175]

Where grew the juniper with berries black,
The sphery mansions of the future gin.
But naught of this decoyed his mind, so bent
On fair Miasma, Saxon-blooded girl,
Who laughed his loving lullabies to scorn,
And would have snatched his hero-sword to deck
Her haughty brow, or warm her hands withal,
So scornful she; and thence Sir Eggnogg cursed
Between his teeth, and chewed his iron boots
In spleen of love.   But ere the morn was high
In the robustious heaven, the postern-tower
Clang to the harsh, discordant, slivering scream
Of the tire-woman, at the window bent
To dress her crispéd hair.   She saw, ah, woe!
The fair Miasma, overbalanced, hurled
O'er the flamboyant parapet which ridged
The muffled coping of the castle's peak,
Prone on the ivory pavement of the court,
Which caught and cleft her fairest skull, and sent
Her rosy brains to fleck the Orient floor.
This saw Sir Eggnogg, in his stirrups poised.
Saw he and cursed, with many a deep-mouthed oath,
And, finding nothing more could reunite
The splintered form of fair Miasma, rode
On his careering palfrey to the wars,
And there found death, another death than hers.

Bayard Taylor.

GODIVA

" I WAITED for the Train at Coventry,"
   The Train was several hundred years too late
   (It had not been invented yet, you see) ;
Such is the Cold Cast Irony of Fate.
At last the Train arrived, and with it too
Your Book — a Precious Package marked " collect."
Raptured I read it through and through, and through,
And then I paused in sadness to reflect —
How that same Book had been a priceless boon,
But for a little accident of Date ;
If only I had not been born so soon,
Or if you had not gone to press so late.
O Book, if only you had come to me
Ere I rode forth upon that morning sad !
In naught but Faith and Hope and Charity,
And other Vague Abstractions thinly clad ;
In whole Editions I would have invested
(I hope you get good Royalties therefrom),
To keep the naughty townfolk interested
And most Particularly, Peeping Tom.

                                   Oliver Herford.

A LAUREATE'S LOG

(Rough-weather notes from the New Birthday-Book)

MONDAY

IF you 're waking, please don't call me, please
    don't call me, Currie dear,
    For they tell me that to-morrow toward the
    open we 're to steer!
No doubt, for you and those aloft, the maddest
    merriest way, —
But I always feel best in a bay, Currie,
I always feel best in a bay.

TUESDAY

    Take, take, take?
    What will I take for tea?
    The thinnest slice — no butter,
    And that 's quite enough for me.

WEDNESDAY

It is the little roll within the berth
That, by and by, will put an end to mirth,
And, never ceasing, slowly prostrate all.

THURSDAY

Let me alone!   What pleasure can you have
In chaffing evil?   Tell me what 's the fun
Of ever climbing up the climbing wave?

[178]

All you, the rest, you know how to behave
In roughish weather! I, for one
Ask for the shore — or death, dark death, —
I am so done.

FRIDAY

Twelve knots an hour!   But what am I ?
   A poet with no land in sight,
   Insisting that he feels " all right,"
With half a smile and half a sigh.

SATURDAY

Comfort?   Comfort scorned of lubbers!   Hear
   this truth the Poet roar,
That a sorrow's crown of sorrows is remembering
   days on shore.
Drug his soda lest he learn it when the foreland
   gleams a speck
In the dead unhappy night, when he can't sit up
   on deck!

SUNDAY

Ah! you 've called me nice and early, nice and
   early, Currie dear!
What?   Really in ?   Well, come, the news I 'm
   precious glad to hear;
For though in such good company I willingly
   would stay —
I 'm glad to be back in the bay, Currie,
I 'm glad to be back in the bay.

                    Punch.

THE RECOGNITION

HOME they brought her sailor son,
　　Grown a man across the sea,
　　Tall and broad and black of beard,
And hoarse of voice as man may be.

Hand to shake and mouth to kiss,
　　Both he offered ere he spoke;
But she said — " What man is this
　　Comes to play a sorry joke?"

Then they praised him — call'd him " smart,"
　　" Tightest lad that ever stept;"
But her son she did not know,
　　And she neither smiled nor wept.

Rose, a nurse of ninety years,
　　Set a pigeon-pie in sight;
She saw him eat — "'T is he! 't is he!"
　　She knew him — by his appetite!

　　　　　　　　　　William Sawyer.

THE HIGHER PANTHEISM IN A
NUTSHELL

ONE, who is not, we see: but one, whom we
　　see not, is;
　　Surely this is not that: but that is assuredly
　　this.

What, and wherefore, and whence? for under is
    over and under;
If thunder could be without lightning, lightning
    could be without thunder.

Doubt is faith in the main: but faith, on the
    whole, is doubt;
We cannot believe by proof: but could we believe
    without?

Why, and whither, and how? for barley and rye
    are not clover;
Neither are straight lines curves: yet over is under
    and over.

Two and two may be four: but four and four are
    not eight;
Fate and God may be twain: but God is the same
    thing as fate.

Ask a man what he thinks, and get from a man
    what he feels;
God, once caught in the fact, shews you a fair
    pair of heels.

Body and spirit are twins: God only knows which
    is which;
The soul squats down in the flesh, like a tinker
    drunk in a ditch.

One and two are not one: but one and nothing is
    two;
Truth can hardly be false, if falsehood cannot be
    true.

Once the mastodon was: pterodactyls were com-
    mon as cocks;
Then the mammoth was God: now is He a
    prize ox.

Parallels all things are: yet many of these are
    askew.
You are certainly I: but certainly I am not you.

Springs the rock from the plain, shoots the stream
    from the rock;
Cocks exist for the hen: but hens exist for the
    cock.

God, whom we see not, is: and God, who is not,
    we see;
Fiddle, we know, is diddle: and diddle, we take
    it, is dee.

Algernon Charles Swinburne.

TIMBUCTOO. — PART I.

The situation.

IN Africa (a quarter of the world),   1
  Men's skins are black, their hair is crisp and
    curl'd,
And somewhere there, unknown to public view,
A mighty city lies, called Timbuctoo.

The natural history.

There stalks the tiger, — there the lion roars,   5
Who sometimes eats the luckless blackamoors;
All that he leaves of them the monster throws
To jackals, vultures, dogs, cats, kites, and crows;
His hunger thus the forest monster gluts,
And then lies down 'neath trees called cocoa-nuts. 10

The lion hunt.

Quick issue out, with musket, torch, and brand,
The sturdy blackamoors, a dusky band!
The beast is found — pop goes the musketoons —
The lion falls covered with horrid wounds.

Their lives at home.

At home their lives in pleasure always flow,   15
But many have a different lot to know!

Abroad.

They're often caught and sold as slaves, alas!

Reflections on the foregoing.

Thus men from highest joy to sorrow pass ;
Yet though thy monarch and thy nobles boil
Rack and molasses in Jamaica's isle,   20
Desolate Africa ! thou art lovely yet !
One heart yet beats which ne'er thee shall forget.

What though thy maidens are a blackish brown,
Does virtue dwell in whiter breasts alone ?
Oh no, oh no, oh no, oh no, oh no !   25
It shall not, must not, cannot, e'er be so.
The day shall come when Albion's self shall feel
Stern Afric's wrath, and writhe 'neath Afric's steel.

I see her tribes the hill of glory mount,
And sell their sugars on their own account ;   30
While round her throne the prostrate nations come,
Sue for her rice, and barter for her rum !

Notes. — Lines 1 and 2. — See Guthrie's Geography.
The site of Timbuctoo is doubtful ; the author has neatly
expressed this in the poem, at the same time giving us some
slight hints relative to its situation.
  Line 5. — So Horace : leonum arida nutrix.
  Line 13. — " Pop goes the musketoons." A learned
friend suggested "Bang" as a stronger expression, but as
African gunpowder is notoriously bad, the author thought
"Pop" the better word.
  Lines 15–18. — A concise but affecting description is
here given of the domestic habits of the people. The
infamous manner in which they are entrapped and sold as
slaves is described, and the whole ends with an appropriate
moral sentiment. The enthusiasm the author feels is beautifully expressed in lines 25 and 26.

W. M. Thackeray.

[184]

AFTER TUPPER

OF FRIENDSHIP

CHOOSE judiciously thy friends; for to dis-
      card them is undesirable,
   Yet it is better to drop thy friends, O my
daughter, than to drop thy H's.
Dost thou know a wise woman? yea, wiser than
   the children of light?
Hath she a position? and a title? and are her
   parties in the *Morning Post?*
If thou dost, cleave unto her, and give up unto her
   thy body and mind;
Think with her ideas, and distribute thy smiles at
   her bidding:
So shalt thou become like unto her; and thy manners shall be "formed,"
And thy name shall be a Sesame, at which the
   doors of the great shall fly open:
Thou shalt know every Peer, his arms, and the
   date of his creation,
His pedigree and their intermarriages, and cousins
   to the sixth remove:
Thou shalt kiss the hand of Royalty, and lo! in
   next morning's papers,
Side by side with rumors of wars, and stories of
   shipwrecks and sieges,

[185]

Shall appear thy name, and the minutiæ of thy
head-dress and petticoat,
For an enraptured public to muse upon over their
matutinal muffin.

Charles S. Calverley.

OF READING

READ not Milton, for he is dry; nor Shakespeare, for he wrote of common life;
Nor Scott, for his romances, though fascinating, are yet intelligible;
Nor Thackeray, for he is a Hogarth, a photogra-
pher who flattereth not;
Nor Kingsley, for he shall teach thee that thou
shouldest not dream, but do.
Read incessantly thy Burke; that Burke who,
nobler than he of old,
Treateth of the Peer and Peeress, the truly Sublime
and Beautiful;
Likewise study the " creations " of " the Prince
of modern Romance; "
Sigh over Leonard the Martyr, and smile on Pel-
ham the puppy;
Learn how " love is the dram-drinking of existence; "
And how we " invoke, in the Gadara of our still
closets,
The beautiful ghost of the Ideal, with the simple
wand of the pen."
Listen how Maltravers and the orphan " forgot all
but love,"

And how Devereux's family chaplain " made and
    unmade kings ; "
How Eugene Aram, though a thief, a liar, and a
    murderer,
Yet, being intellectual, was amongst the noblest
    of mankind ;
So shalt thou live in a world peopled with heroes
    and master spirits
And if thou canst not realize the Ideal, thou shalt
    at least idealize the Real.

Charles S. Calverley.

AFTER THACKERAY

THE WILLOW–TREE

(Another version)

LONG by the willow-trees
     Vainly they sought her,
   Wild rang the mother's screams
 O'er the gray water:
" Where is my lovely one?
 Where is my daughter?

" Rouse thee, Sir Constable —
   Rouse thee and look;
 Fisherman, bring your net,
   Boatman, your hook.
 Beat in the lily-beds,
   Dive in the brook!"

 Vainly the constable
   Shouted and called her;
 Vainly the fisherman
   Beat the green alder;
 Vainly he flung the net,
   Never it hauled her!

Mother beside the fire
   Sat, her nightcap in;
Father, in easy chair,
   Gloomily napping,
When at the window-sill
   Came a light tapping!

And a pale countenance
   Looked through the casement,
Loud beat the mother's heart,
   Sick with amazement,
And at the vision which
   Came to surprise her,
Shrieked in an agony —
   " Lor'! it's Elizar!"

Yes, 't was Elizabeth —
   Yes, 't was their girl;
Pale was her cheek, and her
   Hair out of curl.
" Mother," the loving one,
   Blushing exclaimed,
" Let not your innocent
   Lizzy be blamed.

" Yesterday, going to Aunt
   Jones's to tea,
Mother, dear mother, I
   Forgot the door-key!

And as the night was cold
    And the way steep,
Mrs. Jones kept me to
    Breakfast and sleep."

Whether her Pa and Ma
    Fully believed her,
That we shall never know,
    Stern they received her;
And for the work of that
    Cruel, though short, night
Sent her to bed without
    Tea for a fortnight.

MORAL

Hey diddle diddlety,
    Cat and the fiddlety,
Maidens of England, take caution by she!
    Let love and suicide
    Never tempt you aside,
And always remember to take the door-key.
                                    W. M. Thackeray.

AFTER CHARLES DICKENS

MAN'S PLACE IN NATURE

(*Dedicated to Darwin and Huxley*)

THEY told him gently he was made
    Of nicely tempered mud,
      That man no lengthened part had played
Anterior to the Flood.
'T was all in vain; he heeded not,
    Referring plant and worm,
Fish, reptile, ape, and Hottentot,
    To one primordial germ.

They asked him whether he could bear
    To think his kind allied
To all those brutal forms which were
    In structure Pithecoid;
Whether he thought the apes and us
    Homologous in form;
He said, " Homo and Pithecus
    Came from one common germ."

They called him " atheistical,"
    " Sceptic," and " infidel."
They swore his doctrines without fail
    Would plunge him into hell.

But he with proofs in no way lame,
  Made this deduction firm,
That all organic beings came
  From one primordial germ.

That as for the Noachian flood,
  'T was long ago disproved,
That as for man being made of mud,
  All by whom truth is loved
Accept as fact what, *malgré* strife,
  Research tends to confirm —
That man, and everything with life,
  Came from one common germ.

                              Anonymous.

AFTER ROBERT BROWNING

HOME TRUTHS FROM ABROAD

I

" OH! to be in England
 Now that April's there.
 And whoever wakes in England
Sees some morning " in despair;
There's a horrible fog i' the heart o' the town,
And the greasy pavement is damp and brown,
While the rain-drop falls from the laden bough
 In England —— now !

II

" And after April when May follows,"
How foolish seem the returning swallows.
Hark! how the east wind sweeps along the street,
And how we give one universal sneeze !
The hapless lambs at thought of mint-sauce bleat,
And ducks are conscious of the coming peas.
Lest you should think the Spring is really present,
A biting frost will come to make things pleasant;
And though the reckless flowers begin to blow,
They'd better far have nestled down below;
An English Spring sets men and women frowning,
Despite the rhapsodies of Robert Browning.

Anonymous.

[193]

AFTER BROWNING

NOT that I care for ceremonies — no ;
　　But still there are occasions, as you see
　　(Observe the costumes — gallantly they show
To my poor judgment !) which, twixt you and me,
Not to come forth, one's few remaining hairs,
Or wig, — it matters little, — bravely brushed
And oiled, dress-coated, sprucely-clad, the tears
And tweaks and wrenches, people overflushed
With — well, not wine — oh, no, we 'll rather say
Anticipation, the delight of seeing
No matter what ! inflict upon you (pray
Remove your elbow, friend !) in spite of being
Not quite the man one used to be, and not
So young as once one was, would argue one
Churlish, indifferent, hipped, rheumatic, what
You please to say.

　　　　　　　　So, not to spoil the fun —
Comprenez-vous ? — observe that lady there,
In native worth !　Aha ! you see the jest ?
Not bad, I think.　My own, too !　Woman 's fair,
Or not — the odds so long as she is dressed ?
They 're coming !　Soh !　Ha, Bennett's Bar-
　　　carole —
A poor thing, but mine own !　That minor third
Is not so bad now !　Mum, sirs !　(Bless my soul,
I wonder what her veil cost !)　Mum 's the word !
　　　　　　　　　　　　　　　Anonymous.

[194]

THE COCK AND THE BULL

YOU see this pebble-stone? It's a thing I
   bought
      Of a bit of a chit of a boy i' the mid o' the
      day.
I like to dock the smaller parts o' speech,
As we curtail the already cur-tail'd cur —
(You catch the paronomasia, play 'po' words?)
Did, rather, i' the pre-Landseerian days.
Well, to my muttons. I purchased the concern,
And clapt it i' my poke, having given for same
By way o' chop, swop, barter or exchange —
"Chop" was my snickering dandiprat's own term —
One shilling and fourpence, current coin o' the
      realm.
O-n-e one, and f-o-u-r four
Pence, one and fourpence — you are with me, sir? —
What hour it skills not: ten or eleven o' the clock,
One day (and what a roaring day it was
Go shop or sight-see — bar a spit o' rain!)
In February, eighteen sixty-nine,
Alexandria Victoria, Fidei —
Hm — hm — how runs the jargon? being on the
      throne.

Such, sir, are all the facts, succinctly put,
The basis or substratum — what you will —
Of the impending eighty thousand lines.
"Not much in 'em either," quoth perhaps simple
      Hodge.

But there 's a superstructure.   Wait a bit.
Mark first the rationale of the thing :
Hear logic rivel and levigate the deed.
That shilling — and for matter o' that, the pence —
I had o' course upo' me — wi' me say —
(*Mecum* 's the Latin, make a note o' that)
When I popp'd pen i' stand, scratch'd ear, wiped
    snout,
(Let everybody wipe his own himself)
Sniff'd — tch ! — at snuff-box; tumbled up, ne-
    heed,
Haw-haw'd (not hee-haw'd, that 's another guess
    thing),
Then fumbled at, and stumbled out of, door.
I shoved the timber ope wi' my omoplat;
And *in vestibulo*, i' the lobby to wit
(Iacobi Facciolati's rendering, sir),
Donn'd galligaskins, antigropeloes,
And so forth ; and, complete with hat and gloves,
One on and one a-dangle i' my hand,
And ombrifuge (Lord love you !), case o' rain,
I flopp'd forth, 'sbuddikins ! on my own ten toes
(I do assure you there be ten of them),
And went clump-clumping up hill and down dale
To find myself o' the sudden i' front o' the boy.
But case I had n't 'em on me, could I ha' bought
This sort-o'-kind-o'-what-you-might-call toy,
This pebble thing, o' the boy-thing ?   Q. E. D.
That 's proven without aid from mumping Pope,
Sleek porporate or bloated Cardinal.
(Is n't it, old Fatchaps ?   You 're in Euclid now.)
So, having the shilling — having i' fact a lot —

[196]

And pence and halfpence, ever so many o' them,
I purchased, as I think I said before,
The pebble (*lapis, lapidis,-di,-dem,-de*—
What nouns 'crease short i' the genitive, Fatchaps,
    eh ?)
O' the boy, a bare-legg'd beggarly son of a gun,
For one and fourpence.   Here we are again.

Now Law steps in, bigwigg'd, voluminous-jaw'd ;
Investigates and re-investigates.
Was the transaction illegal ?   Law shakes head.
Perpend, sir, all the bearings of the case.

At first the coin was mine, the chattel his.
But now (by virtue of the said exchange
And barter) *vice versa* all the coin,
Per juris operationem, vests
I' the boy and his assigns till ding o' doom ;
(*In sæcula sæculo-o-o-rum* ;
I think I hear the Abate mouth out that.)
To have and hold the same to him and them.
Confer some idiot on Conveyancing.

Whereas the pebble and every part thereof,
And all that appertaineth thereunto,
Quodcunque pertinet ad eam rem
(I fancy, sir, my Latin 's rather pat),
Or shall, will, may, might, can, could, would or
    should
(*Subaudi cætera* — clap we to the close —
For what 's the good of Law in a case o' the kind),
Is mine to all intents and purposes.
This settled, I resume the thread o' the tale.

Now for a touch o' the vendor's quality.
He says a gen'lman bought a pebble of him
(This pebble i' sooth, sir, which I hold i' my
      hand),
And paid for 't, *like* a gen'lman, on the nail.
" Did I o'ercharge him a ha'penny ?   Devil a bit.
Fiddlepin's end!   Get out, you blazing ass !
Gabble o' the goose.   Don't bugaboo-baby *me !*
Go double or quits?   Yah! tittup! what 's the
      odds ? "
There 's the transaction view'd i' the vendor's light.

Next ask that dumpled hag, stood snuffling by,
With her three frowsy blowsy brats o' babes,
The scum o' the kennel, cream o' the filth-heap —
      Faugh !
Aie, aie, aie, aie ! ὀτοτοτοτοτοῖ
('Stead which we blurt out Hoighty toighty now),
And the baker and candlestickmaker, and Jack and
      Jill,
Blear'd Goody this and queasy Gaffer that.
Ask the schoolmaster.   Take schoolmaster first.

He saw a gentleman purchase of a lad
A stone, and pay for it *rite*, on the square,
And carry it off *per saltum*, jauntily,
Propria quae maribus, gentleman's property now
(Agreeably to the law explain'd above),
In proprium usum, for his private ends,
The boy he chuck'd a brown i' the air, and bit
I' the face the shilling; heaved a thumping stone
At a lean hen that ran cluck clucking by

(And hit her, dead as nail i' post o' door),
Then *abiit* — what 's the Ciceronian phrase ? —
Excessit, evasit, erupit — off slogs boy ;
Off like bird, *avi similis* — you observed
The dative ? Pretty i' the Mantuan !) — *Anglice*
Off in three flea skips. *Hactenus,* so far,
So good, *tam bene. Bene, satis, male,* — .
Where was I with my trope 'bout one in a quag ?
I did once hitch the syntax into verse :
Verbum personale, a verb personal,
Concordat — ay, "agrees," old Fatchaps — *cum*
Nominativo, with its nominative,
Genere, i' point o' gender, *numero,*
O' number, *et persona,* and person. *Ut,*
Instance : *Sol ruit,* down flops sun, *et,* and,
Montes umbrantur, out flounce mountains. Pah !
Excuse me, sir, I think I 'm going mad.
You see the trick on 't though, and can yourself
Continue the discourse *ad libitum.*
It takes up about eighty thousand lines,
A thing imagination boggles at ;
And might, odds-bobs, sir ! in judicious hands,
Extend from here to Mesopotamy.

Charles S. Calverley.

A STACCATO TO O LE LUPE

O LE LUPE, Gelett Burgess, this is very sad
    to find;
In the *Bookman* for September, in a manner
    most unkind,
There appears a half-page picture, makes me think
    I 've lost my mind.

They have reproduced a window, — Doxey's
    window (I dare say
In your rambles you have seen it, passed it twenty
    times a day), —
As " A Novel Exhibition of Examples of Decay."

There is Nordau we all sneer at, and Verlaine we
    all adore,
And a little book of verses with its betters by the
    score,
With three faces on the cover I believe I 've seen
    before.

Well, here 's matter for reflection, makes me won-
    der where I am.
Here is Ibsen the gray lion, linked to Beardsley
    the black lamb.
I was never out of Boston; all that I can say is,
    " Damn !"

Who could think, in two short summers we should
  cause so much remark,
With no purpose but our pastime, and to make
  the public hark,
When I soloed on THE CHAP-BOOK, and you
  answered with THE LARK!

Do young people take much pleasure when they
  read that sort of thing?
"Well, they buy it," answered Doxey, "and I
  take what it will bring.
Publishers may dread extinction — not with such
  fads on the string.

"There is always sale for something, and demand
  for what is new.
These young people who are restless, and have
  nothing else to do,
Like to think there is 'a movement,' just to keep
  themselves in view.

"There is nothing in Decadence but the magic of
  a name.
People talk and papers drivel, scent a vice, and
  hint a shame;
And all that is good for business, helps to boom
  my little game."

But when I sit down to reason, think to stand
  upon my nerve,
Meditate on portly leisure with a balance in reserve,
In he comes with his "Decadence!" like a fly in
  my preserve.

I can see myself, O Burgess, half a century from
    now,
Laid to rest among the ghostly, like a broken toy
    somehow ;
All my lovely songs and ballads vanished with
    your " Purple Cow."

But I will return some morning, though I know it
    will be hard,
To Cornhill among the bookstalls, and surprise
    some minor bard ;
Turning over their old rubbish for the treasures
    we discard.

I shall warn him like a critic, creeping when his
    back is turned :
" Ink and paper, dead and done with ; Doxey spent
    what Doxey earned ;
Poems doubtless are immortal where a poem can
    be discerned ! "

How his face will go to ashes, when he feels his
    empty purse !
How he 'll wish his vogue were greater, — plume
    himself it is no worse ;
Then go bother the dear public with his puny little
    verse !

Don't I know how he will pose it, patronize our
    larger time :
" Poor old Browning ; little Kipling ; what attempts
    they made to rhyme ! "
Just let me have half an hour with that nin-
    compoop sublime !

I will haunt him like a purpose, I will ghost him
    like a fear;
When he least expects my presence, I'll be mum-
    bling in his ear:
"O Le Lupe lived in Frisco, and I lived in Boston
    here.

"Never heard of us? Good heavens, can you
    never have been told
Of the Larks we used to publish, and the Chap-
    Books that we sold?
Where are all our first editions?" I feel damp
    and full of mould.

Bliss Carman.

BY THE SEA

Mutatis Mutandis

IS it life or is it death?
    A whiff of the cool salt scum,
    As the whole sea puffed its breath
Against you, — blind and dumb:
This way it answereth.

Nearer the sands it shows
    Spotted and leprous tints;
But stay! yon fisher knows
    Rock-tokens, which evince
How high the tide arose.

How high?   In you and me
   'T was falling then, I think;
Open your heart's eyes, see
   From just so slight a chink
The chasm that now must be.

You sighed and shivered then.
   Blue ecstasies of June
Around you, shouts of fishermen,
   Sharp wings of sea gulls, soon
To dip — the clock struck ten!

Was it the cup too full,
   To carry it you grew
Too faint, the wine's hue dull
   (Dulness, misjudged untrue!),
Love's flower unfit to cull?

You should have held me fast
   One moment, stopped my pace,
Crushed down the feeble, vast
   Suggestions of embrace,
And so be crowned at last.

But now! Bare-legged and brown
   Bait-diggers delve the sand,
Tramp i' the sunshine down
   Burnt-ochre vestured land,
And yonder stares the town.

A heron screams! I shut
  This book of scurf and scum,
Its final pages uncut;
  The sea-beast, blind and dumb,
Done with his bellowing? All but!

Bayard Taylor.

ANGELO ORDERS HIS DINNER

I, ANGELO, obese, black-garmented,
  Respectable, much in demand, well fed
  With mine own larder's dainties, where, in-
    deed,
Such cakes of myrrh or fine alyssum seed,
Thin as a mallow-leaf, embrowned o' the top.
Which, cracking, lets the ropy, trickling drop
Of sweetness touch your tongue, or potted nests
Which my recondite recipe invests
With cold conglomerate tidbits — ah, the bill!
(You say), but given it were mine to fill
My chests, the case so put were yours, we'll say
(This counter, here, your post, as mine to-day),
And you've an eye to luxuries, what harm
In smoothing down your palate with the charm
Yourself concocted? There we issue take;
And see! as thus across the rim I break
This puffy paunch of glazed embroidered cake,
So breaks, through use, the lust of watering chaps
And craveth plainness: do I so? Perhaps;
But that's my secret. Find me such a man
As Lippo yonder, built upon the plan

[205]

Of heavy storage, double-navelled, fat
From his own giblet's oils, an Ararat
Uplift o'er water, sucking rosy draughts
From Noah's vineyard, — crisp, enticing wafts
Yon kitchen now emits, which to your sense
Somewhat abate the fear of old events,
Qualms to the stomach, — I, you see, am slow
Unnecessary duties to forego, —
You understand ?   A venison haunch, *haut gout.*
Ducks that in Cimbrian olives mildly stew.
And sprigs of anise, might one's teeth provoke
To taste, and so we wear the complex yoke
Just as it suits, — my liking, I confess,
More to receive, and to partake no less,
Still more obese, while through thick adipose
Sensation shoots, from testing tongue to toes
Far off, dim-conscious, at the body's verge,
Where the froth-whispers of its waves emerge
On the untasting sand.   Stay, now ! a seat
Is bare : I, Angelo, will sit and eat.

Bayard Taylor.

THE FLIGHT OF THE BUCKET

*P*RE-ADMONISHETH *the writer:*
    H'm, for a subject it is well enough!
    Who wrote "Sordello" finds no subject
tough.

Well, Jack and Jill — God knows the life they led
(The poet never told us, more 's the pity)

Pent up in some damp kennel of their own,
Beneath the hillside ; but it once befell
That Jack and Jill, niece, cousin, uncle, aunt
(Some one of all the brood), would wash and
      scour,
Rinse out a cess-pit, swab the kennel floor,
And water (*liquor vitae*, Lawson calls,
But I — I hold by whisky.   Never mind ;
I did n't mean to hurt your feelings, sir,
And missed the scrap o' blue at buttonhole),
Spring water was the needful at the time,
So they must climb the hill for 't.   Well and good.
We all climb hills, I take it, on some quest,
Maybe for less than stinking (I forgot !
I mean than wholesome) water. . . . Ferret out
The rotten bucket from the lumber shed,
Weave ropes and splice the handle — off they go
To where the cold spring bubbles up i' the cleft,
And sink the bucket brimful in the spate.
Then downwards — hanging back ?   (You bet
      your life
The girl's share fell upon Jack's shoulders.) Down,
Down to the bottom — all but — trip, slip, squelch !
And guggle-guggle goes the bucketful
Back to the earth, and Jack 's a broken head,
And swears amid the heather does our Jack.
(A man would swear who watched both blood and
      bucket,

One dripping down his forehead, t' other fled
Clinkety-tinkle, to the stones below,
A good half-hour's trudge to get it back.)

Jack, therefore, as I said, exploded straight
In brimstone-flavored language. You, of course,
Maintain he bore it calmly — not a bit.
A good bucolic curse that rent the cliffs
And frightened for a moment quaking Jill
Out of the limp, unmeaning girl's tee-hee
That womankind delight in. . . . Here we end
The first verse — there's a deal to study in't.

So much for Jack — but here's a fate above,
A cosmic force that blunders into right,
Just when the strained sense hints at revolution
Because the world's great fly-wheel runs aslant —
And up go Jill's red kibes. (You think I'm
      wrong;
And Fate was napping at the time; perhaps
You're right.) We'll call it Devil's agency
That sent the shrieking sister on her head,
And knocked the tangled locks against the stones.
Well, down went Jill, but was n't hurt. Oh, no!
The Devil pads the world to suit his own,
And packs the cards according. Down went Jill
Unhurt. And Jack trots off to bed, poor brute,
Fist welted into eyeball, mouth agape
For yelling, — your bucolic always yells,
And out of his domestic pharmacy
Rips forth the cruet-stand, upsets the cat,
And ravages the store-room for his balm.
Eureka! — but he did n't use that word —
A pound of candles, corpse-like, side by side,
Wrapped up in his medicament. Out, knife!

Cut string, and strip the shrouding from the lot!
Steep swift and jam it on the gaping cut;
Then bedward — cursing man and friends alike.

Now back to Jill.   She was n't hurt, I said,
And all the woman's spite was up in arms.
So Jack 's abed.   She slips, peeks through the door,
And sees the split head like a luggage-label,
Halved, quartered, on the pillow.   " Ee-ki-ree,
Tee-hee-hee-hee," she giggles through the crack,
Much   as   the   Roman   ladies   grinned — don't
          smile —
To see the dabbled bodies in the sand,

Appealing to their benches for a sign.
Down thumbs, and giggle louder — so did Jill.
But mark now! Comes the mother round the door,
Red-hot from climbing up the hill herself,
And caught the graceless giggler.   Whack! flack!
          whack!
Here 's Nemesis whichever way you like!
She did n't stop to argue.   Given a head
Broken, a woman chuckling at the door,
And here 's your circumstantial evidence complete.
Whack! while Jack sniffs and sniggers from   the
          bed.
I like that horny-handed mother o' Jill.
The world's best women died, sir, long ago.
Well, Jack 's avenged; as for the other, gr-r-r-r!

Rudyard Kipling.

THE JAM-POT

THE Jam-pot — tender thought!
   I grabbed it — so did you.
    "What wonder while we fought
Together that it flew
In shivers?" you retort.

You should have loosed your hold
   One moment — checked your fist.
But, as it was, too bold
   You grappled and you missed.
More plainly —you were sold.

"Well, neither of us shared
   The dainty."   That your plea?
"Well, neither of us cared,"
   I answer. . . . "Let me see.
How have your trousers fared?"

                 Rudyard Kipling.

IMITATION OF ROBERT BROWNING

BIRTHDAYS? yes, in a general way;
   For the most if not for the best of men.
   You were born (I suppose) on a certain day,
So was I; or perhaps in the night, what then?

Only this : or at least, if more
You must know, not think it, and learn, not
    speak ;
There is truth to be found on the unknown shore,
And many will find where few will seek.

For many are called and few are chosen,
And the few grow many as ages lapse.
But when will the many grow few ; what dozen
Is fused into one by Time's hammer-taps ?

A bare brown stone in a babbling brook, —
It was wanton to hurl it there, you say, —
And the moss, which clung in the sheltered nook
(Yet the stream runs cooler) is washed away.

That begs the question ; many a prater
Thinks such a suggestion a sound " stop thief ! "
Which, may I ask, do you think the greater,
Sergeant-at-arms or a Robber Chief ?

And if it were not so ?   Still you doubt ?
Ah ! yours is a birthday indeed, if so.
That were something to write a poem about,
If one thought a little.   I only know.

P. S.

There's a Me Society down at Cambridge,
Where my works, *cum notis variorum*,
Are talked about ; well, I require the same bridge
That Euclid took toll at as Asinorum.

And, as they have got through several ditties
I thought were as stiff as a brick-built wall,
I 've composed the above, and a stiff one it is,
A bridge to stop asses at, once for all.

J. K. Stephen.

THE LAST RIDE TOGETHER

(*From her Point of View*)

WHEN I had firmly answered " No,"
        And he allowed that that was so,
    I really thought I should be free
For good and all from Mr. B.,
        And that he would soberly acquiesce.
I said that it would be discreet
That for awhile we should not meet;
I promised that I would always feel
A kindly interest in his wea¹;
I thanked him for his amorous zeal;
        In short, I said all I could but " yes."

I said what I 'm accustomed to;
I acted as I always do.
I promised he should find in me
A friend, — a sister, if that might be;
        But he was still dissatisfied.
He certainly was most polite;
He said exactly what was right,

He acted very properly,
Except indeed for this, that he
Insisted on inviting me
    To come with him for " one more last
        ride."

A little while in doubt I stood :
A ride, no doubt, would do me good ;
I had a habit and a hat
Extremely well worth looking at ;
    The weather was distinctly fine.
My horse, too, wanted exercise,
And time, when one is riding, flies ;
Besides, it really seemed, you see,
The only way of ridding me
Of pertinacious Mr. B. ;
    So my head I graciously incline.

I won't say much of what happened next ;
I own I was extremely vexed.
Indeed I should have been aghast
If any one had seen what passed ;
    But nobody need ever know
That, as I leaned forward to stir the fire,
He advanced before I could well retire ;
And I suddenly felt, to my great alarm,
The grasp of a warm, unlicensed arm,
An embrace in which I found no charm ;
    I was awfully glad when he let me go.

Then we began to ride; my steed
Was rather fresh, too fresh indeed,
And at first I thought of little, save
The way to escape an early grave,
    As the dust rose up on either side.
My stern companion jogged along
On a brown old cob both broad and strong.
He looked as he does when he's writing verse,
Or endeavoring not to swear and curse,
Or wondering where he has left his purse;
    Indeed it was a sombre ride.

I spoke of the weather to Mr. B.,
But he neither listened nor spoke to me.
I praised his horse, and I smiled the smile
Which was wont to move him once in a while.
    I said I was wearing his favorite flowers,
But I wasted my words on the desert air,
For he rode with a fixed and gloomy stare.
I wonder what he was thinking about.
As I don't read verse, I shan't find out.
It was something subtle and deep, no doubt,
    A theme to detain a man for hours.

Ah! there was the corner where Mr. S.
So nearly induced me to whisper " yes; "
And here it was that the next but one
Proposed on horseback, or would have done,
    Had his horse not most opportunely shied;
Which perhaps was due to the unseen flick
He received from my whip; 't was a scurvy trick,

But I never could do with that young man, —
I hope his present young woman can.
Well, I must say, never, since time began,
    Did I go for a duller or longer ride.

He never smiles and he never speaks ;
He might go on like this for weeks ;
He rolls a slightly frenzied eye
Towards the blue and burning sky,
    And the cob bounds on with tireless stride.
If we are n't home for lunch at two

I don't know what papa will do ;
But I know full well he will say to me,
" I never approved of Mr. B. ;
It 's the very devil that you and he
    Ride, ride together, forever ride."

                      J. K. Stephen.

UP THE SPOUT

I.

HI ! Just you drop that ! Stop, I say !
    Shirk work, think slink off, twist friend's
        wrist ?
Where that spined sand's lined band 's the bay —
Lined blind with true sea's blue, as due —
    Promising — not to pay ?

II.

For the sea's debt leaves wet the sand;
  Burst worst fate's weight's in one burst gun?
A man's own yacht, blown — What? off land?
  Tack back, or veer round here, then — queer!
Reef points, though — understand?

III.

I'm blest if I do.   Sigh? be blowed!
  Love's doves make break life's ropes, eh? Tropes!
Faith's brig, baulked, sides caulked, rides at road;
    Hope's gropes befogged, storm-dogged and
        bogged —
Clogged, water-logged, her load!

IV.

Stowed, by Jove, right and tight, away.
  No show now how best plough sea's brow,
Wrinkling — breeze quick, tease thick, ere day,
  Clear sheer wave's sheen of green, I mean,
With twinkling wrinkles — eh?

V.

Sea sprinkles wrinkles, tinkles light
  Shells' bells — boy's joys that hap to snap!
It's just sea's fun, breeze done, to spite
  God's rods that scourge her surge, I'd urge —
Not proper, is it — quite?

VI.

See, fore and aft, life's craft undone!
   Crank plank, split spritsail — mark, sea's lark!
That gray cold sea's old sprees, begun
   When men lay dark i' the ark, no spark,
All water — just God's fun!

VII.

Not bright, at best, his jest to these
   Seemed — screamed, shrieked, wreaked on kin
      for sin!
When for mirth's yell earth's knell seemed please
   Some dumb new grim great whim in him
Made Jews take chalk for cheese.

VIII.

Could God's rods bruise God's Jews? Their jowls
   Bobbed, sobbed, gaped, aped, the plaice in face!
None heard, 't is odds, his — God's — folk's howls.
   Now, how must I apply, to try
This hookiest-beaked of owls?

IX.

Well, I suppose God knows — I don't.
   Time's crimes mark dark men's types, in stripes
Broad as fen's lands men's hands were wont
   Leave grieve unploughed, though proud and loud
With birds' words — No! he won't!

[217]

X.

One never should think good impossible.
    Eh? say I'd hide this Jew's oil's cruse —
His shop might hold bright gold, engrossible
    By spy — spring's air takes there no care
To wave the heath-flower's glossy bell!

XI.

But gold bells chime in time there, coined —
    Gold! Old Sphinx winks there — 'Read my
        screed!'
Doctrine Jews learn, use, burn for, joined
    (Through new craft's stealth) with health and
        wealth —
At once all three purloined!

XII.

I rose with dawn, to pawn, no doubt,
    (Miss this chance, glance untried aside?)
John's shirt, my — no! Ay, so — the lout!
    Let yet the door gape, store on floor
And not a soul about?

XIII.

Such men lay traps, perhaps — and I'm
    Weak — meek — mild — child of woe, you
        know!
But theft, I doubt, my lout calls crime.
    Shrink? Think! Love's dawn in pawn —
        you spawn
Of Jewry! Just in time!

Algernon Charles Swinburne.

AFTER WHITMAN

AN AMERICAN, ONE OF THE ROUGHS, A KOSMOS

NATURE, continuous Me!
    Saltness, and vigorous, never torpi-yeast of
      Me!
Florid, unceasing, forever expansive;
Not Schooled, not dizened, not washed and powd-
    ered;
Strait-laced not at all; far otherwise than polite;
Not modest, nor immodest;
Divinely tanned and freckled; gloriously unkempt;
Ultimate yet unceasing; capricious though deter-
    mined;
Speak as thou listeth, and tell the askers that which
    they seek to know.
Thy speech to them will be not quite intelligible.
Never mind! utter thy wild commonplaces;
Yawp them loudly, shrilly;
Silence with shrill noise the lisps of the foo-foos.
Answer in precise terms of barbaric vagueness
The question that the Fun editor hath sparked
    through Atlantic cable
To W . . T W. . TM . . N, the speaker of
    the pass-word primeval;

[219]

The signaller of the signal of democracy;
The seer and hearer of things in general;
The poet translucent; fleshy, disorderly, sensually
  inclined;
Each tag and part of whom is a miracle.
(Thirteen pages of MS. relating to Mr. W. . t
  W. . tm . n are here omitted.)
Rhapsodically state the fact that is and is not;
That is not, being past; that is, being eternal;
If indeed it ever was, which is exactly the point in
  question.

Anonymous.

CAMERADOS

EVERYWHERE, everywhere, following me;
  Taking me by the buttonhole, pulling off my
      boots, hustling me with the elbows;
Sitting down with me to clams and the chowder-
      kettle;
Plunging naked at my side into the sleek, irascible
      surges;
Soothing me with the strain that I neither permit
      nor prohibit;
Flocking this way and that, reverent, eager, orotund,
      irrepressible;
Denser than sycamore leaves when the north-winds
      are scouring Paumanok;
What can I do to restrain them?   Nothing, verily
      nothing.
Everywhere, everywhere, crying aloud for me;

Crying, I hear; and I satisfy them out of my nature;
And he that comes at the end of the feast shall find
    something over.
Whatever they want I give; though it be some-
    thing else, they shall have it.
Drunkard, leper, Tammanyite, small-pox and
    cholera patient, shoddy and codfish million-
    naire,
And the beautiful young men, and the beautiful
    young women, all the same,
Crowding, hundreds of thousands, cosmical multi-
    tudes,
Buss me and hang on my hips and lean up to my
    shoulders,
Everywhere listening to my yawp and glad when-
    ever they hear it;
Everywhere saying, say it, Walt, we believe it:
Everywhere, everywhere.

Bayard Taylor.

IMITATION OF WALT WHITMAN

WHO am I?
    I have been reading Walt Whitman, and
    know not whether he be me, or me he; —
Or otherwise!
Oh, blue skies! oh, rugged mountains! oh, mighty,
    rolling Niagara!
Oh, chaos and everlasting bosh!
I am a poet; I swear it! If you do not believe it
    you are a dolt, a fool, an idiot!

Milton, Shakespere, Dante, Tommy Moore, Pope,
        never, but Byron, too, perhaps, and last,
        not least, Me, and the Poet Close.
We send our resonance echoing down the adaman-
        tine cañons of the future!
We live forever! The worms who criticise us
        (asses!) laugh, scoff, jeer, and babble —
        die!
Serve them right.
What is the difference between Judy, the pride of
        Fleet Street, the glory of Shoe Lane, and
        Walt Whitman?
Start not! 'T is no end of a minstrel show who
        perpends this query;
'T is no brain-racking puzzle from an inner page
        of the Family Herald,
No charade, acrostic (double or single), conun-
        drum, riddle, rebus, anagram, or other guess-
        work.
I answer thus: We both write truths — great, stern,
        solemn, unquenchable truths — couched in
        more or less ridiculous language.
I, as a rule use rhyme, he does not; therefore, I
        am his Superior (which is also a lake in his
        great and glorious country).
I scorn, with the unutterable scorn of the despiser
        of pettiness, to take a mean advantage of
        him.
He writes, he sells, he is read (more or less); why
        then should I rack my brains and my rhym-
        ing dictionary? I will see the public hanged
        first!

I sing of America, of the United States, of the stars
and stripes of Oskhosh, of Kalamazoo, and
of Salt Lake City.
I sing of the railroad cars, of the hotels, of the
breakfasts, the lunches, the dinners, and the
suppers;
Of the soup, the fish, the entrées, the joints, the
game, the puddings and the ice-cream.
I sing all — I eat all — I sing in turn of Dr.
Bluffem's Antibilious Pills.
No subject is too small, too insignificant, for
Nature's poet.
I sing of the cocktail, a new song for every cocktail, hundreds of songs, hundreds of cock-
tails.
It is a great and a glorious land!   The Mississippi,
the Missouri, and a million other torrents
roll their waters to the ocean.
It is a great and glorious land!   The Alleghanies,
the Catskills, the Rockies (see atlas for other
mountain ranges too numerous to mention)
pierce the clouds!
And the greatest and most glorious product of this
great and glorious land is Walt Whitman;
This must be so, for he says it himself.
There is but one greater than he between the rising and the setting sun.
There is but one before whom he meekly bows his
humbled head.
Oh, great and glorious land, teeming producer of
all things, creator of Niagara, and inventor
of Walt Whitman,

Erase your national advertisements of liver pads
and cures for rheumatism from your public
monuments, and inscribe thereon in letters
of gold the name *Judy*.

Judy.

IMITATION OF WALT WHITMAN

THE clear cool note of the cuckoo which has
ousted the legitimate nest-holder,
The whistle of the railway guard despatching
the train to the inevitable collision,
The maiden's monosyllabic reply to a polysyllabic
proposal,
The fundamental note of the last trump, which is
presumably D natural;
All of these are sounds to rejoice in, yea to let your
ribs re-echo with.
But better than all of them is the absolutely last
chord of the apparently inexhaustible piano-
forte player.

J. K. Stephen.

THE POET AND THE WOODLOUSE

SAID a poet to a woodlouse, "Thou art certainly my brother;
I discern in thee the markings of the fingers
of the Whole;

[224]

And I recognize, in spite of all the terrene smut
    and smother,
    In the colors shaded off thee, the suggestions
      of a soul.

" Yea," the poet said, " I smell thee by some pas-
    sive divination,
    I am satisfied with insight of the measure of
      thine house;
What had happened I conjecture, in a blank and
    rhythmic passion,
    Had the æons thought of making thee a man
      and me a louse.

" The broad lives of upper planets, their absorp-
    tion and digestion,
    Food and famine, health and sickness, I can
      scrutinize and test,
Through a shiver of the senses comes a reso-
    nance of question,
    And by proof of balanced answer I decide that
      I am best.

" Man the fleshly marvel always feels a certain
    kind of awe stick
    To the skirts of contemplation, cramped with
      nympholeptic weight;
Feels his faint sense charred and branded by the
    touch of solar caustic,
    On the forehead of his spirit feels the footprint
      of a Fate."

[225]

" Notwithstanding which, O poet," spake the
    woodlouse, very blandly,
  " I am likewise the created, — I the equipoise of
    thee;
I the particle, the atom, I behold on either hand
    lie
  The inane of measured ages that were embryos
    of me.

"I am fed with intimations, I am clothed with
    consequences,
  And the air I breathe is colored with apoca-
    lyptic blush;
Ripest-budded odors blossom out of dim chaotic
    stenches,
  And the Soul plants spirit-lilies in sick leagues
    of human slush.

"I am thrilled half cosmically through by crypto-
    phantic surgings,
  Till the rhythmic hills roar silent through a
    spongious kind of blee;
And earth's soul yawns disembowelled of her pan-
    creatic organs,
  Like a madrepore if mesmerized, in rapt cata-
    lepsy.

" And I sacrifice, a Levite; and I palpitate, a
    poet;
  Can I close dead ears against the rush and reso-
    nance of things?

[226]

Symbols in me breathe and flicker up the heights
    of her heroic ;
  Earth's worst spawn, you said, and cursed me ?
  Look ! approve me ! I have wings.

" Ah, men's poets ! men's conventions crust you
    round and swathe you mist-like,
  And the world's wheels grind your spirits down
    the dust ye overtrod ;
We stand sinlessly stark-naked in effulgence of the
    Christlight,
  And our polecat chokes not cherubs ; and our
    skunk smells sweet to God.

" For he grasps the pale Created by some thousand
    vital handles,
  Till a Godshine, bluely winnowed through the
    sieve of thunder-storms,
Shimmers up the non-existence round the churning
    feet of angels ;
  And the atoms of that glory may be seraphs,
    being worms.

" Friends, your nature underlies us and your pulses
    overplay us ;
  Ye, with social sores unbandaged, can ye sing
    right and steer wrong ?
For the transient cosmic, rooted in imperishable
    chaos,
  Must be kneaded into drastics as material for a
    song.

[227]

" Eyes once purged from homebred vapors through
　　humanitarian passion
　　See that monochrome a despot through a demo-
　　　cratic prism ;
Hands that rip the soul up, reeking from divine
　　evisceration,
　　Not with priestlike oil anoint him, but a
　　stronger-smelling chrism.

" Pass, O poet, retransfigured !　God, the psycho-
　　metric rhapsode,
　　Fills with fiery rhythms the silence, stings the
　　dark with stars that blink ;
All eternities hang round him like an old man's
　　clothes collapsèd,
　　While he makes his mundane music — AND
　　HE WILL NOT STOP, I THINK."

Algernon Charles Swinburne.

AFTER CHARLES KINGSLEY

THREE LITTLE FISHERS

THREE little fishers trudged over the hill,
    Over the hill in the sun's broad glare,
    With rods and crooked pins, to the brook
    by the mill,
While three fond mothers sought them every-
    where.
For boys will go fishing, though mothers deny.
Watching their chance they sneak off on the sly
    To come safely back in the gloaming.

Three mothers waited outside the gate.
    Three little fishers, tired, sunburnt, and worn,
Came into sight as the evening grew late,
    Their chubby feet bleeding, their clothing all torn,
For " boys will be boys " — have a keen eye for
    fun,
While mothers fret, fume, scold, and — succumb,
    And welcome them home in the gloaming.

Three little fishers were called to explain —
    Each stood condemned, with his thumb in his eye,
They promised never to do so again,
    And were hung up in the pantry to dry.
Three mothers heaved great sighs of relief,
An end had been put to their magnified grief,
    When the boys came home in the gloaming.

Frank H. Stauffer.

[229]

THE THREE POETS

THREE poets went sailing down Boston Bay,
  All into the East as the sun went down.
  Each felt that the editors loved him best,
And would welcome spring poetry in Boston town.
For poets must dream, though the editors frown;
Their revel in visions will not be turned down,
  Though the general reader is moaning!

Three editors climbed to the loftiest tower
  That they could find in all Boston town.
And they planned to conceal themselves, hour
      after hour,
  Till the Sun — and the poets — had both gone
      down.
For spring poets must write, though the editors rage.
The artistic nature must thus be engaged,
  Though the publishers all are groaning!

Three corpses lay out on the Back Bay sand
  Just after the first Spring Sun went down,
And the Press sat down to a banquet grand
  In honor of poets no more in the town.
For poets will write while the editors sleep,
Though they've little to earn and nothing to keep,
  And the populace all are moaning!
                                    Lilian Whiting.

AFTER MRS. R. H. STODDARD

THE NETTLE

IF days were nights, I could their weight endure,
  This darkness cannot hide from me the plant
  I seek; I know it by the rasping touch.
The moon is wrapped in bombazine of cloud;
The capes project like crooked lobster-shears
Into the bobbery of the waves; the marsh,
At ebb, has now a miserable smell.
I will not be delayed nor hustled back,
Though every wind should muss my outspread
        hair.
I snatch the plant that seems my coming fate;
I pass the crinkled satin of the rose,
The violets, frightened out of all their wits,
And other flowers, to me so commonplace,
And cursed with showy mediocrity,
To cull the foliage which repels and stings.
Weak hands may bleed; but mine are tough with
        pride,
And I but smile where others sob and screech.
The draggled flounces of the willow lash
My neck; I tread upon the bouncing rake,
Which bangs me sorely, but I hasten on,
With teeth firm-set as biting on a wire,
And feet and fingers clinched in bitter pain.

[231]

This, few would comprehend; but, if they did,
I should despise myself and merit scorn.
We all are riddles which we cannot guess;
Each has his gimcracks and his thingumbobs,
And mine are night and nettles, mud and mist,
Since others hate them, cowardly avoid.
Things are mysterious when you make them so,
And the slow-pacing days are mighty queer;
But Fate is at the bottom of it all,
And something somehow turns up in the end.

Bayard Taylor.

AFTER BAYARD TAYLOR

HADRAMAUT

THE grand conglomerate hills of Araby,
    That stand empanoplied in utmost thought,
  With dazzling ramparts front the Indian sea,
      Down there in Hadramaut.

The sunshine smashes in the doors of morn
    And leaves them open; there the vibrant calm
Of life magniloquent pervades forlorn
      The giant fronds of palm.

The cockatoo upon the upas screams;
    The armadillo fluctuates o'er the hill;
And like a flag, incarnadined in dreams,
      All crimsonly I thrill!

There have iconoclasts no power to harm,
    So, folded grandly in translucent mist,
I let the lights stream down my jasper arm,
      And o'er my opal fist.

An Adamite of old, primeval Earth,
    I see the Sphinx upon the porphyry shore,
Deprived of utterance ages ere her birth,
      As I am, — only more!

Who shall ensnare me with invested gold,
   Or prayer symbols, backed like malachite?
Let gaunt reformers objurgate and scold,
      I gorge me with delight.

I do not yearn for what I covet most;
   I give the winds the passionate gifts I sought;
And slumber fiercely on the torrid coast,
      Down there in Hadramaut!

Bayard Taylor.

AFTER WILLIAM MORRIS

ESTUNT THE GRIFF

*(Argument: Showing how a man of England, hearing
from certain Easterlings of the glories of their
land, set sail to rule it)*

AND so unto the End of Graves came he,
   Where nigh the staging, ready for the sea,
   Oarless and sailless lay the galley's bulk,
Albeit smoke did issue from the hulk
And fell away, across the marshes dun,
Into the visage of the wan-white sun.
And seaward ran the river, cold and gray,
Bearing the brown-sailed Eastland boats away
'Twixt the low shore and shallow sandy spit.
Yet he, being sad, took little heed of it,
But straightly fled toward the misty beach,
And hailed in choked and swiftly spoken speech
A shallop, that for men's conveyance lay
Hard by the margin of that watery way.
Then many that were in like evil plight—
Sad folk, with drawn, dumb lips and faces white,
That writhed themselves into a hopeless smile —
Crowded the shallop, making feint the while
Of merriment and pleasure at that tide,
Though oft upon the laughers' lips there died

The jest, and in its place there came a sigh,
So that men gat but little good thereby,
And, shivering, clad themselves about with furs.
Strange faces of the swarthy outlanders
Looked down upon the shallop as she threw
The sullen waters backward from her screw
And, running forward for some little space,
Stayed featly at the galley's mounting-place,
Where slowly these sad-faced landsmen went
Crabwise and evil-mouthed with discontent,
Holding to sodden rope and rusty chain
And bulwark that was wetted with the rain :
For 'neath their feet the black bows rose and fell,
Nor might a man walk steadfastly or well
Who had not hand upon a rail or rope ;
And Estunt turned him landward, and wan hope
Grew on his spirit as an evil mist,
Thinking of loving lips his lips had kissed
An hour since, and how those lips were sweet
An hour since, far off in Fenchurch Street.
Then, with a deep-drawn breath most like a sigh,
He watched the empty shallop shoreward hie ;
Then turned him round the driving rain to face,
And saw men heave the anchor from its place ;
Whereat, when by the river-mouth, the ship
Began, amid the waters' strife to dip,
His soul was heaved between his jaws that day,
And to the East the good ship took her way.

Rudyard Kipling.

AFTER ALFRED AUSTIN

AN ODE

I SING a song of sixpence, and of rye
    A pocketful — recalling, sad to state,
The niggardly emoluments which I
    Receive as Laureate!

Also I sing of blackbirds — in the mart
    At four-a-penny. Thus, in other words,
The sixpence which I mentioned at the start
    Purchased two dozen birds.

So four-and-twenty birds were deftly hid —
    Or shall we say, were skilfully concealed? —
Within the pie-dish. When they raised the lid,
    What melody forth pealed!

Now I like four-and-twenty blackbirds sing,
    With all their sweetness, all their rapture keen;
And is n't this a pretty little thing
    To set before the Queen?

The money-counting monarch — sordid man! —
    His wife, who robbed the little busy bees,
I disregard. In fact a poet can
    But pity folks like these.

The maid was in the garden.   Happy maid!
   Her choice entitles her to rank above
Master and Mistress.   Gladly she surveyed
   The Garden That I Love!

— Where grow my daffodils, anemones,
   Tulips, auriculas, chrysanthemums,
Cabbages, asparagus, sweet peas,
   With apples, pears, and plums —

(That's a parenthesis.   The very name
   Of garden really carries one astray!)
But suddenly a feathered ruffian came,
   And stole her nose away.

Eight stanzas finished! So my Court costume
   I lay aside: the Laureate, I suppose,
Has done his part; the man may now resume
   His journalistic prose.

Anthony C. Deane.

AFTER W. S. GILBERT

ODE TO A LONDON FOG

ROLL on, thick haze, roll on!
    Through each familiar way
        Roll on!
What though I must go out to-day?
What though my lungs are rather queer?
What though asthmatic ills I fear?
What though my wheeziness is clear?
        Never you mind!
        Roll on!

Roll on, thick haze, roll on!
Through street and square and lane
        Roll on!
It's true I cough and cough again;
It's true I gasp and puff and blow;
It's true my trip may lay me low —
But that's not your affair, you know.
        Never you mind!
        Roll on!

Anonymous.

PRESIDENT GARFIELD

WHEN he was a lad he served a term
On a big canal with a boatman's firm;
With a heart so free and a will so strong,
On the towpath drove two mules along.
And he drove those mules so carefullee
He's a candidate now for the Presidencee.

As a driver boy he made such a mark
He came to the deck of the inland barque
And all of the perils to boat and crew.
He stood at the helm and guided thro'.
He stood at the helm so manfullee
He's a candidate now for the Presidencee.

He did so well with the helm and mules,
They made him a teacher of district schools;
And when from college in a bran new suit,
A Greek Professor at the Institute,
Where Greek and Latin he taught so free
He's a candidate now for the Presidencee.

Now boys who cherish ambitious schemes,
Though now you may be but drivers of teams,
Look well to the work you may chance to do,
And do it with a hand that is kind and true.
Whatever you do, do it faithfullee,
And you may aspire to the Presidencee.

Anonymous.

PROPINQUITY NEEDED

CELESTINE Silvousplait Justine de Mouton
 Rosalie,
 A coryphée who lived and danced in naughty,
 gay Paree,
Was every bit as pretty as a French girl e'er can be
 (Which is n't saying much).

Maurice Boulanger (there's a name that would
 adorn a king),
But Morris Baker was the name they called the
 man I sing.
He lived in New York City in the Street that's
 labeled Spring
 (Chosen because it rhymed).

Now Baker was a lonesome youth and wanted to
 be wed,
And for a wife, all over town he hunted, it is said;
And up and down Fifth Avenue he ofttimes
 wanderéd
 (He was a peripatetic Baker, he was).

And had he met Celestine, not a doubt but Cupid's
 darts
Would in a trice have wounded both of their fond,
 loving hearts;
But he has never left New York to stray in foreign
 parts
 (Because he has n't the price).

And she has never left Paree and so, of course, you
    see
There's not the slightest chance at all she'll marry
    Morris B.
For love to get well started, really needs propinquity
    (Hence my title).

                        Charles Battell Loomis.

AFTER R. H. STODDARD

THE CANTELOPE

SIDE by side in the crowded streets,
　　Amid its ebb and flow,
　　We walked together one autumn morn;
　　　('T was many years ago!)

The markets blushed with fruits and flowers;
　　(Both Memory and Hope!)
You stopped and bought me at the stall,
　　A spicy cantelope.

We drained together its honeyed wine,
　　We cast the seeds away;
I slipped and fell on the moony rinds,
　　And you took me home on a dray!

The honeyed wine of your love is drained;
　　I limp from the fall I had;
The snow-flakes muffle the empty stall,
　　And everything is sad.

The sky is an inkstand, upside down,
　　It splashes the world with gloom;
The earth is full of skeleton bones,
　　And the sea is a wobbling tomb!

Bayard Taylor.

AFTER A. A. PROCTOR

THE LOST VOICE

SEATED at Church in the winter
    I was frozen in every limb;
And the village choir shrieked wildly
    Over a noisy hymn.

I do not know what they were singing,
    For while I was watching them
Our Curate began his sermon
    With the sound of a slight " Ahem ! "

It frightened the female portion,
    Like the storm which succeeds a calm,
Both maidens and matrons heard it
    With a touch of inane alarm.

It told them of pain and sorrow,
    Cold, cough, and neuralgic strife,
Bronchitis, and influenza
    All aimed at our Curate's life.

It linked all perplex'd diseases
    Into one precious frame;
They trembled with rage if a sceptic
    Attempted to ask its name.

[244]

They have wrapped him in mustard plasters,
  Stuffed him with food and wine,
They have fondled, caressed, and nursed him,
  With sympathy divine.

It may be that other Curates
  Will preach in that Church to them,
Will there be every time, Good Heavens!
  Such a fuss for a slight — Ahem!
A. H. S.

THE LOST APE

SEATED one day on an organ,
    A monkey was ill at ease,
    When his fingers wandered idly,
  In search of the busy fleas.
I knew not what he was slaying,
  Or what he was dreaming then,
But a sound burst forth from that organ,
  Not at all like a grand Amen.

It came through the evening twilight
  Like the close of the feline psalm,
But the melody raised by their voices
  Compared to this noise was balm!
It was worse than Salvation's Sorrow,
  With their band of drum and fife,
And cut, like an evening "Echo,"
  The Tit-Bits out of "Life."

I upset my table and tea things,
    And left not one perfect piece;
I gazed at the wreck in silence,
    Not loth, but unable to speak!
Then I sought him, alas! all vainly,
    The source of that terrible whine,
With his cracked and tuneless organ,
    And its melodies undivine.

Of course there was no policeman
    To move him away, — and men
Who grind organs smile demurely
    At your curses, and smile again.
It may be that I could choke him —
    Could kill him — but organ men,
If you kill a dozen to-day,
    To-morrow will come again!

                                    J. W. G. W.

THE LOST WORD

SEATED one day at the typewriter,
    I was weary of a's and e's,
    And my fingers wandered wildly
    Over the consonant keys.

I know not what I was writing,
    With that thing so like a pen;
But I struck one word astounding —
    Unknown to the speech of men.

[246]

It flooded the sense of my verses,
  Like the break of a tinker's dam,
And I felt as one feels when the printer
  Of your " infinite calm " makes clam.

It mixed up s's and x's
  Like an alphabet coming to strife.
It seemed the discordant echo
  Of a row between husband and wife.

It brought a perplexed meaning
  Into my perfect piece,
And set the machinery creaking
  As though it were scant of grease.

I have tried, but I try it vainly,
  The one last word to divine
Which came from the keys of my typewriter
  And so would pass as mine.

It may be some other typewriter
  Will produce that word again,
It may be, but only for others —
  I shall write henceforth with a pen.

                                C. H. Webb.

AFTER GEORGE MEREDITH

AT THE SIGN OF THE COCK

(FRENCH STYLE, 1898)

(*Being an Ode in further* " *Contribution to the Song
of French History,*" *dedicated, without malice or
permission, to Mr. George Meredith*)

I

ROOSTER her sign,
   Rooster her pugnant note, she struts
   Evocative, amazon spurs aprick at heel;
Nid-nod the authentic stump
Of the once ensanguined comb vermeil as wine;
With conspuent doodle-doo
Hails breach o' the hectic dawn of yon New Year,
Last issue up to date
Of quiverful Fate
Evolved spontaneous; hails with tonant trump
The spiriting prime o' the clashed carillon-peal;
Ruffling her caudal plumes derisive of scuts;
Inconscient how she stalks an immarcessibly absurd
Bird.

II

Mark where her Equatorial Pioneer
Delirant on the tramp goes littoralwise.
His Flag at furl, portmanteaued; drains to the dregs

The penultimate brandy-bottle, coal-on-the-head-
    piece gift
Of who avenged the Old Sea-Rover's smirch.
Marchant he treads the all-along of inarable drift
On dubiously connivent legs,
The facile prey of predatory flies;
Panting for further; sworn to lurch
Empirical on to the Menelik-buffered, enhavened
        blue,
Rhyming — see Cantique I. — with doodle-doo.

III

Infuriate she kicked against Imperial fact;
Vulnant she felt
What pin-stab should have stained Another's pelt
Puncture her own Colonial lung-balloon,
Volant to nigh meridian.   Whence rebuffed,
The perjured Scythian she lacked
At need's pinch, sick with spleen of the rudely
    cuffed
Below her breath she cursed; she cursed the hour
When on her spring for him the young Tyrannical
    broke
Amid the unhallowed wedlock's vodka-shower,
She passionate, he dispassionate; tricked
Her wits to eye-blind; borrowed the ready as for
    dower;
Till from the trance of that Hymettus-moon
She woke,
A nuptial-knotted derelict;
Pensioned with Rescripts other aid declined
By the plumped leech saturate urging Peace

In guise of heavy-armed Gospeller to men,
Tyrannical unto fraternal equal liberal, her.   Not
    she;
Not till Alsace her consanguineous find
What red deteutonising artillery
Shall shatter her beer-reek alien police
The just-now pluripollent ; not till then.

IV

More pungent yet the esoteric pain
Squeezing her pliable vitals nourishes feud
Insanely grumous, grumously insane.
For lo !
Past common balmly on the Bordereau,
Churns she the skim o' the gutter's crust
With Anti-Judaic various carmagnole,
Whooped praise of the Anti-Just;
Her boulevard brood
Gyratory in convolvements militant-mad;
Theatrical of faith in the Belliform,
Her Og,
Her Monstrous.   Fled what force she had
To buckle the jaw-gape, wide agog
For the Preconcerted One,
The Anticipated, ripe to clinch the whole ;
Queen-bee to hive the hither and thither volant
    swarm.

Bides she his coming ; adumbrates the new
Expurgatorial Divine,
Her final effulgent Avatar,
Postured outside a trampling mastodon

Black as her Baker's charger; towering; visibly
    gorged
With blood of traitors.   Knee-grip stiff,
Spine straightened, on he rides;
Embossed the Patriot's brow with hieroglyph
Of martial *dossiers*, nothing forged
About him save his armour.   So she bides
Voicing his advent indeterminably far,
Rooster her sign,
Rooster her conspuent doodle-doo.

v

Behold her, pranked with spurs for bloody sport,
How she acclaims,
A crapulous chanticleer,
Breach of the hectic dawn of yon New Year.
Not yet her fill of rumours sucked;
Inebriate of honour; blushfully wroth;
Tireless to play her old primeval games;
Her plumage preened the yet unplucked
Like sails of a galleon, rudder hard amort
With crepitant mast
Fronting the hazard to dare of a dual blast
The intern and the extern, blizzards both.

Owen Seaman.

AFTER DANTE GABRIEL ROSSETTI

A CHRISTMAS WAIL

(*Not by Dante Gabriel Rosetti*)

ON Christmas day I dined with Brown.
　　(*Oh the dinner was fine to see !*)
　I drove to his house, right merrily down,
To a western square of London town.
　　(*And I moan and I cry, Woe's me !*)

We dined off turkey and Christmas beef:
　　(*Oh the dinner was fine to see !*)
My anguish is sore and my comfort's brief,
And nought but blue pills can ease my grief,
　　(*As I moan and I cry, Woe's me !*)

We gorged plum-pudding and hot mince pies,
　　(*Oh the dinner was fine to see !*)
And other nameless atrocities,
The weight of which on my — bosom lies.
　　(*And I moan and I cry, Woe's me !*)

We drank dry Clicquot and rare old port,
　　(*Oh the dinner was fine to see !*)
And I pledged my host for a right good sort
In bumpers of both, for I never thought
　　(*I should moan and cry, Woe's me !*)

But I woke next day with a fearful head,
   (*Oh that dinner was fine to see!*)
And on my chest is a weight like lead,
And I frequently wish that I were dead,
   (*And I moan and I cry, Woe's me!*)

And as for Brown — why the truth to tell —
   (*Oh that dinner was fine to see!*)
I hate him now with the hate of hell,
Though before I loved him passing well,
   (*And I moan and I cry, Woe's me!*)

                   Anonymous.

BALLAD

THE auld wife sat at her ivied door
   (Butter and eggs and a pound of cheese),
   A thing she had frequently done before,
And her spectacles lay on her apron'd knees.

The piper he piped on the hill-top high
  (Butter and eggs and a pound of cheese),
Till the cow said " I die," and the goose ask'd
    " Why ? "
  And the dog said nothing, but search'd for fleas.

The farmer he strode through the square farmyard
  (Butter and eggs and a pound of cheese);
His last brew of ale was a trifle hard —
  The connection of which with the plot one sees.

The farmer's daughter had frank blue eyes
  (Butter and eggs and a pound of cheese);
She hears the rooks caw in the windy skies,
  As she sits at her lattice and shells her peas.

The farmer's daughter hath ripe red lips
    (Butter and eggs and a pound of cheese);
If you try to approach her, away she skips
    Over tables and chairs with apparent ease.

The farmer's daughter hath soft brown hair
    (Butter and eggs and a pound of cheese),
And I met with a ballad, I can't say where,
    Which wholly consisted of lines like these.

Part II

She sat with her hands 'neath her dimpled cheeks
    (Butter and eggs and a pound of cheese),
And spake not a word.   While a lady speaks
    There is hope, but she did n't even sneeze.

She sat, with her hands 'neath her crimson cheeks
    (Butter and eggs and a pound of cheese);
She gave up mending her father's breeks,
    And let the cat roll in her new chemise.

She sat, with her hands 'neath her burning cheeks
    (Butter and eggs and a pound of cheese),
And gazed at the piper for thirteen weeks;
    Then she follow'd him out o'er the misty leas.

Her sheep follow'd her, as their tails did them
    (Butter and eggs and a pound of cheese),
And this song is consider'd a perfect gem,
    And as to the meaning, it's what you please.

                    Charles S. Calverley.

CIMABUELLA

FAIR-TINTED cheeks, clear eyelids drawn
    In crescent curves above the light
    Of eyes, whose dim, uncertain dawn
Becomes not day : a forehead white
Beneath long yellow heaps of hair :
She is so strange she must be fair.

Had she sharp, slant-wise wings outspread,
    She were an angel; but she stands
With flat dead gold behind her head,
    And lilies in her long thin hands :
Her folded mantle, gathered in,
Falls to her feet as it were tin.

Her nose is keen as pointed flame ;
    Her crimson lips no thing express ;
And never dread of saintly blame
    Held down her heavy eyelashes :
To guess what she were thinking of
Precludeth any meaner love.

An azure carpet, fringed with gold,
    Sprinkled with scarlet spots, I laid
Before her straight, cool feet unrolled ;
    But she nor sound nor movement made
(Albeit I heard a soft, shy smile,
Printing her neck a moment's while).

[255]

And I was shamed through all my mind
   For that she spake not, neither kissed,
But stared right past me. Lo! behind
   Me stood, in pink and amethyst,
Sword-girt and velvet-doubleted,
A tall, gaunt youth, with frowzy head.

Wide nostrils in the air, dull eyes,
   Thick lips that simpered, but, ah me!
I saw, with most forlorn surprise,
   He was the Thirteenth Century,
I but the Nineteenth; then despair
Curdled beneath my curling hair.

O Love and Fate! How could she choose
   My rounded outlines, broader brain,
And my resuscitated Muse?
   Some tears she shed, but whether pain
Or joy in him unlocked their source,
I could not fathom which, of course.

But I from missals quaintly bound,
   With cither and with clavichord,
Will sing her songs of sovran sound:
   Belike her pity will afford
Such fain return as suits a saint
So sweetly done in verse and paint.

                             Bayard Taylor.

THE POSTER GIRL

THE blessed Poster girl leaned out
From a pinky-purple heaven.
One eye was red and one was green;
Her bang was cut uneven;
She had three fingers on her hand,
And the hairs on her head were seven.

Her robe, ungirt from clasp to hem,
No sunflowers did adorn,
But a heavy Turkish portière
Was very neatly worn;
And the hat that lay along her back
Was yellow, like canned corn.

It was a kind of wobbly wave
That she was standing on,
And high aloft she flung a scarf
That must have weighed a ton;
And she was rather tall — at least
She reached up to the sun.

She curved and writhed, and then she said,
Less green of speech than blue:
" Perhaps I *am* absurd — perhaps
I *don't* appeal to you;
But my artistic worth depends
Upon the point of view."

I saw her smile, although her eyes
    Were only smudgy smears;
And then she swished her swirling arms,
    And wagged her gorgeous ears.
She sobbed a blue-and-green-checked sob,
    And wept some purple tears.

                    Carolyn Wells.

AFTER JEAN INGELOW

LOVERS, AND A REFLECTION

IN moss-prankt dells which the sunbeams flatter
    (And heaven it knoweth what that may
        mean;
Meaning, however, is no great matter),
    Where woods are a-tremble, with rifts atween;

Thro' God's own heather we wonn'd together,
    I and my Willie (O love my love):
I need hardly remark it was glorious weather,
    And flitterbats waver'd alow, above:

Boats were curtseying, rising, bowing,
    (Boats in that climate are so polite),
And sands were a ribbon of green endowing,
    And oh, the sundazzle on bark and bight!

Thro' the rare red heather we danced together,
    (O love my Willie!) and smelt for flowers:
I must mention again it was gorgeous weather,
    Rhymes are so scarce in this world of ours:

By rises that flush'd with their purple favors,
    Thro' becks that brattled o'er grasses sheen,
We walked and waded, we two young shavers,
    Thanking our stars we were both so green.

[259]

We journeyed in parallels, I and Willie,
  In fortunate parallels !   Butterflies,
Hid in weltering shadows of daffodilly
  Or marjoram, kept making peacock eyes :

Songbirds darted about, some inky
  As coal, some snowy (I ween) as curds ;
Or rosy as pinks, or as roses pinky —
  They reck of no eerie To-come, those birds !

But they skim over bents which the millstream
      washes,
  Or hang in the lift 'neath a white cloud's hem ;
They need no parasols, no goloshes ;
  And good Mrs. Trimmer she feedeth them.

Then we thrid God's cowslips (as erst His heather)
  That endowed the wan grass with their golden
      blooms ;
And snapt — (it was perfectly charming weather) —
  Our fingers at Fate and her goodness-glooms :

And Willie 'gan sing (oh, his notes were fluty ;
  Wafts fluttered them out to the white-winged
      sea) —
Something made up of rhymes that have done much
      duty,
  Rhymes (better to put it) of " ancientry : "

Bowers of flowers encounter'd showers
  In William's carol — (O love my Willie !)
Then he bade sorrow borrow from blithe to-morrow
  I quite forget what — say a daffodilly :

A nest in a hollow, " with buds to follow,"
　　I think occurred next in his nimble strain;
And clay that was " kneaden " of course in Eden —
　　A rhyme most novel, I do maintain:

Mists, bones, the singer himself, love-stories,
　　And all least furlable things got " furled; "
Not with any design to conceal their " glories,"
　　But simply and solely to rhyme with " world."

　　　　.　　.　　.　　.　　.　　.　　.

O if billows and pillows and hours and flowers,
　　And all the brave rhymes of an elder day,
Could be furled together, this genial weather,
　　And carted or carried on " wafts " away,
Nor ever again trotted out — ah me!
How much fewer volumes of verse there 'd be!
　　　　　　　　　　　　　　Charles S. Calverley.

THE SHRIMP – GATHERERS

SCARLET spaces of sand and ocean,
　　Gulls that circle and winds that blow;
Baskets and boats and men in motion,
　　Sailing and scattering to and fro.

Girls are waiting, their wimples adorning
　　With crimson sprinkles the broad gray flood;
And down the beach the blush of the morning
　　Shines reflected from moisture and mud.

Broad from the yard the sail hangs limpy;
  Lightly the steersman whistles a lay;
Pull with a will, for the nets are shrimpy,
  Pull with a whistle, our hearts are gay!

Tuppence a quart; there are more than fifty!
  Coffee is certain, and beer galore;
Coats are corduroy, minds are thrifty,
  Won't we go it on sea and shore!

See, behind, how the hills are freckled
  With low white huts, where the lasses bide!
See, before, how the sea is speckled
  With sloops and schooners that wait the tide!

Yarmouth fishers may rail and roister,
  Tyne-side boys may shout, " Give way ! "
Let them dredge for the lobster and oyster,
  Pink and sweet are our shrimps to-day!

Shrimps and the delicate periwinkle,
  Such are the sea-fruits lasses love;
Ho! to your nets till the blue stars twinkle,
  And the shutterless cottages gleam above!

Bayard Taylor.

AFTER CHRISTINA ROSSETTI

REMEMBER

REMEMBER it, although you 're far away —
    Too far away more fivers yet to land,
    When you no more can proffer notes of hand,
Nor I half yearn to change my yea to nay.
Remember, when no more in airy way,
    You tell me of repayment sagely planned :
    Only remember it, you understand !
It 's rather late to counsel you to pay ;
Yet if you should remember for awhile,
    And then forget it wholly, I should grieve ;
    For, though your light procrastinations leave
    Small remnants of the hope that once I had,
Than that you should forget your debt and smile,
    I 'd rather you 'd remember and be sad.

Judy.

AFTER LEWIS CARROLL

WAGGAWOCKY

'TWAS Maytime, and the lawyer coves
   Did jibe and jabber in the wabe,
All menaced were the Tichborne groves,
   And their true lord, the Babe.

" Beware the Waggawock, my son,
   The eyelid twitch, the knees' incline,
Beware the Baignet network, spun
   For gallant Ballantine."

He took his ton-weight brief in hand,
   Long time the hidden clue he sought,
Then rested he by the Hawkins tree,
   And sat awhile in thought.

And as in toughish thought he rocks,
   The Waggawock, sans truth or shame,
Came lumbering to the witness box,
   And perjured out his Claim.

" Untrue ! untrue ! " Then, through and through
   The weary weeks he worked the rack ;
But March had youth, ere with the Truth
   He dealt the final whack.

[264]

" And hast thou slain the Waggawock
   Come to my arms, my Beamish Boy !
O Coleridge, J. ! Hoorah ! hooray ! "
   Punch chortled in his joy.

Shirley Brooks.

THE VULTURE AND THE HUSBAND–MAN

(*By Louisa Caroline*)

THE rain was raining cheerfully
   As if it had been May,
   The Senate House appeared inside
Unusually gay ;
And this was strange, because it was
   A Viva-Voce day.

The men were sitting sulkily,
   Their paper work was done,
They wanted much to go away
   To ride or row or run ;
" It 's very rude," they said, " to keep
   Us here and spoil our fun."

The papers they had finished lay
   In piles of blue and white,
They answered everything they could,
   And wrote with all their might,
But though they wrote it all by rote,
   They did not write it right.

[265]

The Vulture and the Husbandman
  Besides these piles did stand;
They wept like anything to see
  The work they had in hand:
" If this were only finished up,"
  Said they, " it would be grand ! "

" If seven D's or seven C's
  We give to all the crowd,
Do you suppose," the Vulture said,
  " That we could get them ploughed ? "
" I think so," said the Husbandman,
  " But pray don't talk so loud."

" O Undergraduates, come up,"
  The Vulture did beseech,
" And let us see if you can learn
  As well as we can teach;
We cannot do with more than two,
  To have a word with each."

Two Undergraduates came up,
  And slowly took a seat;
They knit their brows and bit their thumbs,
  As if they found them sweet ;
And this is odd, because, you know,
  Thumbs are not good to eat.

" The time has come," the Vulture said,
  " To talk of many things,
Of Accidence and Adjectives,
  And names of Jewish kings ;
How many notes a sackbut has,
  And whether shawms have strings."

"Please, Sir," the Undergraduates said,
  Turning a little blue,
"We did not know that was the sort
  Of thing we had to do."
"We thank you much," the Vulture said;
  "Send up another two."

Two more came up, and then two more,
  And more, and more, and more,
And some looked upwards at the roof,
  And some down upon the floor,
But none were any wiser than
  The pair that went before.

"I weep for you," the Vulture said;
  "I deeply sympathize!"
With sobs and tears he gave them all
  D's of the largest size,
While at the Husbandman he winked
  One of his streaming eyes.

"I think," observed the Husbandman,
  "We 're getting on too quick;
Are we not putting down the D's
  A little bit too thick?"
The Vulture said with much disgust,
  "Their answers make me sick."

"Now, Undergraduates," he cried,
  "Our fun is nearly done;
Will anybody else come up?"
  But answer came there none;
But this was scarcely odd, because
  They'd ploughed them every one!

A. C. Hilton.

AFTER A. C. SWINBURNE

GILLIAN

JACK and Jille
 I have made me an end of the moods of
  maidens,
  I have loosed me, and leapt from the links
   of love;
 From the kiss that cloys and desire that
  deadens,
  The woes that madden, the words that
   move.
 In the dim last days of a spent September,
  When fruits are fallen, and flies are fain;
 Before you forget, and while I remember,
  I cry as I shall cry never again.

Went up a hylle
 Where the strong fell faints in the lazy levels
  Of misty meadows, and streams that stray;
 We raised us at eve from our rosy revels,
  With the faces aflame for the death of the
   day;
 With pale lips parted, and sighs that shiver,
  Low lids that cling to the last of love:
 We left the levels, we left the river,
  And turned us and toiled to the air above.

To fetch a paile of water,

> By the sad sweet springs that have salved our
> sorrow,
>> The fates that haunt us, the grief that
>> grips —
> Where we walk not to-day nor shall walk not
> to-morrow —
>> The wells of Lethe for wearied lips.
> With souls nor shaken with tears nor laughter,
>> With limp knees loosed as of priests that
>> pray,
> We bowed us and bent to the white well-
> water,
>> We dipped and we drank it and bore away.

Jack felle downe

> The low light trembled on languid lashes,
>> The haze of your hair on my mouth was
>> blown,
> Our love flashed fierce from its fading ashes,
>> As night's dim net on the day was thrown.
> What was it meant for, or made for, that
> minute,
>> But that our lives in delight should be
>> dipt ?
> Was it yours, or my fault, or fate's, that in it
>> Our frail feet faltered, our steep steps slipt.

And brake his crowne, and Jille came tumblynge
after.

[269]

Our linked hands loosened and lapsed in
    sunder,
  Love from our limbs as a shift was shed,
But paused a moment, to watch with wonder
  The pale pained body, the bursten head.
While our sad souls still with regrets are riven,
  While the blood burns bright on our bruised
    brows,
I have set you free, and I stand forgiven —
  And now I had better go call my cows.

Anonymous.

ATALANTA IN CAMDEN-TOWN

AY, 't was here, on this spot,
    In that summer of yore,
  Atalanta did not
  Vote my presence a bore,
Nor reply to my tenderest talk, " She had heard all
that nonsense before."

  She 'd the brooch I had bought
    And the necklace and sash on,
  And her heart, as I thought,
    Was alive to my passion ;
And she 'd done up her hair in the style that the
Empress had brought into fashion.

  I had been to the play
    With my pearl of a Peri —
  But, for all I could say,
    She declared she was weary,
That " the place was so crowded and hot, and she
could n't abide that Dundreary."

[270]

Then I thought, " 'T is for me
That she whines and she whimpers!"
And it soothed me to see
Those sensational simpers,
And I said, " This is scrumptious," — a phrase I
had learned from the Devonshire shrimpers.

And I vowed, " 'T will be said
I 'm a fortunate fellow,
When the breakfast is spread,
When the topers are mellow,
When the foam of the bird-cake is white and the
fierce orange-blossoms are yellow!"

Oh, that languishing yawn!
Oh, those eloquent eyes!
I was drunk with the dawn
Of a splendid surmise —
I was stung by a look, I was slain by a tear, by a
tempest of sighs.

And I whispered, " 'T is time!
Is not Love at its deepest?
Shall we squander Life's prime,
While thou waitest and weepest?
Let us settle it, License or Banns? — though un-
doubtedly Banns are the cheapest."

" Ah, my Hero!" said I,
" Let me be thy Leander!"
But I lost her reply —
Something ending with " gander " —
For the omnibus rattled so loud that no mortal
could quite understand her.

[271]   *Lewis Carroll.*

THE MANLET

IN stature the Manlet was dwarfish —
  No burly big Blunderbore he :
   And he wearily gazed on the crawfish
    His Wifelet had dressed for his tea.
" Now reach me, sweet Atom, my gunlet,
  And hurl the old shoelet for luck ;
Let me hie to the bank of the runlet
    And shoot thee a Duck ! "

She has reached him his minnikin gunlet :
  She has hurled the old shoelet for luck ;
She is busily baking a bunlet,
    To welcome him home with his duck.
On he speeds, never wasting a wordlet,
  Though thoughtlets cling closely as wax,
To the spot where the beautiful birdlet
    So quietly quacks.

Where the Lobsterlet lurks and the Crablet
  So slowly and creepily crawls :
Where the Dolphin 's at home and the Dablet
  Pays long ceremonious calls :
Where the Grublet is sought by the Froglet :
  Where the Frog is pursued by the Duck :
Where the Ducklet is chased by the Doglet —
    So runs the world's luck.

He has loaded with bullet and powder :
  His footfall is noiseless as air :
But the Voices grow louder and louder
  And bellow and bluster and blare.

They bristle before him and after,
   They flutter above and below,
Shrill shriekings of lubberly laughter,
             Weird wailings of woe!

They echo without him, within him:
   They thrill through his whiskers and beard:
Like a teetotum seeming to spin him,
   With sneers never hitherto sneered.
" Avengement," they cry, " on our Foelet!
   Let the Manikin weep for our wrongs!
Let us drench him from toplet to toelet
             With nursery songs!

" He shall muse upon Hey! Diddle! Diddle!
   On the Cow that surmounted the Moon!
He shall rave of the Cat and the Fiddle,
   And the Dish that eloped with the Spoon:
And his soul shall be sad for the Spider,
   When Miss Muffett was sipping her whey,
That so tenderly sat down beside her,
            And scared her away!

" The music of Midsummer-madness
   Shall sting him with many a bite,
Till, in rapture of rollicking sadness,
   He shall groan with a gloomy delight;
He shall swathe him like mists of the morning,
   In platitudes luscious and limp,
Such as deck, with a deathless adorning,
           The Song of the Shrimp!

[273]

" When the Ducklet's dark doom is decided,
    We will trundle him home in a trice :
And the banquet so plainly provided
    Shall round into rosebuds and rice :
In a blaze of pragmatic invention
    He shall wrestle with Fate and shall reign :
But he has not a friend fit to mention,
        So hit him again ! "

He has shot it, the delicate darling !
    And the Voices have ceased from their strife :
Not a whisper of sneering or snarling,
    As he carries it home to his wife :
Then, cheerily champing the bunlet
    His spouse was so skilful to bake,
He hies him once more to the runlet,
        To fetch her the Drake !

                        Lewis Carroll.

IF !

IF life were never bitter,
    And love were always sweet,
    Then who would care to borrow
A moral from to-morrow —
If Thames would always glitter,
    And joy would ne'er retreat,
If life were never bitter,
    And love were always sweet !

If care were not the waiter
    Behind a fellow's chair,
When easy-going sinners
Sit down to Richmond dinners,

And life's swift stream flows straighter,
  By Jove, it would be rare,
If care were not the waiter
  Behind a fellow's chair.

If wit were always radiant,
  And wine were always iced,
And bores were kicked out straightway
Through a convenient gateway;
Then down the year's long gradient
  'T were sad to be enticed,
If wit were always radiant,
  And wine were always iced.

Mortimer Collins.

THE MAID OF THE MEERSCHAUM

NUDE nymph, when from Neuberg's I led
      her
    In velvet enshrined and encased,
When with rarest Virginia I fed her,
  And pampered each maidenly taste
On " Old Judge " and " Lone Jack " and brown
  " Bird's-eye,"
  The best that a mortal might get —
Did she know how, from whiteness of curds, I
  Should turn her to jet?

She was blonde and impassive and stately
  When first our acquaintance began,
When she smiled from the pipe-bowl sedately
  On the " Stunt " who was scarcely a man.

But *labuntur anni fugaces,*
   And changed in due season were we,
For she wears the blackest of faces,
   And I'm a D. C.

Unfailing the comfort she gave me
   In the days when I owned to a heart,
When the charmers that used to enslave me
   For Home or the Hills would depart.
She was Polly or Agnes or Kitty
   (Whoever pro tem. was my flame),
And I found her most ready to pity,
   And — always the same.

At dawn, when the pig broke from cover,
   At noon, when the pleaders were met,
She clung to the lips of her lover
   As never live maiden did yet;
At the Bund, when I waited the far light
   That brought me my Mails o'er the main —
At night, when the tents, in the starlight,
   Showed white on the plain.

And now, though each finely cut feature
   Is flattened and polished away,
I hold her the loveliest creature
   That ever was fashioned from clay.
Let an epitaph thus, then, be wrought for
   Her tomb, when the smash shall arrive:
" *Hic jacet* the life's love I bought for
   Rupees twenty-five."

Rudyard Kipling.

QUAERITUR

DAWN that disheartens the desolate dunes,
    Dulness of day as it bursts on the beach,
    Sea-wind that shrillest the thinnest of tunes,
What is the wisdom thy wailings would teach?
Far, far away, down the foam-frescoed reach,
    Where ravening rocks cleave the crest of the
        seas,
Sigheth the sound of thy sonorous speech,
    As gray gull and guillemot gather their fees;
    Taking toll of the beasts that are bred in the
        seas.

Foam-flakes fly farther than faint eyes can fol-
    low —
    Drop down the desolate dunes and are done;
Fleeter than foam-flowers flitteth the Swallow,
    Sheer for the sweets of the South and the Sun.
What is thy tale?   O thou treacherous Swallow!
    Sing me thy secret, Beloved of the Skies,
That I may gather my garments and follow —
    Flee on the path of thy pinions and rise
    Where strong storms cease and the weary wind
        dies.

Lo! I am bound with the chains of my sorrow;
    Swallow, swift Swallow, ah, wait for a while!
Stay but a moment — it may be to-morrow
    Chains shall be severed and sad souls shall
        smile!

Only a moment — a mere minute's measure —
  How shall it hurt such a swift one as thou?
Pitiless Swallow, full flushed for thy pleasure,
  Canst thou not even one instant allow
    To weak-winged wanderers? Wait for me
    now.

                Rudyard Kipling.

A MELTON MOWBRAY PORK-PIE

STRANGE pie that is almost a passion,
   O passion immoral for pie!
Unknown are the ways that they fashion,
  Unknown and unseen of the eye.
The pie that is marbled and mottled,
  The pie that digests with a sigh:
For all is not Bass that is bottled,
  And all is not pork that is pie.

          Richard Le Gallienne.

FOAM AND FANGS

O NYMPH with the nicest of noses;
   And finest and fairest of forms;
   Lips ruddy and ripe as the roses
  That sway and that surge in the storms;
O buoyant and blooming Bacchante,
  Of fairer than feminine face,
Rush, raging as demon of Dante —
  To this, my embrace!

The foam and the fangs and the flowers,
  The raving and ravenous rage
Of a poet as pinion'd in powers
  As condor confined in a cage!
My heart in a haystack I 've hidden,
  As loving and longing I lie,
Kiss open thine eyelids unbidden —
  I gaze and I die!

I 've wander'd the wild waste of slaughter,
  I 've sniffed up the sepulchre's scent,
I 've doated on devilry's daughter,
  And murmur'd much more than I meant;
I 've paused at Penelope's portal,
  So strange are the sights that I 've seen,
And mighty 's the mind of the mortal
  Who knows what I mean.

                                        Walter Parke.

A SONG OF RENUNCIATION

IN the days of my season of salad,
    When the down was as dew on my cheek,
  And for French I was bred on the ballad,
    For Greek on the writers of Greek, —
Then I sang of the rose that is ruddy,
  Of " pleasure that winces and stings,"
Of white women, and wine that is bloody,
  And similar things.

Of Delight that is dear as Desi-er,
  And Desire that is dear as Delight;
Of the fangs of the flame that is fi-er,
  Of the bruises of kisses that bite;

Of embraces that clasp and that sever,
  Of blushes that flutter and flee
Round the limbs of Dolores, whoever
  Dolores may be.

I sang of false faith that is fleeting
  As froth of the swallowing seas,
Time's curse that is fatal as Keating
  Is fatal to amorous fleas;
Of the wanness of woe that is whelp of
  The lust that is blind as a bat —
By the help of my Muse and the help of
  The relative THAT.

Panatheist, bruiser and breaker
  Of kings and the creatures of kings,
I shouted on Freedom to shake her
  Feet loose of the fetter that clings;
Far rolling my ravenous red eye,
  And lifting a mutinous lid,
To all monarchs and matrons I said I
  Would shock them — and did.

Thee I sang, and thy loves, O Thalassian,
  O " noble and nude and antique ! "
Unashamed in the " fearless old fashion,"
  Ere washing was done by the week ;
When the " roses and rapture " that girt you
  Were visions of delicate vice,
And the " lilies and languors of virtue "
  Not nearly so nice.

O delights of the time of my teething,
    Felise, Fragoletta, Yolande !
Foam-yeast of a youth in its seething
    On blasted and blithering sand !
Snake-crowned on your tresses and belted
    With blossoms that coil and decay,
Ye are gone; ye are lost; ye are melted
    Like ices in May.

Hushed now is the bibulous bubble
    Of " lithe and lascivious " throats;
Long stript and extinct is the stubble
    Of hoary and harvested oats;
From the sweets that are sour as the sorrel's
    The bees have abortively swarmed;
And Algernon's earlier morals
    Are fairly reformed.

I have written a loyal Armada,
    And posed in a Jubilee pose;
I have babbled of babies and played a
    New tune on the turn of their toes;
Washed white from the stain of Astarte,
    My books any virgin may buy;
And I hear I am praised by a party
    Called Something Mackay !

When erased are the records, and rotten
    The meshes of memory's net;
When the grace that forgives has forgotten
    The things that are good to forget;

[281]

When the trill of my juvenile trumpet
    Is dead and its echoes are dead;
Then the laurel shall lie on the crumpet
    And crown of my head !

Owen Seaman.

NEPHELIDIA

FROM the depth of the dreamy decline of the
        dawn through a notable nimbus of
        nebulous moonshine,
    Pallid and pink as the palm of the flag-flower
        that flickers with fear of the flies as they
        float,
Are they looks of our lovers that lustrously lean
        from a marvel of mystic miraculous moon-
        shine,
    These that we feel in the blood of our blushes
        that thicken and threaten with throbs
        through the throat ?
Thicken and thrill as a theatre thronged at appeal
        of an actor's appalled agitation,
    Fainter with fear of the fires of the future than
        pale with the promise of pride in the past;
Flushed with the famishing fulness of fever that
        reddens with radiance of rathe recreation,
    Gaunt as the ghastliest of glimpses that gleam
        through the gloom of the gloaming when
        ghosts go aghast ?
Nay, for the nick of the tick of the time is a trem-
        ulous touch on the temples of terror,

Strained as the sinews yet strenuous with strife
   of the dead who is dumb as the dust-heaps
   of death;
Surely no soul is it, sweet as the spasm of erotic
   emotional exquisite error,
   Bathed in the balms of beatified bliss, beatific
   itself by beatitude's breath.
Surely no spirit or sense of a soul that was soft to
   the spirit and soul of our senses
   Sweetens the stress of surprising suspicion that
   sobs in the semblance and sound of a
   sigh;
Only this oracle opens Olympian, in mystical
   moods and triangular tenses, —
   " Life is the lust of a lamp for the light that is
   dark till the dawn of the day when we die."
Mild is the mirk and monotonous music of memory,
   melodiously mute as it may be,
   While the hope in the heart of a hero is bruised
   by the breach of men's rapiers, resigned to
   the rod;
Made meek as a mother whose bosom-beats bound
   with the bliss-bringing bulk of a balm-
   breathing baby,
   As they grope through the grave-yard of creeds,
   under skies growing green at a groan for
   the grimness of God.
Blank is the book of his bounty beholden of old,
   and its binding is blacker than bluer :
   Out of blue into black is the scheme of the
   skies, and their dews are the wine of the
   bloodshed of things;

Till the darkling desire of delight shall be free as a
fawn that is freed from the fangs that
pursue her,
Till the heart-beats of hell shall be hushed by a
hymn from the hunt that has harried the
kennel of kings.

Algernon Charles Swinburne.

THE LAY OF MACARONI

AS a wave that steals when the winds are
stormy
From creek to cove of the curving shore,
Buffeted, blown, and broken before me,
Scattered and spread to its sunlit core:
As a dove that dips in the dark of maples
To sip the sweetness of shelter and shade,
I kneel in thy nimbus, O noon of Naples,
I bathe in thy beauty, by thee embayed.

What is it ails me that I should sing of her?
The queen of the flashes and flames that were!
Yea, I have felt the shuddering sting of her,
The flower-sweet throat and the hands of her!
I have swayed and sung to the sound of her
psalters,
I have danced her dances of dizzy delight,
I have hallowed mine hair to the horns of her
altars,
Between the nightingale's song and the night!

[284]

What is it, Queen, that now I should do for thee?
What is it now I should ask at thine hands?
Blow of the trumpets thine children once blew for
    thee?
    Break from thine feet and thine bosom the
    bands?
Nay, as sweet as the songs of Leone Leoni,
    And gay as her garments of gem-sprinkled gold,
She gives me mellifluous, mild macaroni,
    The choice of her children when cheeses are old!

And over me hover, as if by the wings of it,
    Frayed in the furnace by flame that is fleet,
The curious coils and the strenuous strings of it,
    Dropping, diminishing down, as I eat;
Lo! and the beautiful Queen, as she brings of it,
    Lifts me the links of the limitless chain,
Bidding mine mouth chant the splendidest things
    of it,
    Out of the wealth of my wonderful brain!

Behold! I have done it: my stomach is smitten
    With sweets of the surfeit her hands have
    unrolled.
Italia, mine cheeks with thine kisses are bitten,
    I am broken with beauty, stabbed, slaughtered,
    and sold!
No man of thy millions is more macaronied,
    Save mighty Mazzini, than musical Me;
The souls of the Ages shall stand as astonied,
    And faint in the flame I am fanning for thee!

                 Bayard Taylor.

AFTER BRET HARTE

THE HEATHEN PASS-EE

By Bred Hard

WHICH I wish to remark,
        And my language is plain,
        That for plots that are dark
And not always in vain
The heathen Pass-ee is peculiar,
And the same I would rise to explain.

I would also premise
    That the term of Pass-ee
Most fitly applies,
    As you probably see,
To one whose vocation is passing
The ordinary B. A. degree.

Tom Crib was his name,
    And I shall not deny
In regard to the same
    What that name might imply;
But his face it was trustful and childlike,
And he had a most innocent eye.

Upon April the First
    The Little-Go fell,
And that was the worst
    Of the gentleman's sell,

For he fooled the Examining Body
In a way I'm reluctant to tell.

The candidates came,
    And Tom Crib soon appeared;
It was Euclid.   The same
    Was "the subject he feared;"
But he smiled as he sat by the table,
With a smile that was wary and weird.

Yet he did what he could,
    And the papers he showed
Were remarkably good,
    And his countenance glowed
With pride when I met him soon after
As he walked down the Trumpington Road.

We did not find him out,
    Which I bitterly grieve,
For I've not the least doubt
    That he'd placed up his sleeve
Mr. Todhunter's excellent Euclid,
The same with intent to deceive.

But I shall not forget
    How the next day at two
A stiff paper was set
    By Examiner U.,
On Euripides' tragedy, Bacchae,
A subject Tom partially knew.

But the knowledge displayed
 By that heathen Pass-ee,
And the answers he made,
 Were quite frightful to see,
For he rapidly floored the whole paper
By about twenty minutes to three.

Then I looked up at U.,
 And he gazed upon me ;
I observed " This won't do ; "
 He replied, " Goodness me ;
We are fooled by this artless young person,"
And he sent for that heathen Pass-ee.

The scene that ensued
 Was disgraceful to view,
For the floor it was strewed
 With a tolerable few
Of the " tips " that Tom Crib had been hiding
For the subject he " partially knew."

On the cuff of his shirt
 He had managed to get
What we hoped had been dirt,
 But which proved, I regret,
To be notes on the rise of the Drama,
A question invariably set.

In his various coats
 We proceeded to seek,
Where we found sundry notes
 And — with sorrow I speak —
One of Bohn's publications, so useful
To the student in Latin or Greek.

In the crown of his cap
  Were the Furies and Fates,
And a delicate map
  Of the Dorian States ;
And we found in his palms, which were hollow,
What are frequent in palms, — that is dates.

Which I wish to remark,
  And my language is plain,
That for plots that are dark
  And not always in vain
The heathen Pass-ee is peculiar,
Which the same I am free to maintain.
                              A. C. Hilton.

DE TEA FABULA

Plain Language from Truthful James

DO I sleep ?   Do I dream ?
    Am I hoaxed by a scout ?
  Are things what they seem,
    Or is Sophists about ?
Is our τὸ τι ἦυ εἶναι a failure, or is Robert Browning
    played out ?

Which expressions like these
    May be fairly applied
By a party who sees
    A Society skied
Upon tea that the Warden of Keble had biled with
    legitimate pride.

[289]

'T was November the third,
  And I says to Bill Nye,
" Which it's true what I've heard :
  If you're, so to speak, fly,
There's a chance of some tea and cheap culture,
  the sort recommended as High."

Which I mentioned its name,
  And he ups and remarks:
" If dress-coats is the game
  And pow-wow in the Parks,
Then I'm nuts on Sordello and Hohenstiel-Schwan-
  gau and similar Snarks."

Now the pride of Bill Nye
  Cannot well be express'd ;
For he wore a white tie
  And a cut-away vest :
Says I, "Solomon's lilies ain't in it, and they was
  reputed well dress'd."

But not far did we wend,
  When we saw Pippa pass
On the arm of a friend
  — Dr. Furnivall 't was,
And he wore in his hat two half-tickets for London,
  return, second-class.

" Well," I thought, " this is odd."
  But we came pretty quick
To a sort of a quad
  That was all of red brick,
And I says to the porter, — " R. Browning : free
  passes ; and kindly look slick."

But says he, dripping tears
    In his check handkerchief,
" That symposium's career 's
    Been regrettably brief,
For it went all its pile upon crumpets and busted
    on gunpowder leaf ! "

Then we tucked up the sleeves
    Of our shirts (that were biled),
Which the reader perceives
    That our feelings were riled,
And we went for that man till his mother had
    doubted the traits of her child.

Which emotions like these
    Must be freely indulged
By a party who sees
    A Society bulged
On a reef the existence of which its prospectus had
    never divulged.

But I ask, — Do I dream ?
    Has it gone up the spout ?
Are things what they seem,
    Or is Sophists about ?
Is our τὸ τι ἦν εἶναι a failure, or is Robert Brown-
    ing played out ?

A. T. Quiller-Couch.

AFTER AUSTIN DOBSON

THE PRODIGALS

*(Dedicated to Mr. Chaplin, M.P., and Mr. Rich-
ard Power, M.P., and 223 who followed him)*

MINISTERS ! you, most serious,
    Critics and statesmen of all degrees,
    Hearken awhile to the motion of us —
Senators keen for the Epsom breeze !
Nothing we ask of poets or fees ;
Worry us not with objections, pray !
    Lo, for the speaker's wig we seize —
Give us, ah ! give us the Derby Day.

Scots most prudent, penurious !
    Irishmen busy as bumblebees !
Hearken awhile to the motion of us —
    Senators keen for the Epsom breeze !
    For Sir Joseph's sake, and his owner's, please !
(Solomon raced like fun, they say.)
    Lo, for we beg on our bended knees —
Give us, ah ! give us the Derby Day.

Campbell — Asheton be generous !
    (But they voted such things were not the cheese.)
Sullivan, hear us, magnanimous !
    (But Sullivan thought with their enemies.)

And shortly they got both of help and ease,
For a mad majority crowded to say,
    " Debate we 've drunk to the dregs and lees :
Give us, ah ! give us the Derby Day."

ENVOI :

Prince, most just was the motion of these,
    And many were seen by the dusty way,
Shouting glad to the Epsom breeze
    Give us, ah ! give us the Derby Day.

Anonymous.

AFTER ANDREW LANG

BO-PEEP

UNHAPPY is Bo-Peep,
　　Her tears profusely flow,
　　Because her precious sheep
　Have wandered to and fro,
　Have chosen far to go,
For " pastures new " inclined,
　(See Lycidas) — and lo !
Their tails are still behind !

How catch them while asleep ?
　(I think Gaboriau
For machinations deep
　Beats Conan Doyle and Co.)
　But none a hint bestow
Save this, on how to find
　The flocks she misses so —
" Their tails are still behind ! "

This simple faith to keep
　Will mitigate her woe,
She is not Joan, to leap
　To arms against the foe
　Or conjugate τύπτω ;
Nay, peacefully resigned
　She waits, till time shall show
Their tails are still behind !

Bo-Peep, rejoice !   Although
  Your sheep appear unkind,
Rejoice at last to know
  Their tails are still behind !
                    Anthony C. Deane.

AFTER W. E. HENLEY

IMITATION

CALM and implacable,
      Eying disdainfully the world beneath,
   Sat Humpty-Dumpty on his mural eminence
In solemn state :
And I relate his story
In verse unfettered by the bothering restrictions of
      rhyme or metre,
In verse (or " rhythm," as I prefer to call it)
Which, consequently, is far from difficult to write.

He sat.   And at his feet
The world passed on — the surging crowd
Of men and women, passionate, turgid, dense,
Keenly alert, lethargic, or obese.
(Those two lines scan !)

Among the rest
He noted Jones ; Jones with his Roman nose,
His eyebrows — the left one streaked with a dash
      of gray —
And yellow boots.
Not that Jones
Has anything in particular to do with the story ;

But a descriptive phrase
Like the above shows that the writer is
A Master of Realism.

Let us proceed.   Suddenly from his seat
Did Humpty-Dumpty slip.   Vainly he clutched
The impalpable air.   Down and down,
Right to the foot of the wall,
Right on to the horribly hard pavement that ran
       beneath it,
Humpty-Dumpty,   the   unfortunate   Humpty-
       Dumpty,
Fell.

And him, alas ! no equine agency,
Him no power of regal battalions —
Resourceful, eager, strenuous —
Could ever restore to the lofty eminence
Which once was his.
Still he lies on the very identical
Spot where he fell — lies, as I said on the ground,
Shamefully and conspicuously abased !
                       Anthony C. Deane.

AFTER R. L. STEVENSON

BED DURING EXAMS

I USED to go to bed at night,
And only worked when day was light.
But now 't is quite the other way,
I never get to bed till day.

I look up from my work and see
The morning light shine in on me,
And listen to the warning knell —
The tinkle of the rising bell.

And does there not seem cause to weep,
When I should like so much to sleep,
I have to sing this mournful lay,
I cannot get to bed till day ?

Clara Warren Vail.

AFTER OSCAR WILDE

MORE IMPRESSIONS
(La Fuite des Oies)

TO outer senses they are geese,
　　Dull drowsing by a weedy pool;
　　But try the impression trick.　Cool!　Cool!
Snow-slumbering sentinels of Peace!

Deep silence on the shadowy flood,
　　Save rare sharp stridence (that means " quack "),
　　Low amber light in Ariel track
Athwart the dun (that means the mud).

And suddenly subsides the sun,
　　Bulks mystic, ghostly, thrid the gloom
　　(That means the white geese waddling home),
And darkness reigns!　(See how it's done?)
　　　　　　　　　　　　Oscuro Wildgoose.

NURSERY RHYMES À LA MODE

*(Our nurseries will soon be too cultured to admit the
old rhymes in their Philistine and unæsthetic garb.
They may be redressed somewhat on this model)*

OH, but she was dark and shrill,
　　(Hey-de-diddle and hey-de-dee!)
　　The cat that (on the first April)
Played the fiddle on the lea.

Oh, and the moon was wan and bright,
  (Hey-de-diddle and hey-de-dee!)
The Cow she looked nor left nor right,
  But took it straight at a jump, pardie!
The hound did laugh to see this thing,
  (Hey-de-diddle and hey-de-dee!)
As it was parlous wantoning,
  (Ah, good my gentles, laugh not ye,)
And underneath a dreesome moon
  Two lovers fled right piteouslie;
A spooney plate with a plated spoon,
  (Hey-de-diddle and hey-de-dee!)

POSTSCRIPT

Then blame me not, altho' my verse
  Sounds like an echo of C. S. C.
Since still they make ballads that worse and worse
  Savor of diddle and hey-de-dee.

                                Anonymous.

A MAUDLE–IN BALLAD

(*To his Lily*)

MY lank limp lily, my long lithe lily,
  My languid lily-love fragile and thin,
  With dank leaves dangling and flower-flap
    chilly,
That shines like the shin of a Highland gilly!
Mottled and moist as a cold toad's skin!
Lustrous and leper-white, splendid and splay!
Art thou not Utter and wholly akin

To my own wan soul and my own wan chin,
And my own wan nose-tip, tilted to sway
The peacock's feather, *sweeter than sin*,
That I bought for a halfpenny yesterday?

My long lithe lily, my languid lily,
My lank limp lily-love, how shall I win —
Woo thee to wink at me?   Silver lily,
How shall I sing to thee, softly or shrilly?
What shall I weave for thee — what shall I spin —
Rondel, or rondeau, or virelai?
Shall I buzz like a bee with my face thrust in
Thy choice, chaste chalice, or choose me a tin
Trumpet, or touchingly, tenderly play
On the weird bird-whistle, *sweeter than sin*,
That I bought for a halfpenny yesterday.

My languid lily, my lank limp lily,
My long lithe lily-love, men may grin —
Say that I'm soft and supremely silly —
What care I while you whisper stilly;
What care I while you smile?   Not a pin!
While you smile, you whisper — 'T is sweet
        to decay?

I have watered with chlorodine, tears of chagrin,
The churchyard mould I have planted thee in,
Upside down in an intense way,
In a rough red flower-pot, *sweeter than sin*,
That I bought for a halfpenny yesterday.

Punch.

QUITE THE CHEESE

(By a Wilde Æsthete)

THERE was once a maiden who loved a
  cheese;
  Sing, hey! potatoes and paint!
She could eat a pound and a half with ease
  Oh, the odorous air was faint!

What was the cheese that she loved the best?
  Sing, hey, red pepper and rags!
You will find it out if you read the rest;
  Oh, the horrors of frowning crags!

Came lovers to woo her from ev'ry land —
  Sing, hey! fried bacon and files!
They asked for her heart, but they meant her
  hand,
  Oh, the joy of the Happy Isles.

A haughty old Don from Oporto came;
  Sing, hey! new carrots and nails!
The Duke of GORGONZOLA, his famous name,
  Oh, the lusciously-scented gales!

Lord STILTON belonged to a mighty line!
  Sing, hey! salt herrings and stones!
He was " Blue " as chine — his taste divine!
  Oh, the sweetness of dulcet tones.

Came stout DOUBLE GLO'STER — a man and wife,
  Sing, hey! post pillars and pies!
And the son was SINGLE, and fair as fate;
  Oh, the purple of sunset skies!

DE CAMEMBERT came from his sunny France,
  Sing, hey! pork cutlets and pearls!
He would talk sweet nothings, and sing and dance,
  Oh, the sighs of the soft sweet girls.

Came GRUYÈRE so pale! a most hole-y man!
  Sing, hey! red sandstone and rice!
But the world saw through him as worldings can,
  Oh, the breezes from Isles of Spice.

But the maiden fair loved no cheese but one!
  Sing, hey! acrostics and ale!
Save for SINGLE GLO'STER she love had none!
  Oh, the roses on fair cheeks pale!

He was fair and single — and so was she!
  Sing, hey! tomatoes and tar!
And so now you know which it is to be!
  Oh, the aid of a lucky star!

They toasted the couple the livelong night,
  Sing, hey! cast iron and carp!
And engaged a poet this song to write.
  Oh, the breathing Æolian harp!

So he wrote this ballad at vast expense!
  Sing, hey! pump-handles and peas!
And, though you may think it devoid of sense,
  Oh, he fancies it QUITE THE CHEESE!
  [303]   *H. C. Waring.*

AFTER WILLIAM WATSON

THE THREE MICE

THREE mice — three sightless mice — averse
from strife,
Peaceful descendants of the Armenian race,
Intent on finding some secluded place
Wherein to pass their inoffensive life;
How little dreamt they of that farmer's wife —
The Porte's malicious minion — giving chase,
And in a moment — ah, the foul disgrace ! —
Shearing their tails off with a carving-knife !

And oh, my unemotional countrymen,
Who choose to dally and to temporize,
When once before with vitriolic pen
I told the tale of Turkish infamies,
Once more I call to vengeance, — now as then,
Shouting the magic word " Atrocities !"
Anthony C. Deane.

AFTER KIPLING

FUZZY WUZZY LEAVES US

WE'VE been visited by men across the seas,
  And some of them could write, and some
      could not;
The English, French, and German — whom you
    please,
But Kipling was the finest of the lot.
In sooth, we're loath to lose him from our list;
Though he's not been wholly kind in all his
    dealings;
Indeed from first to last I must insist,
He has played the cat and banjo with our feelings.

> But here's *to* you, Mr. Kipling, with your
>   comments and your slurs;
> You're a poor, benighted Briton, but the
>   Prince of Raconteurs!
> We'll give you your certificate, and if you
>   want it signed,
> Come back and have a fling at us whenever
>   you're inclined!

You harrowed us with murder and with blood;
You dipped us deep in Simla's petty guile;
Yet we have found ourselves misunderstood
When we served you a sensation in our style;

And though you saw some grewsome pictures
  through
The Windy City's magnifying lens,
Yet we took it just a little hard of *you*,
A-objecting to the slaughter of our pens!

But here's *to* you, Mr. Kipling, and the boys
    of Lung-tung-pen,
And all we have to ask you is, make 'em kill
    again!
For though we're crude in some things here,
    which fact I much deplore,
We know genius when we see it, and we're not
    afraid of gore.

And yet we love you best on Greenough Hill,
By Bisesa and her sisters dark perplext;
In your sermons, which have power to lift and
  thrill
Just because they have the heart of man as text;
And when you bend, the little ones to please,
With Bagheera and Baloo at hide and seek,
Oh! a happy hour with Mowgli in the trees
Sets a little chap a-dreaming for a week.

So, here's *to* you, Mr. Kipling, and to Mowgli and
    Old Kaa,
And to her who loved and waited where the
    Gates of Sorrow are;
For where is brush more potent to paint since
    Art began
The white love of a Woman and the red
    blood of a Man.

So, since to us you 've given such delight,
We hope that you won't think us quite so bad.
You 're all hot sand and ginger, when you write,
But we 're sure you 're only shamming when
    you 're mad.
Yet so you leave us Gunga Din's salaam,
So you incarnate Mulvaney on a spree;
Mr. Kipling, sir, we do not " care a damn "
For the comments you may make on such as we!

    Then here 's *to* you, Mr. Kipling, and
        Columbia avers
    You 're a poor, benighted Briton, but the
        Prince of Raconteurs.
    You may scathe us, and may leave us; still
        in our hearts will stay
    The man who made Mulvaney and the road
        to Mandalay.
                    E. P. C.

A BALLAD

(In the manner of R-dy-rd K-pl-ng)

AS I was walkin' the jungle round, a-killin' of
    tigers an' time;
    I seed a kind of an author man a writin' a
rousin' rhyme;
'E was writin' a mile a minute an' more, an' I sez
    to 'im, " 'Oo are you ? "
Sez 'e, " I 'm a poet — 'er majesty's poet — soldier
    an' sailor, too! "

An 'is poem began in Ispahan an' ended in Kala-
    mazoo,
It 'ad army in it, an' navy in it, an' jungle sprinkled
    through,
For 'e was a poet — 'er majesty's poet — soldier an'
    sailor, too !

An' after, I met 'im all over the world, a doin' of
    things a host;
'E 'ad one foot planted in Burmah, an' one on the
    Gloucester coast ;
'E 's 'alf a sailor an' 'alf a whaler, 'e 's captain,
    cook, and crew,
But most a poet — 'er majesty's poet — soldier an'
    sailor too !
'E 's often Scot an' 'e 's often not, but 'is work is
    never through,
For 'e laughs at blame, an' 'e writes for fame, an'
    a bit for revenoo, —
Bein' a poet — 'er majesty's poet — soldier an' sailor
    too !

'E 'll take you up to the Ar'tic zone, 'e 'll take you
    down to the Nile,
'E 'll give you a barrack ballad in the Tommy
    Atkins style,
Or 'e 'll sing you a Dipsy Chantey, as the bloomin'
    bo'suns do,
For 'e is a poet — 'er majesty's poet — soldier an'
    sailor too.
An' there is n't no room for others, an' there 's
    nothin' left to do;

'E 'as sailed the main from the 'Orn to Spain, 'e
    'as tramped the jungle through,
An' written up all there is to write — soldier an'
    sailor, too !

There are manners an' manners of writin', but 'is
    is the *proper* way,
An' it ain't so hard to be a bard if you 'll imitate
    Rudyard K. ;
But sea an' shore an' peace an' war, an' every-
    thing else in view —
'E 'as gobbled the lot ! — 'er majesty's poet —
    soldier a'n sailor, too.
'E 's not content with 'is Indian 'ome, 'e 's looking
    for regions new,
In another year 'e 'll 'ave swept 'em clear, an'
    what 'll the rest of us do ?
'E's crowdin' us out ! — 'er majesty's poet — soldier
    an' sailor too !

                      Guy Wetmore Carryl.

JACK AND JILL

*HERE is the tale — and you must make the most
    of it !
    Here is the rhyme — ah, listen and attend !
Backwards — forwards — read it all and boast of it
If you are anything the wiser at the end !*

Now Jack looked up — it was time to sup, and the
    bucket was yet to fill ;

And Jack looked round for a space and frowned,
  then beckoned his sister Jill,
And twice he pulled his sister's hair, and thrice he
  smote her side ;
" Ha' done, ha' done with your impudent fun — ha'
  done, with your games ! " she cried ;
" You have made mud-pies of a marvellous size —
  finger and face are black,
You have trodden the Way of the Mire and Clay
  — now up and wash you, Jack !
Or else, or ever we reach our home, there waiteth
  an angry dame —
Well you know the weight of her blow — the
  supperless open shame !
Wash, if you will, on yonder hill — wash if you
  will, at the spring, —
Or keep your dirt, to your certain hurt, and an
  imminent walloping ! "

" You must wash — you must scrub — you must
  scrape ! " growled Jack, " you must traffic
  with can and pails,
Nor keep the spoil of the good brown soil in the
  rim of your fingernails !
The morning path you must tread to your bath —
  you must wash ere the night descends,
And all for the cause of conventional laws and the
  soapmaker's dividends !
But if 't is sooth that our meal in truth depends on
  our washing, Jill,
By the sacred right of our appetite — haste — haste
  to the top of the hill ! "

[310]

They have trodden the Way of the Mire and Clay,
    they have toiled and travelled far,
They have climbed to the brow of the hill-top now,
    where the bubbling fountains are,
They have taken the bucket and filled it up — yea,
    filled it up to the brim ;
But Jack he sneered at his sister Jill, and Jill she
    jeered at him :
" What, blown already ! " Jack cried out (and his
    was a biting mirth !)
" You boast indeed of your wonderful speed — but
    what is the boasting worth ?
Now, if you can run as the antelope runs, and if
    you can turn like a hare,

Come, race me, Jill, to the foot of the hill — and
    prove your boasting fair ! "
" Race ?   What is a race ? " (and a mocking face
    had Jill as she spake the word)
" Unless for a prize the runner tries ?   The truth
    indeed ye heard,
For I can run as the antelope runs, and I can turn
    like a hare : —
The first one down wins half a crown — and I will
    race you there ! "
" Yea, if for the lesson that you will learn (the
    lesson of humbled pride),
The price you fix at two-and-six, it shall not be
    denied ;
Come, take your stand at my right hand, for here
    is the mark we toe :

Now, are you ready, and are you steady ?   Gird
  up your petticoats ?   Go ! ''

And Jill she ran like a winging bolt, a bolt from
  the bow released,
But Jack like a stream of the lightning gleam, with
  its pathway duly greased ;
He ran down hill in front of Jill like a summer
  lightning flash —
Till he suddenly tripped on a stone, or slipped, and
  fell to the earth with a crash.
Then straight did rise on his wondering eyes the
  constellations fair,
Arcturus and the Pleiades, the Greater and Lesser
  Bear,
The swirling rain of a comet's train he saw, as he
  swiftly fell —
And Jill came tumbling after him with a loud,
  triumphant yell:
" You have won, you have won, the race is done !
  And as for the wager laid —
You have fallen down with a broken crown — the
  half-crown debt is paid ! ''

They have taken Jack to the room at the back
  where the family medicines are,
And he lies in bed with a broken head in a halo of
  vinegar ;
While, in that Jill had laughed her fill as her brother
  fell to earth
She had felt the sting of a walloping — she hath
  paid the price of her mirth !

Here is the tale — and now you have the whole of it !
Here is the story, well and wisely planned ;
Beauty — Duty — these make up the soul of it —
But, ah, my little readers, will you mark and
understand ?

Anthony C. Deane.

THE LEGEND OF REALISM

THIS is the sorrowful story,
        Told when the twilight fails,
        And the authors sit together
Reading each other's tales.

" Our fathers lived in the cloudland,
    They were Romanticists,
They went down to the valley
    To play with the Scientists.

" Our fathers murmured of moonshine,
    Our fathers sang to the stars,
Our fathers were playfully prolix,
    Our fathers knew nothing of ' pars.'

" Then came the terrible savants,
    Nothing of play they knew,
Only — they caught our fathers,
    And set them to burrow too.

" Set them to work in the workshop,
    With crucible, test, and scales,
Put them in mud-walled prisons,
    And — cut up their beautiful tales.

" Now we can read our fathers,
    Trenchant, and terse, and cold,
Stooping to dig in dust-heaps,
    Sharing the common mold.

" Driving a quill quotidian,
    Mending a muddy plot,
Sitting in mud-walled prisons,
    Steeping their souls in rot.

" Thus and so do our fathers,
    Thus and so must we do,
For we are the slaves of science,
    And we are Realists too."

This is the horrible story,
    Told as the twilight fails,
And the authors sit together
    Reading each other's tales.

                              Hilda Johnson.

AFTER STEPHEN PHILLIPS

LITTLE JACK HORNER

LITTLÉ JACK HORNER sát in án anglé
         Meditating.
                  Before we go farther,
Please clearly understand this is blank verse.
If it reads strangely, and the accent falls
In unexpected places, do not dare
To criticise.   Remember once for all,
That I and Milton judge questións like that —
Vide my letters to the daily press.
As for my critics — wholesale ignorance
Were a term far too mild to paint their gross
Unintellectuality.   So much said,
I start again.
                  In a cornér he sat,
Remote from comrades.   Resolutely his hand
Clutched a delicious pie.   Anon his thumb
From thé pasty depth próduced á curránt.

(Excuse another interruption, but
Observe the beauty of that ultimate line !
With equal ease I might have written it
" Produced a currant from the pasty depth,"
But I — and Milton in his better moments —

[315]

Prefer to be original.)   In his soul
The obsession of his own superior virtue
Grew and prevailed, till at the last he cried :
" I am a Paragon of Excellence ! "

Happy Jack Horner, thus fully convinced
Of his remarkable superiority !
And happy readers, who peruse his tale
Retold in such magnificent blank verse !

Anthony C. Deane.

AFTER FIONA McLEOD, W. B. YEATS, AND OTHERS

THE CULT OF THE CELTIC

WHEN the eager squadrons of day are faint
        and disbanded,
        And under the wind-swept stars the
    reaper gleans
The petulant passion flowers — although, to be
    candid,
    I haven't the faintest notion what that means —

Surely the Snow-White Bird makes melody sweeter
    High in the air than skimming the clogging
        dust.
(Yes, there's certainly something queer about this
    metre,
    But, as it's Celtic, you and I must take it on ·
    trust.)

And oh, the smile of the Slave as he shakes his
    fetters !
    And oh, the Purple Pig as it roams afar !
And oh, the — something or other in capital let-
    ters —
    As it yields to the magic spell of a wind-swept
    star !

And look at the tricksy Elves, how they leap and
    frolic,
  Ducking the Bad Banshee in the moonlit pool,
Celtic, yet fully content to be " symbolic,"
    Never a thought in their heads about Home
    Rule !

But the wind-swept star — you notice it has to
    figure,
  Taking an average merely, in each alternate verse
Of every Celtic poem — smiles with a palpable
    snigger,
  While the Yellow Wolf-Hound bays his blight-
    ing curse,

And the voices of dead desires in sufferers waken,
  And the voice of the limitless lake is harsh and
    rough,
And the voice of the reader, too, unless I 'm mis-
    taken,
  Is heard to remark that he 's had about enough.

But since the critics have stated with some decision
  That stanzas very like these are simply grand,
Showing " a sense of beauty and intimate vision,"
  Proving a " Celtic Renaissance " close at hand ;

Then, although I admit it 's a terrible tax on
  Powers like mine, yet I sincerely felt
My task, as an unintelligent Saxon,
  Was, at all hazards, to try to copy the Celt !
                Anthony C. Deane.

AFTER VARIOUS WRITERS OF VERS DE SOCIÉTÉ

BEHOLD THE DEEDS!
(*Chant Royal*)

(*Being the Plaint of Adolphe Culpepper Ferguson, Salesman of Fancy Notions, held in durance of his Landlady for a failure to connect on Saturday night*)

I

I WOULD that all men my hard case might know;
  How grievously I suffer for no sin:
I, Adolphe Culpepper Ferguson, for lo!
  I, of my landlady am locked in.
For being short on this sad Saturday,
Nor having shekels of silver wherewith to pay,
She has turned and is departed with my key;
Wherefore, not even as other boarders free,
  I sing (as prisoners to their dungeon stones
When for ten days they expiate a spree):
  Behold the deeds that are done of Mrs. Jones!

II

One night and one day have I wept my woe;
  Nor wot I when the morrow doth begin,
If I shall have to write to Briggs & Co.,
  To pray them to advance the requisite tin

[319]

For ransom of their salesman, that he may
Go forth as other boarders go alway —
As those I hear now flocking from their tea,
Led by the daughter of my landlady
    Pianoward. This day for all my moans,
Dry bread and water have been servèd me.
    Behold the deeds that are done of Mrs. Jones!

III

Miss Amabel Jones is musical, and so
    The heart of the young he-boarder doth win,
Playing "The Maiden's Prayer," adagio —
    That fetcheth him, as fetcheth the banco skin
The innocent rustic. For my part, I pray:
That Badarjewska maid may wait for aye
Ere sits she with a lover, as did we
Once sit together, Amabel! Can it be
    That all of that arduous wooing not atones
For Saturday shortness of trade dollars three?
    Behold the deeds that are done of Mrs. Jones!

IV

Yea! she forgets the arm was wont to go
    Around her waist. She wears a buckle whose
        pin
Galleth the crook of the young man's elbow;
    I forget not, for I that youth have been.
Smith was aforetime the Lothario gay.
Yet once, I mind me, Smith was forced to stay
Close in his room. Not calm, as I, was he;

[320]

But his noise brought no pleasaunce, verily.
  Small ease he gat of playing on the bones,
Or hammering on his stove-pipe, that I see.
  Behold the deeds that are done of Mrs. Jones!

V

Thou, for whose fear the figurative crow
  I eat, accursed be thou and all thy kin!
Thee will I show up — yea, up will I show
  Thy too thick buckwheats, and thy tea too thin.
Ay! here I dare thee, ready for the fray!
Thou dost not keep a first-class house, I say!
It does not with the advertisements agree.
Thou lodgest a Briton with a pugaree,
  And thou hast harbored Jacobses and Cohns,
Also a Mulligan.   Thus denounce I thee!
  Behold the deeds that are done of Mrs. Jones!

ENVOY

Boarders! the worst I have not told to ye:
She hath stole my trousers, that I may not flee
  Privily by the window.   Hence these groans,
There is no fleeing in a *robe de nuit.*
  Behold the deeds that are done of Mrs. Jones!
                                        H. C. Bunner.

CULTURE IN THE SLUMS

(Inscribed to an Intense Poet)

"O CRIKEY, Bill!" she ses to me, she ses,
 "Look sharp," ses she, "with them there
    sossiges.
Yea! sharp with them there bags of mysteree!
For lo!" she ses, "for lo! old pal," ses she,
 "I'm blooming peckish, neither more or less."
Was it not prime — I leave you all to guess
How prime — to have a Jude in love's distress
 Come spooning round, and murmuring balmilee,
    "O crikey, Bill!"

For in such rorty wise doth Love express
His blooming views, and asks for your address,
 And makes it right, and does the gay and free.
I kissed her — I did so! And her and me
Was pals. And if that ain't good business,
    O crikey, Bill!
      W. E. Henley.

A BALLADE OF BALLADE-MONGERS

(After the manner of Master François Villon of Paris)

IN Ballades things always contrive to get lost,
 And Echo is constantly asking where
Are last year's roses and last year's frost?
 And where are the fashions we used to wear?

And what is a "gentleman," and what is a "player"?
   Irrelevant questions I like to ask :
Can you reap the tret as well as the tare?
   And who was the Man in the Iron Mask?

What has become of the ring I tossed
   In the lap of my mistress false and fair?
Her grave is green and her tombstone mossed;
   But who is to be the next Lord Mayor?
And where is King William, of Leicester Square?
   And who has emptied my hunting flask?
And who is possessed of Stella's hair?
   And who was the Man in the Iron Mask?

And what became of the knee I crossed,
   And the rod and the child they would not spare?
And what will a dozen herring cost
   When herring are sold at three halfpence a pair?
And what in the world is the Golden Stair?
   Did Diogenes die in a tub or cask,
Like Clarence, for love of liquor there?
   And who was the Man in the Iron Mask?

ENVOY

   Poets, your readers have much to bear,
     For Ballade-making is no great task,
   If you do not remember, I don't much care
     Who was the man in the Iron Mask.
             Augustus M. Moore.

AFTER VARIOUS POPULAR SONGS

BEAUTIFUL SNOW

(*With a drift*)

OH! the snow, the beautiful snow
 (This is a parody, please, you know;
 Over and over again you may meet
Parodies writ on this poem so sweet;
Rhyming, chiming, skipping along,
Comical bards think they do nothing wrong;
Striving to follow what others have done,
One to the number may keep up the fun).
Beautiful snow, so gently you scud,
Pure for a minute, then dirty as mud!

Oh! the snow, the beautiful snow!
Here's a fine mess you have left us below;
Chilling our feet to the tips of our toes;
Cheekily landing full pert on our nose;
Jinking, slinking, ever you try
'Neath our umbrella to flop in our eye;
Gamins await us at every new street,
Watching us carefully, guiding our feet,
Joking, mocking, ready to throw
A hard-compressed ball of this beautiful snow.

Anonymous.

THE NEWEST THING IN CHRISTMAS CAROLS

GOD rest you, merry gentlemen!
 May nothing you dismay;
  Not even the dyspeptic plats
Through which you 'll eat your way;
Nor yet the heavy Christmas bills
 The season bids you pay;
No, nor the ever tiresome need
 Of being to order gay;

Nor yet the shocking cold you 'll catch
 If fog and slush hold sway;
Nor yet the tumbles you must bear
 If frost should win the day;
Nor sleepless nights — they 're sure to come —
 When " waits " attune their lay;
Nor pantomimes, whose dreariness
 Might turn macassar gray;

Nor boisterous children, home in heaps,
 And ravenous of play;
Nor yet — in fact, the host of ills
 Which Christmases array.
God rest you, merry gentlemen,
 May none of these dismay!

Anonymous.

THE TALE OF LORD LOVELL

LORD LOVELL he stood at his own front
    door,
    Seeking the hole for the key;
His hat was wrecked, and his trousers bore
    A rent across either knee,
When down came the beauteous Lady Jane
    In fair white draperie.

" Oh, where have you been, Lord Lovell ? " she
    said,
    " Oh, where have you been ? " said she ;
" I have not closed an eye in bed,
    And the clock has just struck three.
Who has been standing you on your head
    In the ash-barrel, pardie ? "

" I am not drunk, Lad' Shane," he said :
    " And so late it cannot be ;
The clock struck one as I enteréd —
    I heard it two times or three ;
It must be the salmon on which I fed
    Has been too many for me."

" Go tell your tale, Lord Lovell," she said,
    " To the maritime cavalree,
To your grandmother of the hoary head —
    To any one but me :
The door is not used to be openéd
    With a cigarette for a key."
    Anonymous.

"SONGS WITHOUT WORDS"

I CANNOT sing the old songs,
    Though well I know the tune,
    Familiar as a cradle-song
With sleep-compelling croon;
Yet though I'm filled with music
    As choirs of summer birds,
" I cannot sing the old songs "—
    I do not know the words.

I start on " Hail Columbia,"
    And get to " heav'n-born band,"
And there I strike an up-grade
    With neither steam nor sand;
" Star-Spangled Banner " downs me
    Right in my wildest screaming,
I start all right, but dumbly come
    To voiceless wreck at " streaming."

So when I sing the old songs,
    Don't murmur or complain
If " Ti, diddy ah da, tum dum "
    Should fill the sweetest strain.
I love " Tolly um dum di do,"
    And the " Trilla-la yeep da " birds,
But " I cannot sing the old songs "—
    I do not know the words.
                              Robert J. Burdette.

THE ELDERLY GENTLEMAN

BY the side of a murmuring stream, an elderly
gentleman sat,
   On the top of his head was his wig, and
a-top of his wig was his hat.

The wind it blew high and blew strong, as the
elderly gentleman sat;
And bore from his head in a trice, and plunged in
the river his hat.

The gentleman then took his cane, which lay by
his side as he sat;
And he dropped in the river his wig, in attempt-
ing to get out his hat.

His breast it grew cold with despair, and full in
his eye madness sat;
So he flung in the river his cane to swim with his
wig and his hat.

Cool reflection at last came across, while this
elderly gentleman sat;
So he thought he would follow the stream, and
look for his cane, wig, and hat.

His head, being thicker than common, o'erbalanced
the rest of his fat,
And in plumpt this son of a woman, to follow his
wig, cane, and hat.

George Canning.

TURTLE SOUP

BEAUTIFUL soup, so rich and green,
   Waiting in a hot tureen!
   Who for such dainties would not stoop?
Soup of the evening, beautiful Soup?
Soup of the evening, beautiful Soup?
   Beau—ootiful Soo—oop!
   Beau—ootiful Soo—oop!
Soo—oop of the e—e—evening,
   Beautiful, beautiful Soup!

" Beautiful Soup!   Who cares for fish,
Game, or any other dish?
Who would not give all else for two p
Ennyworth only of beautiful Soup?
Pennyworth only of beautiful soup?
   Beau—ootiful Soo—oop!
   Beau—ootiful Soo—oop!
  Soo—oop of the e—e—evening,
   Beautiful, beauti—FUL SOUP! "

          Lewis Carroll.

SOME DAY

(*To an Extortionate Tailor*)

I KNOW not when your bill I'll see,
   I know not when that bill fell due,
   What interest you will charge to me,
   Or will you take my I. O. U.?

It may not be till years are passed,
  Till chubby children's locks are gray ;
The tailor trusts us, but at last
  His reckoning we must meet some day.
Some day — some day — some day I must meet it,
    Snip, I know not when or how,
    Snip, I know not when or how ;
Only this — only this — this that once you did
    me —
Only this — I 'll do you now — I 'll do you now —
                I 'll do you now !

I know not are you far or near —
  Are you at rest, or cutting still ?
I know not who is held so dear !
  Or who 's to pay your " little bill " !
But when it comes, — some day — some day —
  These eyes an awful tote may see ;
And don't you wish, my tailor gay,
  That you may get your £. s. d. ?
Some day — some day — some day I must meet it,
    Snip, I know not when or how,
    Snip, I know not when or how ;
Only this — only this — this that once you did
    me —
Only this — I 'll do you now — I 'll do you now —
                I 'll do you now !
                        F. P. Doveton.

IF I SHOULD DIE TO-NIGHT

IF I should die to-night
 And you should come to my cold corpse and
   say,
Weeping and heartsick o'er my lifeless clay —
 If I should die to-night,
And you should come in deepest grief and woe —
And say : " Here 's that ten dollars that I owe,"
 I might arise in my large white cravat
 And say, " What 's that ? "

 If I should die to-night
And you should come to my cold corpse and kneel,
Clasping my bier to show the grief you feel,
 I say, if I should die to-night
And you should come to me, and there and then
Just even hint 'bout paying me that ten,
 I might arise the while,
 But I'd drop dead again.

Ben King.

A LOVE SONG

(*In the modern taste*, 1733)

FLUTTERING spread thy purple pinions,
 Gentle Cupid, o'er my heart;
 I, a slave in thy dominions;
 Nature must give way to art.

Mild Arcadians, ever blooming,
    Nightly nodding o'er your flocks,
See my weary days consuming
    All beneath yon flowery rocks.

Thus the Cyprian goddess weeping
    Mourn'd Adonis, darling youth;
Him the boar, in silence creeping,
    Gored with unrelenting tooth.

Cynthia, tune harmonious numbers,
    Fair Discretion, string the lyre;
Soothe my ever-waking slumbers;
    Bright Apollo, lend thy choir.

Gloomy Pluto, king of terrors,
    Arm'd in adamantine chains,
Lead me to the crystal mirrors
    Watering soft Elysian plains.

Mourning cypress, verdant willow,
    Gilding my Aurelia's brows,
Morpheus hovering o'er my pillow,
    Hear me pay my dying vows.

Melancholy smooth Meander,
    Swiftly purling in a round,
On thy margin lovers wander,
With thy flowery chaplets crowned.

Thus when Philomela drooping
    Softly seeks her silent mate,
See the bird of Juno stooping;
    Melody resigns to fate.

                                Dean Swift.

OLD FASHIONED FUN

WHEN that old joke was new,
　　It was not hard to joke,
And puns we now pooh-pooh,
　　Great laughter would provoke.

True wit was seldom heard,
　　And humor shown by few,
When reign'd King George the Third,
　　And that old joke was new.

It passed indeed for wit,
　　Did this achievement rare,
When down your friend would sit,
　　To steal away his chair.

You brought him to the floor,
　　You bruised him black and blue,
And this would cause a roar,
　　When your old joke was new.

W. M. Thackeray.

THEMES WITH VARIATIONS

HOME SWEET HOME WITH VARIATIONS

(*Being suggestions of the various styles in which an old theme might have been treated by certain metrical composers*)

FANTASIA

I

The original theme as John Howard Payne wrote it :

'MID pleasures and palaces though we may
  roam,
   Be it ever so humble, there's no place like
home !
A charm from the skies seems to hallow it there,
Which, seek through the world, is not met with
  elsewhere.

  Home, home ! Sweet, Sweet Home !
  There's no place like Home !

An exile from home, splendor dazzles in vain !
Oh, give me my lowly thatched cottage again !
The birds singing gaily that came at my call !
Give me them ! and the peace of mind, dearer than all.

  Home, home ! Sweet, Sweet Home !
  There's no place like Home !

[334]

II

*(As Algernon Charles Swinburne might have wrapped
it up in variations)*

('Mid pleasures and palaces —)

As sea-foam blown of the winds, as blossom of
    brine that is drifted
Hither and yon on the barren breast of the breeze,
Though we wander on gusts of a god's breath,
    shaken and shifted,
    The salt of us stings and is sore for the sobbing
    seas.
For home's sake hungry at heart, we sicken in
    pillared porches
Of bliss made sick for a life that is barren of bliss,
For the place whereon is a light out of heaven that
    sears not nor scorches,
    Nor elsewhere than this.

(An exile from home, splendor dazzles in vain —)

For here we know shall no gold thing glisten,
    No bright thing burn, and no sweet thing shine ;
Nor love lower never an ear to listen
    To words that work in the heart like wine.
        What time we are set from our land apart,
        For pain of passion and hunger of heart,
Though we walk with exiles fame faints to christen,
    Or sing at the Cytherean's shrine.

(Variation : An exile from home —)

Whether with him whose head
Of gods is honored,
With song made splendent in the sight of men —
  Whose heart most sweetly stout,
  From ravishing France cast out,
Being firstly hers, was hers most wholly then —
  Or where on shining seas like wine
  The dove's wings draw the drooping Erycine.

(Give me my lowly thatched cottage —)

For Joy finds Love grow bitter,
And spreads his wings to quit her,
At thought of birds that twitter
  Beneath the roof-tree's straw —
  Of birds that come for calling,
  No fear or fright appalling,
  When dews of dusk are falling,
Or daylight's draperies draw.

(Give me them, and the peace of mind —)

Give me these things then back, though the giving
  Be at cost of earth's garner of gold;
There is no life without these worth living,
  No treasure where these are not told.
For the heart give the hope that it knows not,
  Give the balm for the burn of the breast —
For the soul and the mind that repose not,
  Oh, give us a rest!

III

(As Mr. Francis Bret Harte might have woven it into a touching tale of a western gentleman in a red shirt)

Brown o' San Juan,
    Stranger, I 'm Brown.
Come up this mornin' from 'Frisco —
    Be'n a-saltin' my specie-stacks down.

Be'n a-knockin' around,
    Fer a man from San Juan,
Putty consid'able frequent —
    Jes' catch onter that streak o' the dawn !

Right thar lies my home —
    Right thar in the red —
I could slop over, stranger, in po'try —
    Would spread out old Shakspoke cold dead.

Stranger, you freeze to this : there ain't no kinder
        gin-palace,
Nor no variety-show lays over a man's own rancho.
Maybe it hain't no style, but the Queen in the
        Tower o' London,
Ain't got naathin' I 'd swop for that house over
        thar on the hill-side.

Thar is my ole gal, 'n' the kids, 'n' the rest o' my
        live-stock ;
Thar my Remington hangs, and thar there's a
        griddle-cake br'ilin' —

For the two of us, pard — and thar, I allow, the
   heavens
Smile more friendly-like than on any other locality.

Stranger, nowhere else I don't take no satisfaction.
Gimme my ranch, 'n' them friendly old Shanghai
   chickens —
I brung the original pair f'm the States in eighteen-
   'n'-fifty —
Gimme me them and the feelin' of solid domestic
   comfort.

   Yer parding, young man —
     But this landscape a kind
   Er flickers — I 'low 't wuz the po'try —
     I thought that my eyes hed gone blind.

   Take that pop from my belt!
     Hi, thar!—gimme yer han'—
   Or I'll kill myself — Lizzie — she's left me —
     Gone off with a purtier man!

   Thar, I'll quit — the ole gal
     An' the kids — run away!
   I be derned! Howsomever, come in, pard —
     The griddle-cake's thar, anyway.

IV

(As Austin Dobson might have translated it from Horace, if it had ever occurred to Horace to write it)

RONDEAU

At home alone, O Nomades,
Although Mæcenas' marble frieze
   Stand not between you and the sky,
   Nor Persian luxury supply
Its rosy surfeit, find ye ease.

Tempt not the far Ægean breeze ;
With home-made wine and books that please,
   To duns and bores the door deny,
       At home, alone.

Strange joys may lure.   Your deities
Smile here alone.   Oh, give me these :
   Low eaves, where birds familiar fly,
   And peace of mind, and, fluttering by,
My Lydia's graceful draperies,
       At home, alone.

V

(As it might have been constructed in 1744, *Oliver Goldsmith, at* 19, *writing the first stanza, and Alexander Pope, at* 52, *the second)*

Home! at the word, what blissful visions rise,
Lift us from earth, and draw toward the skies;
'Mid mirag'd towers, or meretricious joys,
Although we roam, one thought the mind employs:
Or lowly hut, good friend, or loftiest dome,
Earth knows no spot so holy as our Home.
There, where affection warms the father's breast,
There is the spot of heav'n most surely blest.
Howe'er we search, though wandering with the
          wind
Through frigid Zembla, or the heats of Ind,
Not elsewhere may we seek, nor elsewhere know,
The light of heaven upon our dark below.

When from our dearest hope and haven reft,
Delight nor dazzles, nor is luxury left,
We long, obedient to our nature's law,
To see again our hovel thatched with straw:
See birds that know our avenaceous store
Stoop to our hand, and thence repleted soar:
But, of all hopes the wanderer's soul that share,
His pristine peace of mind 's his final prayer.

VI

*(As Walt Whitman might have written all
around it)*

I

You over there, young man with the guide-book,
  red-bound, covered flexibly with red linen,
Come here, I want to talk with you; I, Walt, the
  Manhattanese, citizen of these States, call
  you.
Yes, and the courier, too, smirking, smug-mouthed,
  with oil'd hair; a garlicky look about him
  generally; him, too, I take in, just as I
  would a coyote or a king, or a toad-stool, or
  a ham-sandwich, or anything, or anybody else
  in the world.
Where are you going?
You want to see Paris, to eat truffles, to have a
  good time; in Vienna, London, Florence,
  Monaco, to have a good time; you want to
  see Venice.
Come with me. I will give you a good time; I
  will give you all the Venice you want, and
  most of the Paris.
I, Walt, I call to you. I am all on deck! Come
  and loafe with me! Let me tote you around
  by your elbow and show you things.
You listen to my ophicleide!
Home!

Home, I celebrate. I elevate my fog-whistle, in-
spir'd by the thought of home.
Come in! — take a front seat; the jostle of the
crowd not minding; there is room enough
for all of you.
This is my exhibition — it is the greatest show
on earth — there is no charge for admission.
All you have to pay me is to take in my romanza.

II

1. The brown-stone house; the father coming
   home worried from a bad day's business;
   the wife meets him in the marble pav'd vesti-
   bule; she throws her arms about him; she
   presses him close to her; she looks him full
   in the face with affectionate eyes; the frown
   from his brow disappearing.
   Darling, she says, Johnny has fallen down
   and cut his head; the cook is going away,
   and the boiler leaks.
2. The mechanic's dark little third-story room,
   seen in a flash from the Elevated Railway
   train; the sewing-machine in a corner; the
   small cook-stove; the whole family eating
   cabbage around a kerosene lamp; of the
   clatter and roar and groaning wail of the
   Elevated train unconscious; of the smell of
   the cabbage unconscious.
   Me, passant, in the train, of the cabbage not
   quite so unconscious.
3. The French Flat; the small rooms, all right-

angles, unindividual; the narrow halls; the gaudy, cheap decorations everywhere.

The janitor and the cook exchanging compliments up and down the elevator-shaft; the refusal to send up more coal, the solid splash of the water upon his head, the language he sends up the shaft, the triumphant laughter of the cook, to her kitchen retiring.

4. The widow's small house in the suburbs of the city; the widow's boy coming home from his first day down town; he is flushed with happiness and pride; he is no longer a school-boy, he is earning money; he takes on the airs of a man and talks learnedly of business.

5. The room in the third-class boarding-house; the mean little hard-coal fire, the slovenly Irish servant-girl making it, the ashes on the hearth, the faded furniture, the private provender hid away in the closet, the dreary back-yard out the window; the young girl at the glass, with her mouth full of hairpins, doing up her hair to go downstairs and flirt with the young fellows in the parlor.

6. The kitchen of the old farm-house; the young convict just returned from prison — it was his first offense, and the judges were lenient on him.

He is taking his first meal out of prison; he has been received back, kiss'd, encourag'd to start again; his lungs, his nostrils expand with the big breaths of free air; with shame, with

wonderment, with a trembling joy, his heart
too, expanding.
The old mother busies herself about the table ;
she has ready for him the dishes he us'd to
like ; the father sits with his back to them,
reading the newspaper, the newspaper shaking
and rustling much ; the children hang wondering around the prodigal — they have been
caution'd : Do not ask where our Jim has
been ; only say you are glad to see him.
The elder daughter is there, palefac'd, quiet ; her
young man went back on her four years ago ;
his folks would not let him marry a convict's
sister. She sits by the window, sewing on
the children's clothes, the clothes not only
patching up ; her hunger for children of her
own invisibly patching up.
The brother looks up ; he catches her eye, he fearful, apologetic ; she smiles back at him, not
reproachfully smiling, with loving pretence of
hope smiling — it is too much for him ; he
buries his face in the folds of the mother's
black gown.
7. The best room of the house, on the Sabbath
only open'd ; the smell of horse-hair furniture
and mahogany varnish ; the ornaments on the
what-not in the corner ; the wax fruit, dusty,
sunken, sagged in, consumptive-looking, under a glass globe, the sealing-wax imitation of
coral ; the cigar boxes with shells plastered
over, the perforated card-board motto.
The kitchen ; the housewife sprinkling the clothes

for the fine ironing to-morrow — it is the
Third-day night, and the plain things are
ready iron'd, now in cupboards, in drawers
stowed away.
The wife waiting for the husband — he is at the
tavern, jovial, carousing; she, alone in the
kitchen sprinkling clothes — the little red
wood clock with peaked top, with pendulum
wagging behind a pane of gayly painted glass,
strikes twelve.
The sound of the husband's voice on the still night
air — he is singing : " We won't go home until morning! " — the wife arising, toward the
wood-shed hastily going, stealthily entering,
the voice all the time coming nearer, inebriate,
chantant.
The husband passing the door of the wood-shed;
the club over his head, now with his head in
contact; the sudden cessation of the song;
the benediction of peace over the domestic
foyer temporarily resting.

I sing the soothing influences of home.
You, young man, thoughtlessly wandering, with
courier, with guide-book wandering,
You hearken to the melody of my steam-calliope
Yawp!

Henry Cuyler Bunner.

MODERN VERSIFICATION ON ANCIENT THEMES

GOOSE À LA MODE

— Mary, Mary, quite contrary,
How does your garden grow?

WITHIN the garden's deepness filled of light
Stood Mary, and upon her fair green
gown
Fell glory of gold hair, a stern sweet frown
Was on her forehead, slim cold hands and white
Made ending of her long pale arms' delight.
And questioning, I — " How does your garden
grow?"
Then she — " With bells that ring, and shells that
sing
Of strange gray seas, with fair, strong hands that
cling
Together, stand tall damozels a-row."

Elizabeth Cavazza.

THREE CHILDREN SLIDING

— Three children sliding on the ice
All on a summer's day.

FOUR are the names of the seasons — spring,
summer, autumn, and winter.
Summer is hot and winter is cold, while the
others partake in

Greater or less degree of cold and caloric com-
mingled.
Surely, I think, it is well to be good, and my mind
is astonished
At the exceeding sin of sinfulness, whereof the perils
Shown in my verse are apparent. Three rosy
children were sliding
Over the ice in summer and — fate so decreeing,
it happened —
Fell through the ice and were drowned. Had these
children in winter been sliding
On the bare earth, or had they, by the peaceful
fireside sitting,
Studied their catechism, it were strange — so the
novel thought strikes me —
Even in summer's heat had the ice broken suddenly
under
Avoirdupois of these babes, and diluted the well-
springs of pleasure.

JACK AND JILL

*— Jack and Jill went up a hill
To draw a pail of water.*

WHAT moan is made of the mountain, what
sob of the hillside,
Why a lament of the south wind, and rain-
fall as tears?
Brother and sister, once bodies and spirits together,
Fell as fair ghosts down the sad swift slope of
the years.

Where is the fount on the mount where the thrill
    of water
Sang as a siren its song to the steep beneath?
Where are the feet of the son and the fair-eyed
    daughter,
    Feet drawn aside of Fate, and set in the path-
    way of Death!

Ah cruel earth and hard, ah, pitiless laughter
    Made of the waters, when, shattered his golden
    crown,
Fell the fair boy as a star, and his sister after,
    To the field of the dead, to its cold and the
    darkness unknown!

                                    Elizabeth Cavazza.

JACK AND JILL

(As Austin Dobson might have written it)

THEIR pail they must fill
        In a crystalline springlet,
        Brave Jack and fair Jill.
Their pail they must fill
At the top of the hill,
    Then she gives him a ringlet.
Their pail they must fill
    In a crystalline springlet.

They stumbled and fell,
    And poor Jack broke his forehead,
Oh, how he did yell!
They stumbled and fell,

And went down pell-mell —
By Jove! it was horrid.
They stumbled and fell,
And poor Jack broke his forehead.

(*As Swinburne might have written it*)

The shudd'ring sheet of rain athwart the trees!
The crashing kiss of lightning on the seas!
　The moaning of the night wind on the wold,
That erstwhile was a gentle, murm'ring breeze!

On such a night as this went Jill and Jack
With strong and sturdy strides through dampness
　　black
　To find the hill's high top and water cold,
Then toiling through the town to bear it back.

The water drawn, they rest awhile.　Sweet sips
Of nectar then for Jack from Jill's red lips,
　And then with arms entwined they homeward go;
Till mid the mad mud's moistened mush Jack slips.

Sweet Heaven, draw a veil on this sad plight,
His crazéd cries and cranium cracked; the fright
　Of gentle Jill, her wretchedness and wo!
Kind Phœbus, drive thy steeds and end this night!

(*As Walt Whitman might have written it*)

I celebrate the personality of Jack!
I love his dirty hands, his tangled hair, his locomo-
　tion blundering.

[349]

Each wart upon his hands I sing,
Pæans I chant to his hulking shoulder blades.
Also Jill !
Her I celebrate.
I, Walt, of unbridled thought and tongue,
Whoop her up !
What 's the matter with Jill ?
Oh, she 's all right !
Who 's all right ?
Jill.
Her golden hair, her sun-struck face, her hard and
    reddened hands ;
So, too, her feet, hefty, shambling.
I see them in the evening, when the sun empurples
    the horizon, and through the darkening forest
    aisles are heard the sounds of myriad creatures
    of the night.
I see them climb the steep ascent in quest of water
    for their mother.
Oh, speaking of her, I could celebrate the old lady
    if I had time.
She is simply immense !

But Jack and Jill are walking up the hill.
(I did n't mean that rhyme.)
I must watch them.
I love to watch their walk,
And wonder as I watch ;
He, stoop-shouldered, clumsy, hide-bound,
Yet lusty,
Bearing his share of the 1-lb bucket as though it
    were a paperweight.

She, erect, standing, her head uplifting,
Holding, but bearing not the bucket.
They have reached the spring.
They have filled the bucket.
Have you heard the "Old Oaken Bucket"?
I will sing it : —

Of what countless patches is the bed-quilt of life
    composed!
Here is a piece of lace.   A babe is born.
The father is happy, the mother is happy.
Next black crêpe.   A beldame "shuffles off this
    mortal coil."
Now brocaded satin with orange blossoms,
Mendelssohn's "Wedding March," an old shoe
    missile,
A broken carriage window, the bride in the Bellevue
    sleeping.
Here's a large piece of black cloth!
"Have you any last words to say?"
"No."
"Sheriff, do your work!"
Thus it is: from "grave to gay, from lively to
    severe."

I mourn the downfall of my Jack and Jill.
I see them descending, obstacles not heeding.
I see them pitching headlong, the water from the
    pail outpouring, a noise from leathern lungs
    out-belching.
The shadows of the night descend on Jack, recum-
    bent, bellowing, his pate with gore besmeared.

I love his cowardice, because it is an attribute, just
    like
Job's patience or Solomon's wisdom, and I love
    attributes.
Whoop ! ! !

Charles Battell Loomis.

THE REJECTED "NATIONAL HYMNS"

I

By H—y W. L–NGF—W

BACK in the years when Phlagstaff, the Dane,
        was monarch
    Over the sea-ribb'd land of the fleet-footed
Norsemen,
Once there went forth young Ursa to gaze at the
    heavens —
    Ursa — the noblest of all the kings and horsemen.

Musing, he sat in his stirrups and viewed the horizon,
    Where the Aurora lapt stars in a North-polar
    manner,
Wildly he stared, — for there in the heavens before
    him
    Fluttered and flam'd the original Star Spangled
    Banner.

II

By J–hn Gr—nl—f Wh—t—r

My Native Land, thy Puritanic stock
Still finds its roots firm-bound in Plymouth Rock,
And all thy sons unite in one grand wish —
To keep the virtues of Preservéd Fish.

Preservéd Fish, the Deacon stern and true
Told our New England what her sons should do,
And if they swerve from loyalty and right,
Then the whole land is lost indeed in night.

III

By Dr. Ol–v–r W—nd—l H–lmes

A diagnosis of our history proves
Our native land a land its native loves;
Its birth a deed obstetric without peer,
Its growth a source of wonder far and near.

To love it more, behold how foreign shores
Sink into nothingness beside its stores;
Hyde Park at best — though counted ultra-grand —
The " Boston Common " of Victoria's land.

IV

By Ralph W–ldo Em–r––n

Source immaterial of material naught,
   Focus of light infinitesimal,
Sum of all things by sleepless Nature wrought,
   Of which the normal man is decimal.

Refract, in Prism immortal, from thy stars
   To the stars bent incipient on our flag,
The beam translucent, neutrifying death,
   And raise to immortality the rag.

V

By W–ll––m C–ll–n B–y–nt

The sun sinks softly to his Ev'ning Post,
   The sun swells grandly to his morning crown;
Yet not a star our Flag of Heav'n has lost,
   And not a sunset stripe with him goes down.

So thrones may fall, and from the dust of those,
   New thrones may rise, to totter like the last;
But still our Country's nobler planet glows
   While the eternal stars of Heaven are fast.

VI

By N. P. W—LL IS

One hue of our Flag is taken
    From the cheeks of my blushing Pet,
And its stars beat time, and sparkle
    Like the studs on her chemisette.

Its blue is the ocean shadow
    That hides in her dreamy eyes,
It conquers all men, like her,
    And still for a Union flies.

VII

By Th—m—s B—il—y Ald—ch

The little brown squirrel hops in the corn,
    The cricket quaintly sings,
The emerald pigeon nods his head,
    And the shad in the river springs,
The dainty sunflower hangs its head
    On the shore of the summer sea ;
And better far that I were dead,
    If Maud did not love me.

I love the squirrel that hops in the corn,
    And the cricket that quaintly sings ;
And the emerald pigeon that nods his head,
    And the shad that gaily springs.

I love the dainty sunflower too,
    And Maud with her snowy breast;
I love them all; but I love — I love —
    I love my country best.
                    Robert Henry Newell.
                    (*"Orpheus C. Kerr."*)

A THEME WITH VARIATIONS

THEME

RIDE a cock-horse to Banbury Cross,
    To see a fine lady ride on a white horse;
    With rings on her fingers, and bells on her
        toes,
She shall have music wherever she goes.

(*Variation I. — Edmund Spenser*)

So on he pricked, and loe, he gan espy,
    A market and a crosse of glist'ning stone,
And eke a merrie rablement thereby,
    That with the musik of the strong trombone,
    And shaumes, and trompets made most dyvillish
        mone.
And in their midst he saw a lady sweet,
    That rode upon a milk white steed alone,
In scarlet robe ycladd and wimple meet,
Bedight with rings of gold, and bells about her feet.

Whereat the knight empassioned was so deepe,
    His heart was perst with very agony.
Certes (said he) I will not eat, ne sleepe,
    Till I have seen the royall maid more ny;

[356]

Then will I holde her in fast fealtie,
Whom then a carle adviséd, louting low,
  That little neede there was for him to die,
Sithens in yon pavilion was the show,
Where she did ride, and he for two-and-six mote go.

(*Variation II. — Dr. Jonathan Swift*)

Our Chloe, fresh from London town,
To country B——y comes down.
Furnished with half-a-thousand graces
Of silks, brocades, and hoops, and laces ;
And tired of winning coxcombs' hearts,
On simple bumpkins tries her arts.
Behold her ambling down the street
On her white palfrey, sleek and neat.
(Though rumor talks of gaming-tables,
And says 't was won from C——'s stables.
And that, when duns demand their bill,
She satisfies them at quadrille.)
Her fingers are encased with rings,
Although she vows she hates the things.
(" Oh, la ! Why ever did you buy it ?
Well — it 's a pretty gem — I 'll try it.")
The fine French fashions all combine
To make folk stare, and Chloe shine,
From ribbon'd hat with monstrous feather,
To bells upon her under-leather.
Now Chloe, why, do you suppose,
You wear those bells about your toes ?
Is it, your feet with bells you deck
For want of bows about your neck ?

(Variation III — Sir Walter Scott
From " The Lady of the Cake")

" Who is this maid in wild array,
And riding in that curious way ?
What mean the bells that jingle free
About her as in revelry ? "
" 'T is Madge of Banbury," Roderick said,
" And she 's a trifle off her head,
'T was on her bridal morn, I ween,
When she to Graeme had wedded been,
The man who undertook to bake
Never sent home the wedding cake !
Since then she wears those bells and rings,
Since then she rides — but, hush, she sings."
She sung !   The voice in other days
It had been difficult to praise,
And now it every sweetness lacked,
And voice and singer both were cracked.

SONG

They bid me ride the other way,
    They say my brain is warp'd and wrung,
But, oh ! the bridal bells are gay
    That I about my feet have strung !
And when I face the horse's tail
I see once more in Banbury's vale
My Graeme's white plume before me wave,
So thus I 'll ride until the grave.

They say that this is not my home,
  'Mid Scotland's moors and Scotland's brakes.
But, oh! 't is love that makes me roam
  Forever in the land of cakes!
And woe betide the baker's guile,
Whose blight destroyed the maiden's smile!
O woe the day, and woe the deed,
And woa — gee woa — my bonnie steed!
                                    Barry Pain.

THE POETS AT TEA

1. — (*Macaulay, who made it*)

POUR, varlet, pour the water,
    The water steaming hot!
  A spoonful for each man of us,
    Another for the pot!
We shall not drink from amber,
  Nor Capuan slave shall mix
For us the snows of Athos
  With port at thirty-six;
Whiter than snow the crystals,
  Grown sweet 'neath tropic fires,
More rich the herbs of China's field,
The pasture-lands more fragrance yield;
For ever let Britannia wield
  The tea-pot of her sires!

2. — (*Tennyson, who took it hot*)

I think that I am drawing to an end:
For on a sudden came a gasp for breath,

And stretching of the hands, and blinded eyes,
And a great darkness falling on my soul.
O Hallelujah! . . . Kindly pass the milk.

3. — (*Swinburne, who let it get cold*)

As the sin that was sweet in the sinning
  Is foul in the ending thereof,
As the heat of the summer's beginning
  Is past in the winter of love:
O purity, painful and pleading!
  O coldness, ineffably gray!
Oh, hear us, our handmaid unheeding,
  And take it away!

4. — (*Cowper, who thoroughly enjoyed it*)

The cosy fire is bright and gay,
The merry kettle boils away
    And hums a cheerful song.
I sing the saucer and the cup;
Pray, Mary, fill the tea-pot up,
    And do not make it strong.

5. — (*Browning, who treated it allegorically*)

Tut! Bah! We take as another case —
  Pass the bills on the pills on the window-sill;
    notice the capsule
(A sick man's fancy, no doubt, but I place
  Reliance on trade-marks, Sir) — so perhaps
    you 'll

Excuse the digression — this cup which I hold
  Light-poised — Bah, it's spilt in the bed! —
    well, let's on go —
Hold Bohea and sugar, Sir; if you were told
The sugar was salt, would the Bohea be Congo?

6. — (Wordsworth, who gave it away)

" Come, little cottage girl, you seem
  To want my cup of tea;
And will you take a little cream?
  Now tell the truth to me."

She had a rustic, woodland grin,
  Her cheek was soft as silk,
And she replied, " Sir, please put in
  A little drop of milk."

" Why, what put milk into your head?
  'T is cream my cows supply;"
And five times to the child I said,
  " Why, pig-head, tell me, why?"

" You call me pig-head," she replied;
  " My proper name is Ruth.
I called that milk " — she blushed with pride —
  " You bade me speak the truth."

7. — (*Poe, who got excited over it*)

Here's a mellow cup of tea, golden tea!
What a world of rapturous thought its fragrance
      brings to me!
  Oh, from out the silver cells
  How it wells!
  How it smells!
Keeping tune, tune, tune
To the tintinnabulation of the spoon.
And the kettle on the fire
Boils its spout off with desire,
With a desperate desire
And a crystalline endeavour
Now, now to sit, or never,
On the top of the pale-faced moon,
But he always came home to tea, tea, tea, tea, tea,
     Tea to the n—th.

8. — (*Rossetti, who took six cups of it*)

The lilies lie in my lady's bower
(O weary mother, drive the cows to roost),
They faintly droop for a little hour;
My lady's head droops like a flower.

She took the porcelain in her hand
(O weary mother, drive the cows to roost);
She poured; I drank at her command;
Drank deep, and now — you understand!
(O weary mother, drive the cows to roost.)

9. — (*Burns, who liked it adulterated*)

Weel, gin ye speir, I 'm no inclined,
Whusky or tay — to state my mind,
    Fore ane or ither;
For, gin I tak the first, I 'm fou,
And gin the next, I 'm dull as you,
    Mix a' thegither.

10. — (*Walt Whitman, who did n't stay more than a minute*)

One cup for my self-hood,
Many for you.   Allons, camerados, we will drink together,
O hand-in-hand!   That tea-spoon, please, when you 've done with it.
What butter-colour'd hair you 've got.   I don't want to be personal.
All right, then, you need n't.   You 're a stale-cadaver.
Eighteen-pence if the bottles are returned.
Allons, from all bat-eyed formula.

Barry Pain.

THE POETS AT A HOUSE-PARTY

(*A modern mortal having inadvertently stumbled in upon a house-party of poets given on Mount Olympus, being called upon to justify his presence there by writing a poem, offered a Limerick. Whereupon each poet scoffed, and the mortal, offended, challenged them to do better with the same theme)*

The Limerick

A SCHOLARLY person named Finck
　　Went mad in the effort to think
　　Which were graver misplaced,
　To dip pen in his paste,
Or dip his paste-brush in the ink.

(*Omar Khayyam's version*)

Stay, fellow-traveler, let us stop and think,
Pause and reflect on the abysmal brink;
　　Say, would you rather thrust your pen in paste,
Or dip your paste-brush carelessly in ink?

(*Rudyard Kipling's version*)

Here is a theme that is worthy of our cognizance,
　　A theme of great importance and a question for
　　　　your ken;
Would you rather — stop and think well —
Dip your paste-brush in your ink-well,
　　Or in your pesky pasting-pot immerse your inky
　　　　pen?

(*Walt Whitman's version*)

Hail, Camerados!
I salute you,
Also I salute the sewing-machine, and the flour-
　　barrel, and the feather-duster.

What is an aborigine, anyhow ?
I see a paste-pot.
Ay, and a well of ink.
Well, well !
Which shall I do ?
Ah, the immortal fog.
What am I myself
But a meteor
In the fog ?

(Chaucer's version)

A mayde ther ben, a wordy one and wyse,
Who wore a paire of gogles on her eyes.
O'er theemes of depest thogt her braine she werked,
Nor ever any knoty problemme sherked.
Yette when they askt her if she 'd rather sinke
Her penne in payste, or eke her brushe in inke,
" Ah," quo' the canny mayde, " now wit ye wel,
I 'm wyse enow to know — too wyse to tel."

(Henry James' version)

    She luminously wavered, and I tentatively in-
ferred that she would soon perfectly reconsider her
not altogether unobvious course. Furiously, though
with a tender, ebbing similitude, across her mental
consciousness stole a re-culmination of all the
truths she had ever known concerning, or even
remotely relating to, the not-easily fathomed qualities of paste and ink. So she stood, focused in an
intensity of soul-quivers, and I, all unrelenting,
waited, though of a dim uncertainty whether, after
all, it might not be only a dubitant problem.

(*Swinburne's version*)

Shall I dip, shall I dip it, Dolores,
    This luminous paste-brush of thine?
Shall I sully its white-breasted glories,
    Its fair, foam-flecked figure divine?
Or shall I — abstracted, unheeding —
    Swish swirling this pen in my haste,
And, deaf to thy pitiful pleading,
    Just jab it in paste?

(*Eugene Field's version*)

See the Ink Bottle on the Desk! It is full of
Nice Black Ink. Why, the Paste-Pot is there,
Too! Let us watch Papa as he sits down to
write. Oh, he is going to paste a Second-hand
Stamp on a Letter. See, he has dipped his Brush
in the Ink by Mistake. Oh, what a Funny Mistake! Now, although it is Winter, we may have
to Endure the Heated Term.

(*Stephen Crane's version*)

I stood upon a church spire,
A slender, pointed spire,
And I saw
Ranged in solemn row before me,
A paste-pot and an ink-pot.
I held in my either hand
A pen and a brush.
Ay, a pen and a brush.

[366]

Now this is the strange part ;
I stood upon a church spire,
A slender, pointed spire,
Glad, exultant,
Because
The choice was mine !
Ay, mine !
As I stood upon a church spire,
A slender, pointed spire.

(*Mr. Dooley's version*)

" I see by th' pa-apers, Hennessy," said Mr.
Dooley, " that they'se a question up for dee-bate."
" What 's a dee-bate ? " asked Mr. Hennessy.
" Well, it 's different from a fish-bait," returned
Mr. Dooley, " an' it 's like this, if I can bate it
into the thick head of ye. A lot of people argyfies
an' argyfies to decide, as in the prisint instance,
whether a man 'd rayther shtick his pastin'-brush in
his ink-shtand, or if he 'd like it betther to be afther
dippin' his pen in his pashte-pot."
" Thot," said Mr. Hennessy, " is a foolish
question, an' only fools wud argyfy about such a
thing as thot."
" That 's what makes it a dee-bate," said Mr.
Dooley.

Carolyn Wells.

AN OLD SONG BY NEW SINGERS

(In the original)

MARY had a little lamb,
   Its fleece was white as snow, —
   And everywhere that Mary went
   The lamb was sure to go.

(As Austin Dobson writes it)

TRIOLET

A little lamb had Mary, sweet,
   With a fleece that shamed the driven snow.
Not alone Mary went when she moved her feet
(For a little lamb had Mary, sweet),
And it tagged her 'round with a pensive bleat,
   And wherever she went it wanted to go;
A little lamb had Mary, sweet,
   With a fleece that shamed the driven snow.

(As Mr. Browning has it)

You knew her ? — Mary the small,
How of a summer, — or, no, was it fall ?
You 'd never have thought it, never believed,
But the girl owned a lamb last fall.

Its wool was subtly, silky white,
Color of lucent obliteration of night,
Like the shimmering snow or — our Clothild's
   arm !

You've seen her arm — her right, I mean —
The other she scalded a-washing, I ween —
How white it is and soft and warm?

Ah, there was soul's heart-love, deep, true, and
    tender,
Wherever went Mary, the maiden so slender,
There followed, his all-absorbed passion, inciting,
That passionate lambkin — her soul's heart de-
    lighting —
Ay, every place that Mary sought in,
That lamb was sure to soon be caught in.

(*As Longfellow might have done it*)

Fair the daughter known as Mary,
Fair and full of fun and laughter,
Owned a lamb, a little he-goat,
Owned him all herself and solely.
White the lamb's wool as the Gotchi —
The great Gotchi, driving snowstorm.
Hither Mary went and thither,
But went with her to all places,
Sure as brook to run to river,
Her pet lambkin following with her.

(*How Andrew Lang sings it*)

RONDEAU

A wonderful lass was Marie, petite,
And she looked full fair and passing sweet —
    And, oh ! she owned — but cannot you guess
    What pet can a maiden so love and caress
[369]

As a tiny lamb with a plaintive bleat,
And mud upon his dainty feet,
And a gentle veally odour of meat,
   And a fleece to finger and kiss and press —
      White as snow ?

Wherever she wandered, in lane or street,
As she sauntered on, there at her feet
   She would find that lambkin — bless
   The dear ! — treading on her dainty dress,
Her dainty dress, fresh and neat —
      White as snow !

(*Mr. Algernon C. Swinburne's idea*)

VILLANELLE

Dewy-eyed with shimmering hair,
   Maiden and lamb were a sight to see,
For her pet was white as she was fair.

And its lovely fleece was beyond compare,
   And dearly it loved its Mistress Marie,
Dewy-eyed, with shimmering hair.

Its warpéd wool was an inwove snare,
   To tangle her fingers in, where they could be
(For her pet was white as she was fair).

Lost from sight, both so snow-white were,
   And the lambkin adored the maiden wee,
Dewy-eyed with shimmering hair.

Th' impassioned incarnation of rare,
  Of limpid-eyed, luscious-lipped, loved beauty,
And her pet was white as she was fair.

Wherever she wandered, hither and there,
  Wildly that lambkin sought with her to be,
With the dewy-eyed, with shimmering hair,
And a pet as white as its mistress was fair.
                          A. C. Wilkie.

INDEX OF TITLES

[373]

Index of Titles

[375]

Index of Titles

Index of Titles

INDEX OF AUTHORS

Index of Authors

INDEX OF AUTHORS
PARODIED

A CATALOGUE OF SELECTED DOVER BOOKS
IN ALL FIELDS OF INTEREST

A CATALOGUE OF SELECTED DOVER BOOKS
IN ALL FIELDS OF INTEREST

AMERICA'S OLD MASTERS, James T. Flexner. Four men emerged unexpectedly from provincial 18th century America to leadership in European art: Benjamin West, J. S. Copley, C. R. Peale, Gilbert Stuart. Brilliant coverage of lives and contributions. Revised, 1967 edition. 69 plates. 365pp. of text.
21806-6 Paperbound $2.75

FIRST FLOWERS OF OUR WILDERNESS: AMERICAN PAINTING, THE COLONIAL PERIOD, James T. Flexner. Painters, and regional painting traditions from earliest Colonial times up to the emergence of Copley, West and Peale Sr., Foster, Gustavus Hesselius, Feke, John Smibert and many anonymous painters in the primitive manner. Engaging presentation, with 162 illustrations. xxii + 368pp.
22180-6 Paperbound $3.50

THE LIGHT OF DISTANT SKIES: AMERICAN PAINTING, 1760-1835, James T. Flexner. The great generation of early American painters goes to Europe to learn and to teach: West, Copley, Gilbert Stuart and others. Allston, Trumbull, Morse; also contemporary American painters—primitives, derivatives, academics—who remained in America. 102 illustrations. xiii + 306pp. 22179-2 Paperbound $3.00

A HISTORY OF THE RISE AND PROGRESS OF THE ARTS OF DESIGN IN THE UNITED STATES, William Dunlap. Much the richest mine of information on early American painters, sculptors, architects, engravers, miniaturists, etc. The only source of information for scores of artists, the major primary source for many others. Unabridged reprint of rare original 1834 edition, with new introduction by James T. Flexner, and 394 new illustrations. Edited by Rita Weiss. 6⅝ x 9⅝.
21695-0, 21696-9, 21697-7 Three volumes, Paperbound $13.50

EPOCHS OF CHINESE AND JAPANESE ART, Ernest F. Fenollosa. From primitive Chinese art to the 20th century, thorough history, explanation of every important art period and form, including Japanese woodcuts; main stress on China and Japan, but Tibet, Korea also included. Still unexcelled for its detailed, rich coverage of cultural background, aesthetic elements, diffusion studies, particularly of the historical period. 2nd, 1913 edition. 242 illustrations. lii + 439pp. of text.
20364-6, 20365-4 Two volumes, Paperbound $5.00

THE GENTLE ART OF MAKING ENEMIES, James A. M. Whistler. Greatest wit of his day deflates Oscar Wilde, Ruskin, Swinburne; strikes back at inane critics, exhibitions, art journalism; aesthetics of impressionist revolution in most striking form. Highly readable classic by great painter. Reproduction of edition designed by Whistler. Introduction by Alfred Werner. xxxvi + 334pp.
21875-9 Paperbound $2.25

VISUAL ILLUSIONS: THEIR CAUSES, CHARACTERISTICS, AND APPLICATIONS, Matthew Luckiesh. Thorough description and discussion of optical illusion, geometric and perspective, particularly; size and shape distortions, illusions of color, of motion; natural illusions; use of illusion in art and magic, industry, etc. Most useful today with op art, also for classical art. Scores of effects illustrated. Introduction by William H. Ittleson. 100 illustrations. xxi + 252pp.

21530-X Paperbound $1.50

A HANDBOOK OF ANATOMY FOR ART STUDENTS, Arthur Thomson. Thorough, virtually exhaustive coverage of skeletal structure, musculature, etc. Full text, supplemented by anatomical diagrams and drawings and by photographs of undraped figures. Unique in its comparison of male and female forms, pointing out differences of contour, texture, form. 211 figures, 40 drawings, 86 photographs. xx + 459pp. 5⅜ x 8⅜.

21163-0 Paperbound $3.00

150 MASTERPIECES OF DRAWING, Selected by Anthony Toney. Full page reproductions of drawings from the early 16th to the end of the 18th century, all beautifully reproduced: Rembrandt, Michelangelo, Dürer, Fragonard, Urs, Graf, Wouwerman, many others. First-rate browsing book, model book for artists. xviii + 150pp. 8⅜ x 11¼.

21032-4 Paperbound $2.00

THE LATER WORK OF AUBREY BEARDSLEY, Aubrey Beardsley. Exotic, erotic, ironic masterpieces in full maturity: Comedy Ballet, Venus and Tannhauser, Pierrot, Lysistrata, Rape of the Lock, Savoy material, Ali Baba, Volpone, etc. This material revolutionized the art world, and is still powerful, fresh, brilliant. With *The Early Work*, all Beardsley's finest work. 174 plates, 2 in color. xiv + 176pp. 8⅛ x 11.

21817-1 Paperbound $3.00

DRAWINGS OF REMBRANDT, Rembrandt van Rijn. Complete reproduction of fabulously rare edition by Lippmann and Hofstede de Groot, completely reedited, updated, improved by Prof. Seymour Slive, Fogg Museum. Portraits, Biblical sketches, landscapes, Oriental types, nudes, episodes from classical mythology—All Rembrandt's fertile genius. Also selection of drawings by his pupils and followers. "Stunning volumes," *Saturday Review*. 550 illustrations. lxxviii + 552pp. 9⅛ x 12¼.

21485-0, 21486-9 Two volumes, Paperbound $6.50

THE DISASTERS OF WAR, Francisco Goya. One of the masterpieces of Western civilization—83 etchings that record Goya's shattering, bitter reaction to the Napoleonic war that swept through Spain after the insurrection of 1808 and to war in general. Reprint of the first edition, with three additional plates from Boston's Museum of Fine Arts. All plates facsimile size. Introduction by Philip Hofer, Fogg Museum. v + 97pp. 9⅜ x 8¼.

21872-4 Paperbound $1.75

GRAPHIC WORKS OF ODILON REDON. Largest collection of Redon's graphic works ever assembled: 172 lithographs, 28 etchings and engravings, 9 drawings. These include some of his most famous works. All the plates from *Odilon Redon: oeuvre graphique complet,* plus additional plates. New introduction and caption translations by Alfred Werner. 209 illustrations. xxvii + 209pp. 9⅛ x 12¼.

21966-8 Paperbound $4.00

DESIGN BY ACCIDENT; A BOOK OF "ACCIDENTAL EFFECTS" FOR ARTISTS AND DESIGNERS, James F. O'Brien. Create your own unique, striking, imaginative effects by "controlled accident" interaction of materials: paints and lacquers, oil and water based paints, splatter, crackling materials, shatter, similar items. Everything you do will be different; first book on this limitless art, so useful to both fine artist and commercial artist. Full instructions. 192 plates showing "accidents," 8 in color. viii + 215pp. 8⅜ x 11¼. 21942-9 Paperbound $3.50

THE BOOK OF SIGNS, Rudolf Koch. Famed German type designer draws 493 beautiful symbols: religious, mystical, alchemical, imperial, property marks, runes, etc. Remarkable fusion of traditional and modern. Good for suggestions of timelessness, smartness, modernity. Text. vi + 104pp. 6⅛ x 9¼. 20162-7 Paperbound $1.25

HISTORY OF INDIAN AND INDONESIAN ART, Ananda K. Coomaraswamy. An unabridged republication of one of the finest books by a great scholar in Eastern art. Rich in descriptive material, history, social backgrounds; Sunga reliefs, Rajput paintings, Gupta temples, Burmese frescoes, textiles, jewelry, sculpture, etc. 400 photos. viii + 423pp. 6⅜ x 9¾. 21436-2 Paperbound $3.50

PRIMITIVE ART, Franz Boas. America's foremost anthropologist surveys textiles, ceramics, woodcarving, basketry, metalwork, etc.; patterns, technology, creation of symbols, style origins. All areas of world, but very full on Northwest Coast Indians. More than 350 illustrations of baskets, boxes, totem poles, weapons, etc. 378 pp. 20025-6 Paperbound $2.50

THE GENTLEMAN AND CABINET MAKER'S DIRECTOR, Thomas Chippendale. Full reprint (third edition, 1762) of most influential furniture book of all time, by master cabinetmaker. 200 plates, illustrating chairs, sofas, mirrors, tables, cabinets, plus 24 photographs of surviving pieces. Biographical introduction by N. Bienenstock. vi + 249pp. 9⅞ x 12¾. 21601-2 Paperbound $3.50

AMERICAN ANTIQUE FURNITURE, Edgar G. Miller, Jr. The basic coverage of all American furniture before 1840. Individual chapters cover type of furniture—clocks, tables, sideboards, etc.—chronologically, with inexhaustible wealth of data. More than 2100 photographs, all identified, commented on. Essential to all early American collectors. Introduction by H. E. Keyes. vi + 1106pp. 7⅞ x 10¾. 21599-7, 21600-4 Two volumes, Paperbound $7.50

PENNSYLVANIA DUTCH AMERICAN FOLK ART, Henry J. Kauffman. 279 photos, 28 drawings of tulipware, Fraktur script, painted tinware, toys, flowered furniture, quilts, samplers, hex signs, house interiors, etc. Full descriptive text. Excellent for tourist, rewarding for designer, collector. Map. 146pp. 7⅞ x 10¾. 21205-X Paperbound $2.00

EARLY NEW ENGLAND GRAVESTONE RUBBINGS, Edmund V. Gillon, Jr. 43 photographs, 226 carefully reproduced rubbings show heavily symbolic, sometimes macabre early gravestones, up to early 19th century. Remarkable early American primitive art, occasionally strikingly beautiful; always powerful. Text. xxvi + 207pp. 8⅜ x 11¼. 21380-3 Paperbound $3.00

ALPHABETS AND ORNAMENTS, Ernst Lehner. Well-known pictorial source for decorative alphabets, script examples, cartouches, frames, decorative title pages, calligraphic initials, borders, similar material. 14th to 19th century, mostly European. Useful in almost any graphic arts designing, varied styles. 750 illustrations. 256pp. 7 x 10. 21905-4 Paperbound $3.50

PAINTING: A CREATIVE APPROACH, Norman Colquhoun. For the beginner simple guide provides an instructive approach to painting: major stumbling blocks for beginner; overcoming them, technical points; paints and pigments; oil painting; watercolor and other media and color. New section on "plastic" paints. Glossary. Formerly *Paint Your Own Pictures*. 221pp. 22000-1 Paperbound $1.75

THE ENJOYMENT AND USE OF COLOR, Walter Sargent. Explanation of the relations between colors themselves and between colors in nature and art, including hundreds of little-known facts about color values, intensities, effects of high and low illumination, complementary colors. Many practical hints for painters, references to great masters. 7 color plates, 29 illustrations. x + 274pp.
20944-X Paperbound $2.50

THE NOTEBOOKS OF LEONARDO DA VINCI, compiled and edited by Jean Paul Richter. 1566 extracts from original manuscripts reveal the full range of Leonardo's versatile genius: all his writings on painting, sculpture, architecture, anatomy, astronomy, geography, topography, physiology, mining, music, etc., in both Italian and English, with 186 plates of manuscript pages and more than 500 additional drawings. Includes studies for the Last Supper, the lost Sforza monument, and other works. Total of xlvii + 866pp. 7⅞ x 10¾.
22572-0, 22573-9 Two volumes, Paperbound $10.00

MONTGOMERY WARD CATALOGUE OF 1895. Tea gowns, yards of flannel and pillow-case lace, stereoscopes, books of gospel hymns, the New Improved Singer Sewing Machine, side saddles, milk skimmers, straight-edged razors, high-button shoes, spittoons, and on and on . . . listing some 25,000 items, practically all illustrated. Essential to the shoppers of the 1890's, it is our truest record of the spirit of the period. Unaltered reprint of Issue No. 57, Spring and Summer 1895. Introduction by Boris Emmet. Innumerable illustrations. xiii + 624pp. 8½ x 11⅝.
22377-9 Paperbound $6.95

THE CRYSTAL PALACE EXHIBITION ILLUSTRATED CATALOGUE (LONDON, 1851). One of the wonders of the modern world—the Crystal Palace Exhibition in which all the nations of the civilized world exhibited their achievements in the arts and sciences—presented in an equally important illustrated catalogue. More than 1700 items pictured with accompanying text—ceramics, textiles, cast-iron work, carpets, pianos, sleds, razors, wall-papers, billiard tables, beehives, silverware and hundreds of other artifacts—represent the focal point of Victorian culture in the Western World. Probably the largest collection of Victorian decorative art ever assembled—indispensable for antiquarians and designers. Unabridged republication of the Art-Journal Catalogue of the Great Exhibition of 1851, with all terminal essays. New introduction by John Gloag, F.S.A. xxxiv + 426pp. 9 x 12.
22503-8 Paperbound $4.50

A HISTORY OF COSTUME, Carl Köhler. Definitive history, based on surviving pieces of clothing primarily, and paintings, statues, etc. secondarily. Highly readable text, supplemented by 594 illustrations of costumes of the ancient Mediterranean peoples, Greece and Rome, the Teutonic prehistoric period; costumes of the Middle Ages, Renaissance, Baroque, 18th and 19th centuries. Clear, measured patterns are provided for many clothing articles. Approach is practical throughout. Enlarged by Emma von Sichart. 464pp. 21030-8 Paperbound $3.00

ORIENTAL RUGS, ANTIQUE AND MODERN, Walter A. Hawley. A complete and authoritative treatise on the Oriental rug—where they are made, by whom and how, designs and symbols, characteristics in detail of the six major groups, how to distinguish them and how to buy them. Detailed technical data is provided on periods, weaves, warps, wefts, textures, sides, ends and knots, although no technical background is required for an understanding. 11 color plates, 80 halftones, 4 maps. vi + 320pp. 6⅛ x 9⅛. 22366-3 Paperbound $5.00

TEN BOOKS ON ARCHITECTURE, Vitruvius. By any standards the most important book on architecture ever written. Early Roman discussion of aesthetics of building, construction methods, orders, sites, and every other aspect of architecture has inspired, instructed architecture for about 2,000 years. Stands behind Palladio, Michelangelo, Bramante, Wren, countless others. Definitive Morris H. Morgan translation. 68 illustrations. xii + 331pp. 20645-9 Paperbound $2.50

THE FOUR BOOKS OF ARCHITECTURE, Andrea Palladio. Translated into every major Western European language in the two centuries following its publication in 1570, this has been one of the most influential books in the history of architecture. Complete reprint of the 1738 Isaac Ware edition. New introduction by Adolf Placzek, Columbia Univ. 216 plates. xxii + 110pp. of text. 9½ x 12¾. 21308-0 Clothbound $10.00

STICKS AND STONES: A STUDY OF AMERICAN ARCHITECTURE AND CIVILIZATION, Lewis Mumford.One of the great classics of American cultural history. American architecture from the medieval-inspired earliest forms to the early 20th century; evolution of structure and style, and reciprocal influences on environment. 21 photographic illustrations. 238pp. 20202-X Paperbound $2.00

THE AMERICAN BUILDER'S COMPANION, Asher Benjamin. The most widely used early 19th century architectural style and source book, for colonial up into Greek Revival periods. Extensive development of geometry of carpentering, construction of sashes, frames, doors, stairs; plans and elevations of domestic and other buildings. Hundreds of thousands of houses were built according to this book, now invaluable to historians, architects, restorers, etc. 1827 edition. 59 plates. 114pp. 7⅞ x 10¾. 22236-5 Paperbound $3.00

DUTCH HOUSES IN THE HUDSON VALLEY BEFORE 1776, Helen Wilkinson Reynolds. The standard survey of the Dutch colonial house and outbuildings, with constructional features, decoration, and local history associated with individual homesteads. Introduction by Franklin D. Roosevelt. Map. 150 illustrations. 469pp. 6⅝ x 9¼. 21469-9 Paperbound $3.50

THE ARCHITECTURE OF COUNTRY HOUSES, Andrew J. Downing. Together with Vaux's *Villas and Cottages* this is the basic book for Hudson River Gothic architecture of the middle Victorian period. Full, sound discussions of general aspects of housing, architecture, style, decoration, furnishing, together with scores of detailed house plans, illustrations of specific buildings, accompanied by full text. Perhaps the most influential single American architectural book. 1850 edition. Introduction by J. Stewart Johnson. 321 figures, 34 architectural designs. xvi + 560pp.
22003-6 Paperbound $3.50

LOST EXAMPLES OF COLONIAL ARCHITECTURE, John Mead Howells. Full-page photographs of buildings that have disappeared or been so altered as to be denatured, including many designed by major early American architects. 245 plates. xvii + 248pp. 7⅞ x 10¾.
21143-6 Paperbound $3.00

DOMESTIC ARCHITECTURE OF THE AMERICAN COLONIES AND OF THE EARLY REPUBLIC, Fiske Kimball. Foremost architect and restorer of Williamsburg and Monticello covers nearly 200 homes between 1620-1825. Architectural details, construction, style features, special fixtures, floor plans, etc. Generally considered finest work in its area. 219 illustrations of houses, doorways, windows, capital mantels. xx + 314pp. 7⅞ x 10¾.
21743-4 Paperbound $3.50

EARLY AMERICAN ROOMS: 1650-1858, edited by Russell Hawes Kettell. Tour of 12 rooms, each representative of a different era in American history and each furnished, decorated, designed and occupied in the style of the era. 72 plans and elevations, 8-page color section, etc., show fabrics, wall papers, arrangements, etc. Full descriptive text. xvii + 200pp. of text. 8⅜ x 11¼.
21633-0 Paperbound $4.00

THE FITZWILLIAM VIRGINAL BOOK, edited by J. Fuller Maitland and W. B. Squire. Full modern printing of famous early 17th-century ms. volume of 300 works by Morley, Byrd, Bull, Gibbons, etc. For piano or other modern keyboard instrument; easy to read format. xxxvi + 938pp. 8⅜ x 11.
21068-5, 21069-3 Two volumes, Paperbound $8.00

HARPSICHORD MUSIC, Johann Sebastian Bach. Bach Gesellschaft edition. A rich selection of Bach's masterpieces for the harpsichord: the six English Suites, six French Suites, the six Partitas (Clavierübung part I), the Goldberg Variations (Clavierübung part IV), the fifteen Two-Part Inventions and the fifteen Three-Part Sinfonias. Clearly reproduced on large sheets with ample margins; eminently playable. vi + 312pp. 8⅛ x 11.
22360-4 Paperbound $5.00

THE MUSIC OF BACH: AN INTRODUCTION, Charles Sanford Terry. A fine, nontechnical introduction to Bach's music, both instrumental and vocal. Covers organ music, chamber music, passion music, other types. Analyzes themes, developments, innovations. x + 114pp.
21075-8 Paperbound $1.25

BEETHOVEN AND HIS NINE SYMPHONIES, Sir George Grove. Noted British musicologist provides best history, analysis, commentary on symphonies. Very thorough, rigorously accurate; necessary to both advanced student and amateur music lover. 436 musical passages. vii + 407 pp.
20334-4 Paperbound $2.25

JOHANN SEBASTIAN BACH, Philipp Spitta. One of the great classics of musicology, this definitive analysis of Bach's music (and life) has never been surpassed. Lucid, nontechnical analyses of hundreds of pieces (30 pages devoted to St. Matthew Passion, 26 to B Minor Mass). Also includes major analysis of 18th-century music. 450 musical examples. 40-page musical supplement. Total of xx + 1799pp.
(EUK) 22278-0, 22279-9 Two volumes, Clothbound $15.00

MOZART AND HIS PIANO CONCERTOS, Cuthbert Girdlestone. The only full-length study of an important area of Mozart's creativity. Provides detailed analyses of all 23 concertos, traces inspirational sources. 417 musical examples. Second edition. 509pp. (USO) 21271-8 Paperbound $3.50

THE PERFECT WAGNERITE: A COMMENTARY ON THE NIBLUNG'S RING, George Bernard Shaw. Brilliant and still relevant criticism in remarkable essays on Wagner's Ring cycle, Shaw's ideas on political and social ideology behind the plots, role of Leitmotifs, vocal requisites, etc. Prefaces. xxi + 136pp.
21707-8 Paperbound $1.50

DON GIOVANNI, W. A. Mozart. Complete libretto, modern English translation; biographies of composer and librettist; accounts of early performances and critical reaction. Lavishly illustrated. All the material you need to understand and appreciate this great work. Dover Opera Guide and Libretto Series; translated and introduced by Ellen Bleiler. 92 illustrations. 209pp.
21134-7 Paperbound $1.50

HIGH FIDELITY SYSTEMS: A LAYMAN'S GUIDE, Roy F. Allison. All the basic information you need for setting up your own audio system: high fidelity and stereo record players, tape records, F.M. Connections, adjusting tone arm, cartridge, checking needle alignment, positioning speakers, phasing speakers, adjusting hums, trouble-shooting, maintenance, and similar topics. Enlarged 1965 edition. More than 50 charts, diagrams, photos. iv + 91pp. 21514-8 Paperbound $1.25

REPRODUCTION OF SOUND, Edgar Villchur. Thorough coverage for laymen of high fidelity systems, reproducing systems in general, needles, amplifiers, preamps, loudspeakers, feedback, explaining physical background. "A rare talent for making technicalities vividly comprehensible," R. Darrell, *High Fidelity.* 69 figures. iv + 92pp. 21515-6 Paperbound $1.00

HEAR ME TALKIN' TO YA: THE STORY OF JAZZ AS TOLD BY THE MEN WHO MADE IT, Nat Shapiro and Nat Hentoff. Louis Armstrong, Fats Waller, Jo Jones, Clarence Williams, Billy Holiday, Duke Ellington, Jelly Roll Morton and dozens of other jazz greats tell how it was in Chicago's South Side, New Orleans, depression Harlem and the modern West Coast as jazz was born and grew. xvi + 429pp.
21726-4 Paperbound $2.00

FABLES OF AESOP, translated by Sir Roger L'Estrange. A reproduction of the very rare 1931 Paris edition; a selection of the most interesting fables, together with 50 imaginative drawings by Alexander Calder. v + 128pp. 6½x9¼.
21780-9 Paperbound $1.25

AGAINST THE GRAIN (A REBOURS), Joris K. Huysmans. Filled with weird images, evidences of a bizarre imagination, exotic experiments with hallucinatory drugs, rich tastes and smells and the diversions of its sybarite hero Duc Jean des Esseintes, this classic novel pushed 19th-century literary decadence to its limits. Full unabridged edition. Do not confuse this with abridged editions generally sold. Introduction by Havelock Ellis. xlix + 206pp. 22190-3 Paperbound $2.00

VARIORUM SHAKESPEARE: HAMLET. Edited by Horace H. Furness; a landmark of American scholarship. Exhaustive footnotes and appendices treat all doubtful words and phrases, as well as suggested critical emendations throughout the play's history. First volume contains editor's own text, collated with all Quartos and Folios. Second volume contains full first Quarto, translations of Shakespeare's sources (Belleforest, and Saxo Grammaticus), Der Bestrafte Brudermord, and many essays on critical and historical points of interest by major authorities of past and present. Includes details of staging and costuming over the years. By far the best edition available for serious students of Shakespeare. Total of xx + 905pp. 21004-9, 21005-7, 2 volumes, Paperbound $5.25

A LIFE OF WILLIAM SHAKESPEARE, Sir Sidney Lee. This is the standard life of Shakespeare, summarizing everything known about Shakespeare and his plays. Incredibly rich in material, broad in coverage, clear and judicious, it has served thousands as the best introduction to Shakespeare. 1931 edition. 9 plates. xxix + 792pp. (USO) 21967-4 Paperbound $3.75

MASTERS OF THE DRAMA, John Gassner. Most comprehensive history of the drama in print, covering every tradition from Greeks to modern Europe and America, including India, Far East, etc. Covers more than 800 dramatists, 2000 plays, with biographical material, plot summaries, theatre history, criticism, etc. "Best of its kind in English," *New Republic*. 77 illustrations. xxii + 890pp. 20100-7 Clothbound $7.50

THE EVOLUTION OF THE ENGLISH LANGUAGE, George McKnight. The growth of English, from the 14th century to the present. Unusual, non-technical account presents basic information in very interesting form: sound shifts, change in grammar and syntax, vocabulary growth, similar topics. Abundantly illustrated with quotations. Formerly *Modern English in the Making*. xii + 590pp. 21932-1 Paperbound $3.50

AN ETYMOLOGICAL DICTIONARY OF MODERN ENGLISH, Ernest Weekley. Fullest, richest work of its sort, by foremost British lexicographer. Detailed word histories, including many colloquial and archaic words; extensive quotations. Do not confuse this with the Concise Etymological Dictionary, which is much abridged. Total of xxvii + 830pp. 6½ x 9¼. 21873-2, 21874-0 Two volumes, Paperbound $5.50

FLATLAND: A ROMANCE OF MANY DIMENSIONS, E. A. Abbott. Classic of science-fiction explores ramifications of life in a two-dimensional world, and what happens when a three-dimensional being intrudes. Amusing reading, but also useful as introduction to thought about hyperspace. Introduction by Banesh Hoffmann. 16 illustrations. xx + 103pp. 20001-9 Paperbound $1.00

POEMS OF ANNE BRADSTREET, edited with an introduction by Robert Hutchinson. A new selection of poems by America's first poet and perhaps the first significant woman poet in the English language. 48 poems display her development in works of considerable variety—love poems, domestic poems, religious meditations, formal elegies, "quaternions," etc. Notes, bibliography. viii + 222pp.
22160-1 Paperbound $2.00

THREE GOTHIC NOVELS: THE CASTLE OF OTRANTO BY HORACE WALPOLE; VATHEK BY WILLIAM BECKFORD; THE VAMPYRE BY JOHN POLIDORI, WITH FRAGMENT OF A NOVEL BY LORD BYRON, edited by E. F. Bleiler. The first Gothic novel, by Walpole; the finest Oriental tale in English, by Beckford; powerful Romantic supernatural story in versions by Polidori and Byron. All extremely important in history of literature; all still exciting, packed with supernatural thrills, ghosts, haunted castles, magic, etc. xl + 291pp.
21232-7 Paperbound $2.00

THE BEST TALES OF HOFFMANN, E. T. A. Hoffmann. 10 of Hoffmann's most important stories, in modern re-editings of standard translations: Nutcracker and the King of Mice, Signor Formica, Automata, The Sandman, Rath Krespel, The Golden Flowerpot, Master Martin the Cooper, The Mines of Falun, The King's Betrothed, A New Year's Eve Adventure. 7 illustrations by Hoffmann. Edited by E. F. Bleiler. xxxix + 419pp.
21793-0 Paperbound $2.25

GHOST AND HORROR STORIES OF AMBROSE BIERCE, Ambrose Bierce. 23 strikingly modern stories of the horrors latent in the human mind: The Eyes of the Panther, The Damned Thing, An Occurrence at Owl Creek Bridge, An Inhabitant of Carcosa, etc., plus the dream-essay, Visions of the Night. Edited by E. F. Bleiler. xxii + 199pp.
20767-6 Paperbound $1.50

BEST GHOST STORIES OF J. S. LEFANU, J. Sheridan LeFanu. Finest stories by Victorian master often considered greatest supernatural writer of all. Carmilla, Green Tea, The Haunted Baronet, The Familiar, and 12 others. Most never before available in the U. S. A. Edited by E. F. Bleiler. 8 illustrations from Victorian publications. xvii + 467pp.
20415-4 Paperbound $2.50

THE TIME STREAM, THE GREATEST ADVENTURE, AND THE PURPLE SAPPHIRE— THREE SCIENCE FICTION NOVELS, John Taine (Eric Temple Bell). Great American mathematician was also foremost science fiction novelist of the 1920's. *The Time Stream,* one of all-time classics, uses concepts of circular time; *The Greatest Adventure,* incredibly ancient biological experiments from Antarctica threaten to escape; The *Purple Sapphire,* superscience, lost races in Central Tibet, survivors of the Great Race. 4 illustrations by Frank R. Paul. v + 532pp.
21180-0 Paperbound $2.50

SEVEN SCIENCE FICTION NOVELS, H. G. Wells. The standard collection of the great novels. Complete, unabridged. *First Men in the Moon, Island of Dr. Moreau, War of the Worlds, Food of the Gods, Invisible Man, Time Machine, In the Days of the Comet.* Not only science fiction fans, but every educated person owes it to himself to read these novels. 1015pp.
20264-X Clothbound $5.00

LAST AND FIRST MEN AND STAR MAKER, TWO SCIENCE FICTION NOVELS, Olaf Stapledon. Greatest future histories in science fiction. In the first, human intelligence is the "hero," through strange paths of evolution, interplanetary invasions, incredible technologies, near extinctions and reemergences. Star Maker describes the quest of a band of star rovers for intelligence itself, through time and space: weird inhuman civilizations, crustacean minds, symbiotic worlds, etc. Complete, unabridged. v + 438pp. 21962-3 Paperbound $2.00

THREE PROPHETIC NOVELS, H. G. WELLS. Stages of a consistently planned future for mankind. *When the Sleeper Wakes,* and *A Story of the Days to Come,* anticipate *Brave New World* and *1984,* in the 21st Century; *The Time Machine,* only complete version in print, shows farther future and the end of mankind. All show Wells's greatest gifts as storyteller and novelist. Edited by E. F. Bleiler. x + 335pp. (USO) 20605-X Paperbound $2.00

THE DEVIL'S DICTIONARY, Ambrose Bierce. America's own Oscar Wilde— Ambrose Bierce—offers his barbed iconoclastic wisdom in over 1,000 definitions hailed by H. L. Mencken as "some of the most gorgeous witticisms in the English language." 145pp. 20487-1 Paperbound $1.25

MAX AND MORITZ, Wilhelm Busch. Great children's classic, father of comic strip, of two bad boys, Max and Moritz. Also Ker and Plunk (Plisch und Plumm), Cat and Mouse, Deceitful Henry, Ice-Peter, The Boy and the Pipe, and five other pieces. Original German, with English translation. Edited by H. Arthur Klein; translations by various hands and H. Arthur Klein. vi + 216pp. 20181-3 Paperbound $1.50

PIGS IS PIGS AND OTHER FAVORITES, Ellis Parker Butler. The title story is one of the best humor short stories, as Mike Flannery obfuscates biology and English. Also included, That Pup of Murchison's, The Great American Pie Company, and Perkins of Portland. 14 illustrations. v + 109pp. 21532-6 Paperbound $1.00

THE PETERKIN PAPERS, Lucretia P. Hale. It takes genius to be as stupidly mad as the Peterkins, as they decide to become wise, celebrate the "Fourth," keep a cow, and otherwise strain the resources of the Lady from Philadelphia. Basic book of American humor. 153 illustrations. 219pp. 20794-3 Paperbound $1.25

PERRAULT'S FAIRY TALES, translated by A. E. Johnson and S. R. Littlewood, with 34 full-page illustrations by Gustave Doré. All the original Perrault stories— Cinderella, Sleeping Beauty, Bluebeard, Little Red Riding Hood, Puss in Boots, Tom Thumb, etc.—with their witty verse morals and the magnificent illustrations of Doré. One of the five or six great books of European fairy tales. viii + 117pp. 8⅛ x 11. 22311-6 Paperbound $2.00

OLD HUNGARIAN FAIRY TALES, Baroness Orczy. Favorites translated and adapted by author of the *Scarlet Pimpernel.* Eight fairy tales include "The Suitors of Princess Fire-Fly," "The Twin Hunchbacks," "Mr. Cuttlefish's Love Story," and "The Enchanted Cat." This little volume of magic and adventure will captivate children as it has for generations. 90 drawings by Montagu Barstow. 96pp. (USO) 22293-4 Paperbound $1.95

THE RED FAIRY BOOK, Andrew Lang. Lang's color fairy books have long been children's favorites. This volume includes Rapunzel, Jack and the Bean-stalk and 35 other stories, familiar and unfamiliar. 4 plates, 93 illustrations x + 367pp.
21673-X Paperbound $1.95

THE BLUE FAIRY BOOK, Andrew Lang. Lang's tales come from all countries and all times. Here are 37 tales from Grimm, the Arabian Nights, Greek Mythology, and other fascinating sources. 8 plates, 130 illustrations. xi + 390pp.
21437-0 Paperbound $1.95

HOUSEHOLD STORIES BY THE BROTHERS GRIMM. Classic English-language edition of the well-known tales — Rumpelstiltskin, Snow White, Hansel and Gretel, The Twelve Brothers, Faithful John, Rapunzel, Tom Thumb (52 stories in all). Translated into simple, straightforward English by Lucy Crane. Ornamented with head-pieces, vignettes, elaborate decorative initials and a dozen full-page illustrations by Walter Crane. x + 269pp.
21080-4 Paperbound $2.00

THE MERRY ADVENTURES OF ROBIN HOOD, Howard Pyle. The finest modern versions of the traditional ballads and tales about the great English outlaw. Howard Pyle's complete prose version, with every word, every illustration of the first edition. Do not confuse this facsimile of the original (1883) with modern editions that change text or illustrations. 23 plates plus many page decorations. xxii + 296pp.
22043-5 Paperbound $2.00

THE STORY OF KING ARTHUR AND HIS KNIGHTS, Howard Pyle. The finest children's version of the life of King Arthur; brilliantly retold by Pyle, with 48 of his most imaginative illustrations. xviii + 313pp. 6⅛ x 9¼.
21445-1 Paperbound $2.00

THE WONDERFUL WIZARD OF OZ, L. Frank Baum. America's finest children's book in facsimile of first edition with all Denslow illustrations in full color. The edition a child should have. Introduction by Martin Gardner. 23 color plates, scores of drawings. iv + 267pp.
20691-2 Paperbound $1.95

THE MARVELOUS LAND OF OZ, L. Frank Baum. The second Oz book, every bit as imaginative as the Wizard. The hero is a boy named Tip, but the Scarecrow and the Tin Woodman are back, as is the Oz magic. 16 color plates, 120 drawings by John R. Neill. 287pp.
20692-0 Paperbound $1.75

THE MAGICAL MONARCH OF MO, L. Frank Baum. Remarkable adventures in a land even stranger than Oz. The best of Baum's books not in the Oz series. 15 color plates and dozens of drawings by Frank Verbeck. xviii + 237pp.
21892-9 Paperbound $2.00

THE BAD CHILD'S BOOK OF BEASTS, MORE BEASTS FOR WORSE CHILDREN, A MORAL ALPHABET, Hilaire Belloc. Three complete humor classics in one volume. Be kind to the frog, and do not call him names . . . and 28 other whimsical animals. Familiar favorites and some not so well known. Illustrated by Basil Blackwell. 156pp.
(USO) 20749-8 Paperbound $1.25

EAST O' THE SUN AND WEST O' THE MOON, George W. Dasent. Considered the best of all translations of these Norwegian folk tales, this collection has been enjoyed by generations of children (and folklorists too). Includes True and Untrue, Why the Sea is Salt, East O' the Sun and West O' the Moon, Why the Bear is Stumpy-Tailed, Boots and the Troll, The Cock and the Hen, Rich Peter the Pedlar, and 52 more. The only edition with all 59 tales. 77 illustrations by Erik Werenskiold and Theodor Kittelsen. xv + 418pp.　　　　　22521-6 Paperbound $3.00

GOOPS AND HOW TO BE THEM, Gelett Burgess. Classic of tongue-in-cheek humor, masquerading as etiquette book. 87 verses, twice as many cartoons, show mischievous Goops as they demonstrate to children virtues of table manners, neatness, courtesy, etc. Favorite for generations. viii + 88pp. 6½ x 9¼.
　　　　　　　　　　　　　　　　　　22233-0 Paperbound $1.25

ALICE'S ADVENTURES UNDER GROUND, Lewis Carroll. The first version, quite different from the final *Alice in Wonderland,* printed out by Carroll himself with his own illustrations. Complete facsimile of the "million dollar" manuscript Carroll gave to Alice Liddell in 1864. Introduction by Martin Gardner. viii + 96pp. Title and dedication pages in color.　　　　　21482-6 Paperbound $1.25

THE BROWNIES, THEIR BOOK, Palmer Cox. Small as mice, cunning as foxes, exuberant and full of mischief, the Brownies go to the zoo, toy shop, seashore, circus, etc., in 24 verse adventures and 266 illustrations. Long a favorite, since their first appearance in St. Nicholas Magazine. xi + 144pp. 6⅝ x 9¼.
　　　　　　　　　　　　　　　　　　21265-3 Paperbound $1.75

SONGS OF CHILDHOOD, Walter De La Mare. Published (under the pseudonym Walter Ramal) when De La Mare was only 29, this charming collection has long been a favorite children's book. A facsimile of the first edition in paper, the 47 poems capture the simplicity of the nursery rhyme and the ballad, including such lyrics as I Met Eve, Tartary, The Silver Penny. vii + 106pp. 21972-0 Paperbound $1.25

THE COMPLETE NONSENSE OF EDWARD LEAR, Edward Lear. The finest 19th-century humorist-cartoonist in full: all nonsense limericks, zany alphabets, Owl and Pussycat, songs, nonsense botany, and more than 500 illustrations by Lear himself. Edited by Holbrook Jackson. xxix + 287pp.　　　(USO) 20167-8 Paperbound $1.75

BILLY WHISKERS: THE AUTOBIOGRAPHY OF A GOAT, Frances Trego Montgomery. A favorite of children since the early 20th century, here are the escapades of that rambunctious, irresistible and mischievous goat—Billy Whiskers. Much in the spirit of *Peck's Bad Boy,* this is a book that children never tire of reading or hearing. All the original familiar illustrations by W. H. Fry are included: 6 color plates, 18 black and white drawings. 159pp.　　　　22345-0 Paperbound $2.00

MOTHER GOOSE MELODIES. Faithful republication of the fabulously rare Munroe and Francis "copyright 1833" Boston edition—the most important Mother Goose collection, usually referred to as the "original." Familiar rhymes plus many rare ones, with wonderful old woodcut illustrations. Edited by E. F. Bleiler. 128pp. 4½ x 6⅜.　　　　　　　　　　　　　　22577-1 Paperbound $1.25

Two Little Savages; Being the Adventures of Two Boys Who Lived as Indians and What They Learned, Ernest Thompson Seton. Great classic of nature and boyhood provides a vast range of woodlore in most palatable form, a genuinely entertaining story. Two farm boys build a teepee in woods and live in it for a month, working out Indian solutions to living problems, star lore, birds and animals, plants, etc. 293 illustrations. vii + 286pp.

20985-7 Paperbound $2.50

Peter Piper's Practical Principles of Plain & Perfect Pronunciation. Alliterative jingles and tongue-twisters of surprising charm, that made their first appearance in America about 1830. Republished in full with the spirited woodcut illustrations from this earliest American edition. 32pp. 4½ x 6⅜.

22560-7 Paperbound $1.00

Science Experiments and Amusements for Children, Charles Vivian. 73 easy experiments, requiring only materials found at home or easily available, such as candles, coins, steel wool, etc.; illustrate basic phenomena like vacuum, simple chemical reaction, etc. All safe. Modern, well-planned. Formerly *Science Games for Children*. 102 photos, numerous drawings. 96pp. 6⅛ x 9¼.

21856-2 Paperbound $1.25

An Introduction to Chess Moves and Tactics Simply Explained, Leonard Barden. Informal intermediate introduction, quite strong in explaining reasons for moves. Covers basic material, tactics, important openings, traps, positional play in middle game, end game. Attempts to isolate patterns and recurrent configurations. Formerly *Chess*. 58 figures. 102pp.   (USO) 21210-6 Paperbound $1.25

Lasker's Manual of Chess, Dr. Emanuel Lasker. Lasker was not only one of the five great World Champions, he was also one of the ablest expositors, theorists, and analysts. In many ways, his Manual, permeated with his philosophy of battle, filled with keen insights, is one of the greatest works ever written on chess. Filled with analyzed games by the great players. A single-volume library that will profit almost any chess player, beginner or master. 308 diagrams. xli x 349pp.

20640-8 Paperbound $2.50

The Master Book of Mathematical Recreations, Fred Schuh. In opinion of many the finest work ever prepared on mathematical puzzles, stunts, recreations; exhaustively thorough explanations of mathematics involved, analysis of effects, citation of puzzles and games. Mathematics involved is elementary. Translated by F. Göbel. 194 figures. xxiv + 430pp.   22134-2 Paperbound $3.00

Mathematics, Magic and Mystery, Martin Gardner. Puzzle editor for Scientific American explains mathematics behind various mystifying tricks: card tricks, stage "mind reading," coin and match tricks, counting out games, geometric dissections, etc. Probability sets, theory of numbers clearly explained. Also provides more than 400 tricks, guaranteed to work, that you can do. 135 illustrations. xii + 176pp.

20338-2 Paperbound $1.50

MATHEMATICAL PUZZLES FOR BEGINNERS AND ENTHUSIASTS, Geoffrey Mott-Smith. 189 puzzles from easy to difficult—involving arithmetic, logic, algebra, properties of digits, probability, etc.—for enjoyment and mental stimulus. Explanation of mathematical principles behind the puzzles. 135 illustrations. viii + 248pp.
20198-8 Paperbound $1.25

PAPER FOLDING FOR BEGINNERS, William D. Murray and Francis J. Rigney. Easiest book on the market, clearest instructions on making interesting, beautiful origami. Sail boats, cups, roosters, frogs that move legs, bonbon boxes, standing birds, etc. 40 projects; more than 275 diagrams and photographs. 94pp.
20713-7 Paperbound $1.00

TRICKS AND GAMES ON THE POOL TABLE, Fred Herrmann. 79 tricks and games— some solitaires, some for two or more players, some competitive games—to entertain you between formal games. Mystifying shots and throws, unusual caroms, tricks involving such props as cork, coins, a hat, etc. Formerly *Fun on the Pool Table*. 77 figures. 95pp.
21814-7 Paperbound $1.00

HAND SHADOWS TO BE THROWN UPON THE WALL: A SERIES OF NOVEL AND AMUSING FIGURES FORMED BY THE HAND, Henry Bursill. Delightful picturebook from great-grandfather's day shows how to make 18 different hand shadows: a bird that flies, duck that quacks, dog that wags his tail, camel, goose, deer, boy, turtle, etc. Only book of its sort. vi + 33pp. 6½ x 9¼. 21779-5 Paperbound $1.00

WHITTLING AND WOODCARVING, E. J. Tangerman. 18th printing of best book on market. "If you can cut a potato you can carve" toys and puzzles, chains, chessmen, caricatures, masks, frames, woodcut blocks, surface patterns, much more. Information on tools, woods, techniques. Also goes into serious wood sculpture from Middle Ages to present, East and West. 464 photos, figures. x + 293pp.
20965-2 Paperbound $2.00

HISTORY OF PHILOSOPHY, Julián Marías. Possibly the clearest, most easily followed, best planned, most useful one-volume history of philosophy on the market; neither skimpy nor overfull. Full details on system of every major philosopher and dozens of less important thinkers from pre-Socratics up to Existentialism and later. Strong on many European figures usually omitted. Has gone through dozens of editions in Europe. 1966 edition, translated by Stanley Appelbaum and Clarence Strowbridge. xviii + 505pp. 21739-6 Paperbound $2.75

YOGA: A SCIENTIFIC EVALUATION, Kovoor T. Behanan. Scientific but non-technical study of physiological results of yoga exercises; done under auspices of Yale U. Relations to Indian thought, to psychoanalysis, etc. 16 photos. xxiii + 270pp.
20505-3 Paperbound $2.50

Prices subject to change without notice.
Available at your book dealer or write for free catalogue to Dept. GI, Dover Publications, Inc., 180 Varick St., N. Y., N. Y. 10014. Dover publishes more than 150 books each year on science, elementary and advanced mathematics, biology, music, art, literary history, social sciences and other areas.